CAMBRIDGE TEXTS IN THE
HISTORY OF PHILOSOPHY

FRIEDRICH NIETZSCHE
The Gay Science

CAMBRIDGE TEXTS IN THE
HISTORY OF PHILOSOPHY

Series editor
KARL AMERIKS
Professor of Philosophy at the University of Notre Dame
DESMOND M. CLARKE
Professor of Philosophy at University College Cork

The main objective of Cambridge Texts in the History of Philosophy is to expand the range, variety and quality of texts in the history of philosophy which are available in English. The series includes texts by familiar names (such as Descartes and Kant) and also by less well-known authors. Wherever possible, texts are published in complete and unabridged form, and translations are specially commissioned for the series. Each volume contains a critical introduction together with a guide to further reading and any necessary glossaries and textual apparatus. The volumes are designed for student use at undergraduate and postgraduate level and will be of interest not only to students of philosophy, but also to a wider audience of readers in the history of science, the history of theology and the history of ideas.

For a list of titles published in the series, please see end of book.

FRIEDRICH NIETZSCHE

The Gay Science

With a Prelude in German Rhymes and an Appendix of Songs

EDITED BY

BERNARD WILLIAMS

All Souls College, Oxford

TRANSLATED BY

JOSEFINE NAUCKHOFF

Wake Forest University

POEMS TRANSLATED BY

ADRIAN DEL CARO

University of Colorado at Boulder

CAMBRIDGE
UNIVERSITY PRESS

PUBLISHED BY THE PRESS SYNDICATE OF THE UNIVERSITY OF CAMBRIDGE
The Pitt Building, Trumpington Street, Cambridge, United Kingdom

CAMBRIDGE UNIVERSITY PRESS
The Edinburgh Building, Cambridge CB2 2RU, UK
40 West 20th Street, New York, NY 10011–4211, USA
10 Stamford Road, Oakleigh, Melbourne 3166, Australia
Ruiz de Alarcón 13, 28014 Madrid, Spain
Dock House, The Waterfront, Cape Town 8001, South Africa

http://www.cambridge.org

First published 2001

Printed in the United Kingdom at the University Press, Cambridge

Typeset in Ehrhardt 11/13 pt   System 3b2   [CE]

A catalogue record for this book is available from the British Library

Library of Congress cataloguing in publication data

Nietzsche, Friedrich Wilhelm, 1844–1900.
[Fröhliche Wissenschaft. English]
The gay science: with a prelude in German rhymes and an appendix of songs / Friedrich Nietzsche;
edited by Bernard Williams; translated by Josefine Nauckhoff; poems translated by Adrian Del Caro.
p.   cm. – (Cambridge texts in the history of philosophy)
Includes bibliographical references (p.) and index.
ISBN 0 521 63159 9 (hardback) – ISBN 0 521 63645 0 (paperback)
I. Philosophy.   I. Williams, Bernard Arthur Owen.   II. Nauckhoff, Josefine.
III. Del Caro, Adrian, 1952– .   IV. Title.   V. Series.
B3313.F72 E5 2001
193–dc21   2001025408

ISBN 0 521 63159 9 hardback
ISBN 0 521 63645 0 paperback

Contents

Introduction

The Gay Science is a remarkable book, both in itself and as offering a way into some of Nietzsche's most important ideas. The history of its publication is rather complex, and it throws some light on the development of his thought and of his methods as a writer. He published the first edition of it in 1882. In that version, it consisted of only four books, and had no Preface, though it did have the 'Prelude in Rhymes'. A second edition appeared in 1887, which added a fifth book, the Preface, and an Appendix of further poems. This is the work as we now know it, and which is translated here.

Between the two editions of *The Gay Science*, Nietzsche wrote two of his best-known works, *Thus Spoke Zarathustra* (1883–5) and *Beyond Good and Evil* (1886); the last section of Book Four of *The Gay Science* (342)[1] is indeed virtually the same as the first section of *Zarathustra*. So the complete *Gay Science* brackets these two books, which are different from it and from each other. (*Zarathustra*, which is a peculiar literary experiment in a rhetoric drawn from the Bible, was once one of Nietzsche's most popular works, but it has worn less well than the others.) Book Five of *The Gay Science* anticipates, in turn, some of the themes of another famous book which was to follow in 1887, *On the Genealogy of Morality*, which is again different in tone, sustaining a more continuous theoretical argument.

The Gay Science is a prime example of what is often called Nietzsche's 'aphoristic' style. It consists of a sequence of sections which are not obviously tied to one another except, sometimes, in general content, and

---

[1] References to *The Gay Science*, and to other works by Nietzsche, are to numbered sections.

which do not offer a connected argument. The second half of Book Three, in particular, consists of many very short paragraphs of this kind. Elsewhere, however, there are longer passages, and in fact the arrangement of the shorter sections is not as fortuitous as it may look. It is often designed to gather thoughts which will, so to speak, circle in on some central theme or problem.

In his earlier works, Nietzsche had moved gradually towards this style. He had been appointed in 1869 as a professor of classical philology at the University of Basle, at the extraordinarily early age of twenty-four. He served in this position for ten years, resigning in 1879 because of the ill health which was to persist throughout his life. (The last letter he wrote, when in 1889 he broke down into insanity and a silence which lasted until his death in 1900, was to his distinguished colleague at Basle, Jacob Burckhardt, in which he said that he would rather have been a Swiss professor than God, but he had not dared to push egoism so far.) In his years at Basle he published first *The Birth of Tragedy*, which has the form, if not the content or the tone, of a treatise, and a set of four long essays collected as *Untimely Meditations*. In 1878–9 he brought out two books forming *Human, All Too Human*, followed in 1880 by a further part called 'The Wanderer and his Shadow', and in these writings he moved from continuous exposition and argument to setting out a sequence of thoughts which were not necessarily tied discursively to their neighbours, a style that allowed him to approach a question from many different directions. In *Daybreak*, which came out in 1881, the style is fully developed. As late as 25 January 1882 he still referred to what were to be the first books of *The Gay Science* as a continuation of *Daybreak*; by June they had acquired their separate title.

When he made that decision, he sensed that Book Four, which is called 'Sanctus Januarius' and invokes the spirit of the New Year, might be found obscure, and he was anxious about whether his correspondent, Peter Gast, would understand it. He knew that this was not just a set of penetrating, perhaps rather cynical, *aperçus*. 'Aphorism', the standard term which I have already mentioned, implies too strongly that each is supposed to be a squib, or a compact expression of a truth (often in the form of an exaggerated falsehood) in the style of the French writers La Rochefoucault and Chamfort, whom Nietzsche indeed admired, but whom he did not simply follow in giving a self-conscious exposé of some human failing, foible or piece of self-deception. There is a certain amount of that, particularly in the earlier books, but he was very aware of the risk that such aphorisms run of sliding from the daring through the knowing to the self-satisfied (it is not merely cynicism that he intends when he says in 379 that 'we are artists of contempt'). His ambitions are deeper; the effect is meant to be cumulative, and its aim is more systematically subversive. A philosopher who had a similar intention, though in totally different connections, is the later Wittgenstein, and Nietzsche might have called the sections of this book, as Wittgenstein called the paragraphs of his manuscripts, 'remarks'.

His remarks cover very various subjects. Many of them touch on what may be called moral psychology, and sometimes he does claim to detect an egoistic origin of some ethically approved reaction (as he does, for example, in the shrewd observation about magnanimity and revenge at section 49). The search for the 'shameful origin' of our moral sentiments was later to become an important principle of his genealogical method. But he is very clear that mere reductionism, the readily cynical explanation of all such attitudes in terms of self-interest, is a mistake. Partly this is because he does not think that self-interest is an individual's basic motive anyway, and this book contains some quite complex, if unresolved, reflections on that question, in particular when he considers whether the virtues have a value for the individual who possesses them, or for the group. But, more broadly, Nietzsche thinks that the reductive spirit itself can be in error, a form of vulgarity (3), and that the 'realists' who congratulate themselves on having the measure of human unreason and self-deception are usually themselves in the grip of some ancient fantasy (57).

Above all, it is simply not enough, in Nietzsche's view, to 'unmask' some supposedly honourable sentiment or opinion and leave it at that. 'Only as creators can we destroy', he very significantly says (58). What things are *called* is fundamentally important, but a conventional set of names – as we may say, an interpretation – can be replaced only by another, more powerful, interpretation. When we say that one interpretation is more powerful than another, it is vitally important what counts as 'power'. It is often said that Nietzsche explains everything in terms of power. This says something about the way in which he saw these problems, but it is wrong if it is supposed to state his solution to it. The point is very clear in *On the Genealogy of Morality*. There he tells a story of how a certain outlook or interpretation, embodying metaphysical illusions, came into existence as a psychological compensation for the weakness of people who were powerless, and how this outlook triumphed over the conventionally strong and their view of the world. The question must be, how could this have come about? What was the source of this new power? There had to be *something to* this new way of describing the world which accounted in naturalistic terms for its triumph, and Nietzsche fully accepts this, even if he does not have a very rich vocabulary of social explanation in which he can discuss what it might be. 'Let us . . . not forget', he goes on in section 58 of *The Gay Science*, 'that in the long run it is enough to create new names and valuations and appearances of truth in order to create new "things"'. Indeed, but this immediately raises the question, one to which Nietzsche returned in many different connections: what must someone do to 'create' new names?

The words 'The Gay Science' translate the German title 'Die Fröhliche Wissenschaft'. No one, presumably, is going to be misled by the more recent associations of the word 'gay' – it simply means joyful, light-hearted, and above all, lacking in solemnity (section 327, on taking things seriously, says something about this). 'Science' has its own difficulties. The word 'Wissenschaft', unlike the English word 'science' in its modern use, does not mean simply the natural and biological sciences – they are, more specifically, 'Naturwissenschaft'. It means any organized study or body of knowledge, including history, philology, criticism and generally what we call 'the humanities', and that is often what Nietzsche has in mind when he uses the word in the text (it is often translated as 'science', for want of a brief alternative). But in the title itself there is an idea still broader than this. It translates a phrase, 'gai saber', or, as Nietzsche writes on his title page, 'gaya scienza', which referred to the art of song cultivated by the medieval troubadours of Provence, and with that, as he explains in *Beyond Good and Evil* (260), it invokes an aristocratic culture of courtly love. As he made clear, this association comes out in the fact that the book contains poems. But the title has other implications as well. One – particularly important to understanding this book and Nietzsche more generally – is that, just as the troubadours possessed not so much a body of information as an art, so Nietzsche's 'gay science' does not in the first place consist of a doctrine, a theory or body of knowledge. While it involves and encourages hard and rigorous thought, and to this extent the standard implications of 'Wissenschaft' are in place, it is meant to convey a certain spirit, one that in relation to understanding and criticism could defy the 'spirit of gravity' as lightly as the troubadours, supposedly, celebrated their loves. This is why the original publisher could announce at the beginning of the book that it brought to a conclusion a series of Nietzsche's writings (including *Human, All Too Human* and *Daybreak*) which shared the aim of setting out 'a new image and ideal of the free spirit'.

He said that it was the most personal of his books, meaning that in part it was explicitly about his own life: some of it is like a diary. It is not irrelevant that the 'gai saber' belonged to the south of Europe, to the Mediterranean. Nietzsche spent much of his time in the last years of his working life in Italy (in places such as those he praises in sections 281 and 291), and he was very conscious of the contrast between overcast German earnestness and Southern sun and freedom, an idea which had a long literary history and had been most famously expressed, perhaps, in Goethe's *Italian Journey*. That is a recurrent contrast in *The Gay Science*, but, as so often with Nietzsche, it is not one contrast, and his reflections on the German spirit in philosophy and religion are specially nuanced in this book, for instance in his discussion (357) of 'What is German?'

Nietzsche's general reflections, here as elsewhere, have some recurrent weaknesses. There are cranky reflections on diet and climate. His opinions about women and sex, even if they include (as at 71) one or two shrewd and compassionate insights into the conventions of his time, are often shallow and sometimes embarrassing; they were, biographically, the product of an experience which had been drastically limited and disappointing. However, what is most significant for his thought as a whole is the fact that his resources for thinking about modern society and politics, in particular about the modern state, were very thin. The point is not that he was opposed to a free society, equal rights, and other typically modern aspirations (though he certainly was, as section 377, for instance, makes clear). In fact, Nietzsche has by no means been a hero exclusively of the political Right, and many radical, socialist and even feminist groups in the last century found support in his writings.[2]

[2] A very interesting study in this connection is Steven E. Ascheim, *The Nietzsche Legacy in Germany 1890–1990* (Berkeley: University of California Press, 1992). A helpful discussion of Nietzsche's political thought is Bruce Detwiler, *Nietzsche and the Politics of Aristocratic Radicalism*

This was possible just because the deeply radical spirit of his work was combined with a lack of effective political and social ideas, leaving a blank on which many different aspirations could be projected. His clearly aristocratic sympathies are, in political connections, not so much reactionary as archaic, and while he has many illuminating things to say about the religious and cultural history of Europe, his conception of social relations owes more to his understanding of the ancient world than to a grasp of modernity. The idea of nihilism which is so important in his later works is undeniably relevant to modern conditions, but his discussions of such subjects as 'corruption' (in section 23 of this book) borrow a lot from the rhetoric of the Roman Empire and the disposition of its writers to praise the largely imaginary virtues of the vanished Republic.

The Gay Science marks a decisive step beyond the books that came before it because it introduces two of what were to become Nietzsche's best-known themes, the Death of God and the Eternal Recurrence. The idea that God is dead occurs first at 108, in association with the image of the Buddha's shadow, still to be seen in a cave for centuries after his death. This is followed at 125 by the haunting story of a madman with a lantern in the bright morning, looking for God. He is met by ridicule, and he concludes that he has 'come too early', that the news of God's death has not yet reached humanity, even though they have killed him themselves. This idea recurs in more literal terms in 343, the first section of Book Five (published, we may recall, five years later). The death of God is identified there as the fact that 'the belief in . . . God has become unbelievable': this, 'the greatest recent event', is beginning to cast its shadow across Europe. Once this event is fully recognized, it will have incalculable consequences, in particular for European morality. Some of these consequences will be melancholy, and indeed elsewhere Nietzsche struggles with the question of what act of creation, by whom, might overcome the emptiness left by the collapse of traditional illusions. But here the news brings, at least in the short term, only joy, a sense of daybreak and freedom, the promise of an open sea: 'maybe there has never been such an "open sea" '.

(University of Chicago Press, 1990). Mark Warren, in *Nietzsche and Political Thought* (Boston: MIT Press, 1988), well brings out the limitations of Nietzsche's social ideas, but is over-optimistic in thinking that if his philosophy were true to itself, it would offer a basis for liberalism.

Nietzsche continued to think that the death of God would have vast and catastrophic consequences. But on the account that he himself gave of Christian belief and its origins (in this book and in *Beyond Good and Evil*, but above all in *On the Genealogy of Morality*), should he really have thought this? He believed that the faith in the Christian God, and more generally in a reassuring metaphysical structure of the world, was a projection of fear and resentment, representing a victory of the weak over the strong. That metaphysical belief has died; it has been destroyed, as Nietzsche often points out, by itself, by the belief in truthfulness – and we shall come back to that – which was itself part of the metaphysical faith. But how much difference should he expect its death to make? He shares with another nineteenth-century subverter, Marx (with whom he shares little else), the idea that religious belief is a consequence, an expression of social and psychological forces. If those forces remain, and the Christian expression of them collapses, then surely other expressions will take its place. If need secretes thought, and the need remains, then it will secrete new thoughts.

Indeed, Nietzsche does think this: he thinks that liberalism, socialism, Utilitarianism and so on are just secularized expressions of those same forces. But he thinks that they are too manifestly close to the original, and that our growing understanding that the world has no metaphysical structure whatsoever must discredit them as well. The death of God is the death of those gods, too. He has a particular contempt for benign freethinkers who hope to keep all the ethical content of Christianity without its theology: George Eliot is the unlucky target when the point is spelled out very clearly in *The Twilight of the Idols* (the section called 'Expeditions of an Untimely Man'). But that is not the most important point. Even if the content of our morality changes noticeably, as for instance attitudes towards sex have done in recent times, much more basic and structural elements of it, its humanitarianism and its professed belief in equal respect for everyone, are in Nietzsche's view too bound up with the mechanisms that generated Christianity, and will inevitably go the same way that it has gone. It is too soon, surely, to say that he was wrong.

For Nietzsche himself there was another dimension as well, one immediately connected with his own values. He saw the unravelling of Christianity as part of the phenomenon that he called European nihilism, the loss of any sense of depth or significance to life. The world might conceivably avoid destruction and overt hatred by organizing a pleasantly undemanding and unreflective way of life, a dazed but adequately efficient consumerism. Nietzsche probably did not think that such a society could survive in the long run, but in any case he could not reconcile himself to such a prospect or regard it as anything but loathsome. Contempt was one of his readier emotions, and nothing elicited it more than what he sometimes calls 'the last man', the contented, unadventurous, philistine product of such a culture. This book, like all his others, makes it clear that any life worth living must involve daring, individuality and creative bloody-mindedness. This is indeed expressed in the 'gaiety' of its title. Gaiety can encompass contentment, as it does on New Year's Day at the beginning of Book Four, but when that is so, it is a particular achievement and a piece of good luck. Gaiety is not itself contentment, and while it rejects solemnity and the spirit of gravity, it does so precisely because it is the only way of taking life seriously.

Nietzsche has been thought by some people to have had a brutal and ruthless attitude to the world; sometimes, perhaps, he wished that he had. But in fact, one personal feature which, together with his illness and his loneliness, contributed to his outlook was a hyper-sensitivity to suffering. It was linked to a total refusal to forget, not only the existence of suffering, but the fact that suffering was necessary to everything that he and anyone else valued. 'All good things come from bad things' is one of his fundamental tenets: it signals his rejection of what he calls 'the fundamental belief of the metaphysicians, *the belief in the opposition of values*' (*Beyond Good and Evil*, 2). This is, for him, a principle of interpretation, but it presents itself in the first instance simply as a fact, which he thought no honest understanding of the world could evade. If a sense of the world's achievements and glories – art, self-understanding, nobility of character – cannot in common honesty be separated from the knowledge of the horrors that have been involved in bringing these things about, then there is a question that cannot, Nietzsche supposed, simply be ignored: whether it has all been worth it.

Thinkers in the past have supposed that the question could be answered, and answered positively. Leibniz, with his famous doctrine that this is the best of all possible worlds, believed in a cosmic cost-benefit analysis which would vindicate God's mysterious management. Hegel had told a progressive metaphysical story of the historical development of freedom and reason, which represented the horrors as all dialectically necessary to the eventual outcome, so that we could be sure that none of them was meaningless. Neither of these fantasies, Nietzsche reasonably thought, could be taken seriously in the late 19th century. Nor, he came to think, could one take altogether seriously someone who answered the same question, but in the negative. In his earlier years he had been very impressed, as Wagner was, by the philosophy of Schopenhauer, and his references to Schopenhauer in this book are mostly respectful (more so than those to Wagner), but he came to be very sceptical about Schopenhauer's so-called pessimism, which had been expressed in the judgement (for instance) that the world's 'non-existence would be preferable to its existence'.[3] 'We take care not to say that the world is worth *less*', he says at 346:

> The whole attitude of man. . .as judge of the world who finally places existence itself on his scales and finds it too light – the monstrous stupidity of this attitude has finally dawned on us and we are sick of it.

Nietzsche recognizes that his own *Birth of Tragedy* had been full of the Schopenhauerian spirit. Taken in that spirit, the question of 'the value of life', he came to think, had no answer and was indeed not a question. Yet it did not simply go away, because there remained what seemed to Nietzsche, at least, to be a fact, that anyone who really understood and held in his mind the horrors of the world would be crushed or choked by them. That fact left, if not a question to be answered, at least a problem to be overcome. Nietzsche presents the problem, and his way of overcoming it, in the form of the thought-experiment of the Eternal Recurrence, which appears for the first time in *The Gay Science*.[4] In the startling words of 341, what would you think if a demon told you that everything in life would recur over and over again eternally? How would you answer the question 'Do you want this again and innumerable times again?'? This question, Nietzsche says, 'would lie on your actions as the heaviest weight'. It tests your ability not to be overcome by the world's horror and meaninglessness.

[3] *The World as Will and Representation*, trans. E. F. J. Payne (2 vols., New York: Dover, 1969), vol. II, chapter 46, p. 576

[4] The *phrase* 'eternal recurrence' occurs first at sec 285, but in a more limited connection, of recognizing that there is no perpetual peace, but only (as the pre-Socratic philosopher Heraclitus taught) a cycle of war and peace.

There is no *belief* which could 'justify the world': confronted with the question of its value, or rather with the replacement for that question, which is the prospect of being crushed by the consciousness of what the world is like, the only issue is (as Nietzsche also puts it) whether one can say 'yes' to it, and the test of that is whether seriously and in the fullest consciousness you could will that the course of everything should happen over and over again, including not just its pain and cruelty and humiliation, but also its triviality, emptiness and ugliness, the last man and everything that goes with him.

This is an entirely hypothetical question, a thought-experiment. It is not a matter, as I read him, of Nietzsche's believing in a *theory* of eternal recurrence. The idea (which does not occur in *Beyond Good and Evil* or *The Genealogy of Morality*) appears in *Zarathustra* in a form similar to that of *The Gay Science*, and Nietzsche mentions its importance in *The Twilight of the Idols* and in *Ecce Homo* (the intellectual autobiography that he wrote on the verge of insanity). There are some places in which it is treated as a theoretical idea, but they are largely confined to his unpublished notes (his *Nachlass*), some of which, particularly from his last years, were published in *The Will to Power*, which is not a book by Nietzsche at all, but a selection from these notes tendentiously put together by his sister.

But if the idea of the Eternal Recurrence is a thought-experiment, how can answering its question lie on our actions 'as the heaviest weight'? If it is a mere fantasy, then how can 'willing' the Eternal Recurrence cost one anything at all? It seems as simple as saying 'yes'. But one has to recall that in facing the question one is supposed to have a real and live consciousness of everything that has led to this moment, in particular to what we value. We would have to think in vivid detail, if we could, of every dreadful happening that has been necessary to create Venice, or Newton's science, or whatever one thinks best of in our morality. Then we would have not simply to say 'yes', but to say 'yes' and mean it. That does not seem exactly weightless. What perhaps does less work in the thought-experiment is the element, which Nietzsche certainly thought essential to it, of *eternity*. If there is anything in this test at all, why would willing one recurrence not be enough? If you could overcome the 'nausea', as Zarathustra repeatedly puts it, of the prospect that the horrors and the last man and all the rest will come round again *even once*, and say 'yes' to it, you would have taken the essential step: could willing all those further recurrences cost you very much more?

There is another, very natural, reaction to the problem, which is almost everyone's reaction: to forget about it. One can forget that the horrors exist, and also, if one has a taste for metaphysical consolations, that God is dead. The narrator of Scott Fitzgerald's *The Great Gatsby* says of Tom and Daisy that they 'retreated back into their money and their vast carelessness, or whatever it was that held them together', and that is, roughly speaking, the remedy that the 'last man' finds for Nietzsche's problem. David Hume spoke of 'carelessness and inattention' as the only remedy for sceptical doubts; but that is not the same, because Hume thought that sceptical doubts were *unreal*. Nietzsche knew that the considerations we all forget were not unreal, and he held obstinately to an idea of truthfulness that would not allow us to falsify them. In this book, he calls on honesty and intellectual conscience at 319 and (as we shall see) at 344; at 284 he speaks of those who have to have an argument against the sceptic inside themselves – 'the great self-dissatisfied people'. In *The Anti-Christ* (50), at the very end of his active life, he wrote:

> Truth has had to be fought for every step of the way, almost everything else dear to our hearts, on which our love and our trust in life depend, has had to be sacrificed to it. Greatness of soul is needed for it, the service of truth is the hardest service. – For what does it mean to be *honest* in intellectual things? That one is stern towards one's heart, that one despises 'fine feelings', that one makes every Yes and No a question of conscience!

The value of truthfulness embraces the need to find out the truth, to hold on to it, and to tell it – in particular, to oneself. But Nietzsche's own dedication to this value, he saw, immediately raised the question of what this value is. We have taken it for granted, he thinks, and we have seriously misunderstood it: as he says in *Beyond Good and Evil* (177), 'Perhaps nobody yet has been truthful enough about what "truthfulness" is.'

Section 344 of *The Gay Science* (the second section of Book Five) gives one of Nietzsche's most important and illuminating statements of this question:

> This unconditional will to truth – what is it? Is it the will not to let oneself be deceived? Is it the will *not to deceive*? For the will to

truth could be interpreted in this second way, too – if 'I do not want to deceive *myself*' is included as a special case under the generalization 'I do not want to deceive'. But why not deceive? But why not allow oneself to be deceived?

The reasons for not wanting to be deceived, he goes on to say, are prudential; seen in that light, wanting to get things right in our intellectual studies and in practical life will be a matter of utility. But those considerations cannot possibly sustain an *unconditional* value for truth: much of the time it is more useful to believe falsehoods. Our belief in the unconditional will to truth

> must have originated *in spite of* the fact that the disutility and dangerousness of 'the will to truth' or 'truth at any price' is proved to it constantly. 'At any price': we understand this well enough once we have offered and slaughtered one faith after another on this altar! Consequently, 'will to truth' does *not* mean 'I do not want to let myself be deceived' but – there is no alternative – 'I will not deceive, not even myself'; *and with that we stand on moral ground.*
> . . .you will have gathered what I am getting at, namely, that it is still a *metaphysical faith* upon which our faith in science rests – that even we knowers of today, we godless anti-metaphysicians, still take *our* fire, too, from the flame lit by the thousand-year-old faith, the Christian faith which was also Plato's faith, that God is truth; that truth is divine. . .

The title of the section is 'In what way we, too, are still pious'. The idea is developed further in Book III of *On the Genealogy of Morality*, where the 'ascetic ideal' which has received an unflattering genealogical explanation is discovered to lie at the root of the will to truth, which powered the need to discover that very explanation. But that does not overthrow the will to truth: 'I have every respect for the ascetic ideal *in so far as it is honest!*' (III.26).

The 'unconditional will to truth' does not mean that we want to believe any and every truth. It does mean that we want to understand who we are, to correct error, to avoid deceiving ourselves, to get beyond comfortable falsehood. The value of truthfulness, so understood, cannot lie just in its consequences, as Nietzsche repeatedly points out. Earlier in this book (121), he says that various beliefs may be necessary for our life, but that does not show them to be true: 'life is not an argument'.

xviii

Already in *Human, All Too Human* (517) he had noted: '*Fundamental Insight:* There is no pre-established harmony between the furthering of truth and the well-being of humanity.' Again, in *Beyond Good and Evil* (11) he says that we must understand that there are some judgements which 'must be *believed* to be true, for the sake of preservation of creatures like ourselves, though they might, of course, be false judgements for all that'.

Truth may be not just unhelpful, but destructive. In particular the truths of Nietzsche's own philosophy, which discredit the metaphysical world, can (as we have seen) destructively lead to nihilism if they come to be accepted. In the *Nachlass* (*The Will to Power* 5) there is a revealing note, which mentions the way in which the idea of truthfulness has turned against the morality which fostered it, and ends with the remark:

> This antagonism – *not* to esteem what we know, and not to be *allowed* any longer to esteem the lies we should like to tell ourselves – results in a process of dissolution.

In what ways are we 'not allowed' to esteem these lies? To some degree, Nietzsche thought that this was already in his time a historical or social necessity: that, at least among thoughtful people, these beliefs simply could not stand up much longer or have much life to them. It is a good question whether this was right, indeed whether it is right today – particularly when we recall the secularized, political, forms which are now taken, as Nietzsche supposed, by the same illusions. What is certainly true is that Nietzsche took it to be an *ethical* necessity, for himself and anyone he was disposed to respect, not to esteem these illusions. He did think that there were things which, even for honest and reflective people, could rightly compensate in some ways for the loss of the illusions; it is in this spirit that he remarks elsewhere in the *Nachlass* (*The Will to Power* 822) 'We possess *art* lest *we perish of the truth.*' He does not mean that we possess art in place of the truth; he means that we possess art so that we can possess the truth and not perish of it.

There continue to be complex debates about what Nietzsche understood truth to be. Quite certainly, he did not think, in pragmatist spirit, that beliefs are true if they serve our interests or welfare: we have already seen some of his repeated denials of this idea. A more recently fashionable view of him is that he shared, perhaps founded, a kind of deconstructive scepticism to the effect that there is no such thing as truth, or that truth is what anyone thinks it is, or that it is a boring category that we can do without. This is also wrong, and more deeply so. As we have seen, Nietzsche did not think that the ideal of truthfulness went into retirement when its metaphysical origins were discovered, and he did not suppose, either, that truthfulness could be detached from a concern for the truth. Truthfulness as an ideal retains its power, and so far from truth being dispensable or malleable, his main question is how it can be made bearable. Repeatedly Nietzsche – the 'old philologist', as he called himself – reminds us that, quite apart from any question about philosophical interpretations, including his own, there are facts to be respected. In *The Anti-Christ* (59) he praises the ancient world for having invented 'the incomparable art of reading well, the prerequisite for all systematic knowledge', and with that 'the *sense for facts*, the last-developed and most valuable of all the senses'. At the beginning of *On the Genealogy of Morality*, he tells us that 'the English psychologists' should not be dismissed as old, cold, boring frogs; rather, they are brave animals,

> who have been taught to sacrifice desirability to truth, every truth, even a plain, bitter, ugly, foul, unchristian, immoral truth. . .Because there are such truths –

He keenly detects elements in our intellectual structures which we mistake for truths. In *The Gay Science* he stresses the importance of 'a law of agreement', which regulates people's thoughts and provides intellectual security (76). He stresses the historical, indeed the continuing, importance of these conceptions, but he does not think that they are the truth, or that they are immune to the discovery of truth. They are *contrasted* with the truth, and the question is, what will emerge from a battle between them and a growing awareness of the truth: as he asks at 110, 'to what extent can truth stand to be incorporated?'

In his earliest writings about truth and error, Nietzsche sometimes spoke as though he could compare the entire structure of our thought to the 'real' nature of things and find our thought defective. It is as though the business of using concepts at all falsified a reality which in itself was – what? Formless, perhaps, or chaotic, or utterly unstructured. Later, he rightly rejected this picture, with its implication that we can somehow look round our the edge of our concepts at the world to which we are applying them and grasp it as entirely unaffected by any descriptions (including, we would be forced to admit, the descriptions 'formless', 'chaotic', and so on).[5] There are passages in *The Gay Science* where it is unclear whether he is still attached to this picture. He discusses fictions, the practice of regarding things as equal or identical or mathematically structured when they are not so or only approximately so (110, 121). He is making the point, certainly, that mathematical representations which are offered by the sciences are in various ways idealizations, and this is entirely intelligible. There is greater ambiguity when he suggests that nothing is really 'identical' or 'the same'. To take an example: the concept 'snake' allows us to classify various individual things as 'the same animal', and to recognize one individual thing as 'the same snake'. It is trivially true that 'snake' is a human concept, a cultural product. But it is a much murkier proposition that its use somehow *falsifies* reality – that 'in itself' the world does not contain snakes, or indeed anything else you might mention. Nietzsche came to see that this idea of the world 'in itself' was precisely a relic of the kind of metaphysics that he wanted to overcome. As a remark in the *Nachlass* puts it (*The Will to Power* 567): 'The antithesis of the apparent world and the true world is reduced to the antithesis "world" and "nothing".'

It is less than clear, and also well worth considering, how far the formulations of *The Gay Science* still commit him to the murky metaphysical picture. Some of the same problems affect another idea which appears in the book, and which was to be important in works he wrote after it, the idea of 'a perspective'. Our interpretative outlook, our particular 'take' on the world, is modelled on the analogy of a literal, visual, perspective, and this analogy has two implications: that we understand that there can be alternative perspectives, and, importantly, that these will be alternative perspectives *on the same reality*. In later works, Nietzsche is often less than definite about what is involved in this second implication, but he is very clear about the first implication, and indeed urges us to combine perspectives, or move between them, which shows that we not only know *that* there are other perspectival views, but that we know what some of them are. In *The Gay Science*, he seems on the very edge of stepping into this problem. Section 299, for instance, suggests that we can make use of different perspectives. But at 374,

---

[5] This is well argued by Maudemarie Clark, *Nietzsche on Truth and Philosophy* (Cambridge University Press, 1991).

where he says 'we cannot reject the possibility that it [the world] includes infinite interpretations', the idea of the 'alternatives' seems to remain an entirely abstract possibility: 'we cannot look around our corner'.

The 'Greeks were superficial – out of profundity', he says in the Preface (and he repeated the remark later, in the epilogue to *Nietzsche contra Wagner*). But the Greeks in their time could straightforwardly display a delight in surfaces and appearances which was indeed profound. That is not possible for us, after so much history: any such attitude for us will be a different and more sophisticated thing, and it will represent an achievement. At the very end of the book, he returns to the gaiety of the gay science, and calls up the ideal of 'a spirit that plays naively, i.e. not deliberately but from overflowing abundance and power, with everything that was hitherto called holy, good, untouchable, divine. . .' This might seem even inhuman in comparison to conventional forms of seriousness, that is to say, solemnity,

> and in spite of all this, it is perhaps only with it that *the great seriousness* really emerges; that the real question mark is posed for the first time; that the destiny of the soul changes; the hand of the clock moves forward. . .

Then he adds, at the end of that section, '. . .the tragedy begins'. But immediately there comes the last section of all, *Epilogue*, in which the spirits of his own book tell him to stop these gloomy noises, these 'voices from the crypt, and marmot whistles'. 'Nicht solche Töne!' they cry in an echo of Schiller's *Ode to Joy*, 'Not such sounds!' He says he will give them something else – the poems, presumably, with which he ends the book. But he does so with a final question, and it is a question which he wanted his readers to ask themselves not just at the end of this book, but throughout it and indeed throughout all his books – 'Is that what you *want*?'

Chronology

1844 Born in Röcken, a small village in the Prussian province of Saxony, on 15 October.

1846 Birth of his sister Elisabeth.

1848 Birth of his brother Joseph.

1849 His father, a Lutheran minister, dies at age thirty-six of 'softening of the brain'.

1850 Brother dies; family moves to Naumburg to live with father's mother and her sisters.

1858 Begins studies at Pforta, Germany's most famous school for education in the classics.

1864 Graduates from Pforta with a thesis in Latin on the Greek poet Theognis; enters the University of Bonn as a theology student.

1865 Transfers from Bonn, following the classical philologist Friedrich Ritschl to Leipzig where he registers as a philology student; reads Schopenhauer's *The World as Will and Representation*.

1866 Reads Friedrich Lange's *History of Materialism*.

1868 Meets Richard Wagner.

1869 On Ritschl's recommendation is appointed professor of classical philology at Basle at the age of twenty-four before completing his doctorate (which is then conferred without a dissertation); begins frequent visits to the Wagner residence at Tribschen.

1870 Serves as a medical orderly in the Franco-Prussian war; contracts a serious illness and so serves only two months. Writes 'The Dionysiac World View'.

1872 Publishes his first book, *The Birth of Tragedy*; its dedicatory preface to Richard Wagner claims for art the role of 'the highest task and truly metaphysical activity of his life'; devastating reviews follow.

1873 Publishes 'David Strauss, the Confessor and the Writer', the first of his *Untimely Meditations*; begins taking books on natural science out of the Basle library, whereas he had previously confined himself largely to books on philological matters. Writes 'On Truth and Lying in a Non-Moral Sense'.

1874 Publishes two more *Meditations*, 'The Uses and Disadvantages of History for Life' and 'Schopenhauer as Educator'.

1876 Publishes the fourth *Meditation*, 'Richard Wagner in Bayreuth', which already bears subtle signs of his movement away from Wagner.

1878 Publishes *Human, All Too Human* (dedicated to the memory of Voltaire); it praises science over art as the high culture and thus marks a decisive turn away from Wagner.

1879 Terrible health problems force him to resign his chair at Basle (with a small pension); publishes 'Assorted Opinions and Maxims', the first part of vol. II of *Human, All Too Human*; begins living alone in Swiss and Italian boarding-houses.

1880 Publishes 'The Wanderer and His Shadow', which becomes the second part of vol. II of *Human, All Too Human*.

1881 Publishes *Daybreak*.

1882 Publishes *Idylls of Messina* (eight poems) in a monthly magazine; publishes *The Gay Science* (first edition); friendship with Paul Ree and Lou Andreas-Salomé ends badly, leaving Nietzsche devastated.

1883 Publishes the first two parts of *Thus Spoke Zarathustra*; learns of Wagner's death just after mailing part one to the publisher.

1884 Publishes the third part of *Thus Spoke Zarathustra*.

1885 Publishes the fourth part of *Zarathustra* for private circulation only.

1886 Publishes *Beyond Good and Evil*; writes prefaces for new releases of: *The Birth of Tragedy*, *Human, All Too Human* vols. I, II, and *Daybreak*.

1887 Publishes expanded edition of *The Gay Science* with a new preface, a fifth book, and an appendix of poems; publishes *Hymn to Life*, a musical work for chorus and orchestra; publishes *On the Genealogy of Morality*.

1888   Publishes *The Case of Wagner*, composes a collection of poems, *Dionysian Dithyrambs*, and four short books: *Twilight of Idols*, *The Antichrist, Ecce Homo*, and *Nietzsche contra Wagner*.

1889   Collapses physically and mentally in Turin on 3 January; writes a few lucid notes but never recovers sanity; is briefly institutionalized; spends remainder of his life as an invalid, living with his mother and then his sister, who also gains control of his literary estate.

1900   Dies in Weimar on 25 August.

Further reading

The standard biography of Nietzsche in English is R. J. Hollingdale, *Nietzsche: The Man and his Philosophy*, recently published in a revised and updated second edition (Cambridge University Press, 1999). Lesley Chamberlain's *Nietzsche in Turin: An Intimate Biography* (Picador, 1997) gives a vivid picture of his life in the period during which he was at work on *The Gay Science*. There are two excellent general introductions to Nietzsche's philosophy, a short book by Michael Tanner, *Nietzsche* (Oxford University Press, 1995) and a slightly longer and more technical book by Henry Staten, *Nietzsche's Voice* (Cornell University Press, 1990). Readers interested in Nietzsche's epistemology and metaphysics should consult Maudemarie Clark's *Nietzsche on Truth and Philosophy* (Cambridge University Press, 1991), John T. Wilcox, *Truth and Value in Nietzsche: A Study of his Metaethics and Epistemology* (University of Michigan Press, 1974), and Ken Gemes, 'Nietzsche's Critique of Truth', *Philosophy and Phenomenological Research*, 52 (1992), 47–66. Those with an interest in Nietzsche's moral philosophy should consult Alexander Nehamas, *Nietzsche: Life as Literature* (Harvard University Press, 1987). There are two recent helpful discussions of Nietzsche's political and social thought: Bruce Detwiler, *Nietzsche and the Politics of Aristocratic Radicalism* (University of Chicago Press, 1990) and Mark Warren, *Nietzsche and Political Thought* (MIT Press, 1988). See also Peter Bergmann, *Nietzsche, 'the Last Unpolitical German'* (Indiana University Press, 1987). For an interesting discussion of some aspects of Nietzsche's legacy, see Steven E. Ascheim, *The Nietzsche Legacy in Germany 1890–1990* (University of California Press, 1992).

Note on the text

The text used for this translation is printed in the now standard edition of Nietzsche's works edited by Giorgio Colli and Mazzino Montinari (Berlin, de Gruyter, 1967–77). Their edition, and that of Peter Pütz (Munich, Goldmann, 1994), have been used in the preparation of the footnotes to this edition.

The Gay Science
('La gaya scienza')

This house is my own and here I dwell,
I've never aped nothing from no one
and – laugh at each master, mark me well,
who at himself has not poked fun.

Over my front door.

The title is a translation into German (in our edition, into English) of the Provençal subtitle. *Gaya scienza* ('joyful, cheerful, or gay science') was a term used by the troubadours in the twelfth to fourteenth centuries to refer to the art of poetry. In *Ecce Homo* Nietzsche writes that he has used the term *gaya scienza* here to designate the specific unity of 'singer, knight, and free spirit' which was characteristic of early Provençal culture.

Preface to the second edition

This book might need more than one preface; and in the end there would still be room for doubting whether someone who has not experienced something similar could, by means of prefaces, be brought closer to the *experiences* of this book. It seems to be written in the language of the wind that brings a thaw: it contains high spirits, unrest, contradiction, and April weather, so that one is constantly reminded of winter's nearness as well as of the *triumph* over winter that is coming, must come, perhaps has already come. . .Gratitude flows forth incessantly, as if that which was most unexpected had just happened – the gratitude of a convalescent – for *recovery* was what was most unexpected. 'Gay Science': this signifies the saturnalia[1] of a mind that has patiently resisted a terrible, long pressure – patiently, severely, coldly, without yielding, but also without hope – and is now all of a sudden attacked by hope, by hope for health, by the *intoxication* of recovery. Is it any wonder that in the process much that is unreasonable and foolish comes to light, much wanton tenderness, lavished even on problems that have a prickly hide, not made to be fondled and lured? This entire book is really nothing but an amusement after long privation and powerlessness, the jubilation of returning strength, of a reawakened faith in a tomorrow and a day after tomorrow, of a sudden sense and anticipation of a future, of impending adventures, of reopened seas, of goals that are permitted and believed in again. How many and what

---

[1] Roman winter festival at which usual bonds of social order were thrown off, social roles were reversed, etc.

sorts of things did not lie behind me then! This stretch of desert, exhaustion, loss of faith, icing-up in the midst of youth; this onset of dotage at the wrong time; this tyranny of pain surpassed still by the tyranny of a pride that refused the *conclusions* of pain – and conclusions are consolations; this radical seclusion as a self-defence against a pathologically clairvoyant contempt for humanity, this limitation in principle to what was bitter, harsh, painful to know, as prescribed by the *nausea* that had gradually developed from an incautious and excessively luxurious spiritual diet – one calls it romanticism – oh, who could re-experience all of this as I did? But if anyone could, he would surely pardon even more than a bit of foolishness, exuberance, 'gay science' – for example, the handful of songs that have been added to the book this time, songs in which a poet makes fun of all poets in a manner that is hard to forgive. Alas, it is not only the poets and their beautiful 'lyrical sentiments' on whom this resurrected author has to vent his malice: who knows what kind of victim he is looking for, what kind of monster will stimulate him to pardon it? *Incipit tragoedia*,[2] we read at the end of this suspiciously innocent book. Beware! Something utterly wicked and mischievous is being announced here: *incipit parodia*,[3] no doubt.

2

But let us leave Mr. Nietzsche: what is it to us that Mr Nietzsche has got well again?. . .A psychologist knows few questions as attractive as that concerning the relation between health and philosophy; and should he himself become ill, he will bring all of his scientific curiosity into the illness. For assuming that one is a person, one necessarily also has the philosophy of that person; but here there is a considerable difference. In some, it is their weaknesses that philosophize; in others, their riches and strengths. The former *need* their philosophy, be it as a prop, a sedative, medicine, redemption, elevation, or self-alienation; for the latter, it is only a beautiful luxury, in the best case the voluptuousness of a triumphant gratitude that eventually has to inscribe itself in cosmic capital letters on the heaven of concepts. In the former, more common case, however, when it is distress that philosophizes, as in all sick thinkers – and perhaps sick thinkers are in the majority in the history of

---

[2] 'the tragedy begins'
[3] 'the parody begins'

philosophy – what will become of the thought that is itself subjected to
the *pressure* of illness? This is the question that concerns the psychologist, and here an experiment is possible. Just like a traveller who resolves
to wake up at a certain hour and then calmly gives himself up to sleep,
so too we philosophers, should we become ill, temporarily surrender
with body and soul to the illness – we shut our eyes to ourselves, as it
were. And as the traveller knows that something is *not* asleep, something
that will count the hours and wake him up, we, too, know that the
decisive moment will find us awake, that something will then leap
forward and catch the mind *in the act*, i.e. in its weakness or repentance
or hardening or gloom, and whatever else the pathological states of the
mind are called that on healthy days are opposed by the *pride* of the
mind (for the old saying still holds: 'the proud mind, the peacock, and
the horse are the three proudest animals on earth'). After such self-
questioning, self-temptation, one acquires a subtler eye for all philosophizing to date; one is better than before at guessing the involuntary
detours, alleyways, resting places, and *sunning* places of thought to
which suffering thinkers are led and misled on account of their
suffering; one now knows where the sick *body* and its needs uncon-
sciously urge, push, and lure the mind – towards sun, stillness,
mildness, patience, medicine, balm in some sense. Every philosophy
that ranks peace above war, every ethic with a negative definition of
happiness, every metaphysics and physics that knows some *finale*, a final
state of some sort, every predominantly aesthetic or religious craving for
some Apart, Beyond, Outside, Above, permits the question whether it
was not illness that inspired the philosopher. The unconscious disguise
of physiological needs under the cloaks of the objective, ideal, purely
spiritual goes frighteningly far – and I have asked myself often enough
whether, on a grand scale, philosophy has been no more than an
interpretation of the body and a *misunderstanding of the body*. Behind the
highest value judgements that have hitherto guided the history of
thought are concealed misunderstandings of the physical constitution –
of individuals or classes or even whole races. All those bold lunacies of
metaphysics, especially answers to the question about the *value* of
existence, may always be considered first of all as symptoms of certain
bodies; and if such world affirmations or world negations lack altogether
any grain of significance when measured scientifically, they give the
historian and psychologist all the more valuable hints as symptoms

of the body, of its success or failure, its fullness, power and high-handedness in history, or of its frustrations, fatigues, impoverishments, its premonitions of the end, its will to an end. I am still waiting for a philosophical *physician* in the exceptional sense of the term – someone who has set himself the task of pursuing the problem of the total health of a people, time, race or of humanity – to summon the courage at last to push my suspicion to its limit and risk the proposition: what was at stake in all philosophizing hitherto was not at all 'truth' but rather something else – let us say health, future, growth, power, life. . .

3

– One might guess that I do not want to take my leave ungratefully from that time of severe illness whose profits I have not yet exhausted even today: I am well aware of the advantages that my erratic health gives me over all burly minds. A philosopher who has passed through many kinds of health, and keeps passing through them again and again, has passed through an equal number of philosophies; he simply *cannot* but translate his state every time into the most spiritual form and distance – this art of transfiguration just *is* philosophy. We philosophers are not free to separate soul from body as the common people do; we are even less free to separate soul from spirit. We are no thinking frogs, no objectifying and registering devices with frozen innards – we must constantly give birth to our thoughts out of our pain and maternally endow them with all that we have of blood, heart, fire, pleasure, passion, agony, conscience, fate, and disaster. Life – to us, that means constantly transforming all that we are into light and flame, and also all that wounds us; we simply *can do* no other. And as for illness: are we not almost tempted to ask whether we can do without it at all? Only great pain is the liberator of the spirit, as the teacher of *the great suspicion* that turns every U into an X,[4] a real, proper X, that is, the penultimate one before the final one. Only great pain, that long, slow pain that takes its time and in which we are burned, as it were, over green wood, forces us philosophers to descend into our ultimate depths and put aside all trust, everything good-natured, veiling, mild, average – things in which formerly we may have found our humanity. I doubt that such pain

---

[4] 'to make a U out to be an X' is a standard German expression for trying to pretend that one thing is something completely different.

makes us 'better' – but I know that it makes us *deeper*. Whether we learn to pit our pride, our scorn, our willpower against it, like the savage who, however badly tormented, repays his tormentor with the malice of his tongue; or whether we withdraw before pain into the Oriental Nothingness – called Nirvana – into mute, rigid, deaf self-surrender, self-forgetting, self-extinction: one emerges from such dangerous exercises in self-mastery as a different person, with a few more question marks, above all with the *will* henceforth to question further, more deeply, severely, harshly, evilly, and quietly than one had previously questioned. The trust in life is gone: life itself has become a *problem*. Yet one should not jump to the conclusion that this necessarily makes one sullen. Even love of life is still possible – only one loves differently. It is like the love for a woman who gives us doubts. . .But the attraction of everything problematic, the delight in an X, is so great in highly spiritual, spiritualized people such as these that this delight flares up like bright embers again and again over all the distress of what is problematic, over all the danger of uncertainty, and even over the jealousy of the lover. We know a new happiness. . .

4

Finally, lest what is most important remain unsaid: from such abysses, from such severe illness, also from the illness of severe suspicion, one returns *newborn*, having shed one's skin, more ticklish and malicious, with a more delicate taste for joy, with a more tender tongue for all good things, with merrier senses, joyful with a more dangerous second innocence, more childlike, and at the same time a hundred times subtler than one had ever been before. How repulsive enjoyment is to us now, that crude, muggy, brown enjoyment as understood by those who enjoy it, our 'educated', our rich, and our rulers! How maliciously we nowadays listen to the great fairground boom-boom with which the 'educated person' and urbanite today allows art, books and music – aided by spirituous beverages – to rape him for 'forms of spiritual enjoyment'! How the theatrical cry of passion now hurts our ears; that whole romantic uproar and tumult of the senses that is loved by the educated mob together with its aspirations towards the sublime, the elevated, the distorted, how foreign it has become to our taste! No, if we convalescents still need art, it is *another kind* of art – a mocking, light, fleeting, divinely untroubled, divinely artificial art that, like a bright flame, blazes into an unclouded sky! Above all: an art for artists, only for artists! In addition we will know better what is first and foremost needed *for that*: cheerfulness – any cheerfulness, my friends! As artists, too, we will know this – I would like to prove it. There are some things we now know too well, we knowing ones: oh, how we nowadays learn as artists to forget well, to be good at *not* knowing! And as for our future, one will hardly find us again on the paths of those Egyptian youths[5] who make temples unsafe at night, embrace statues, and want by all means to unveil, uncover, and put into a bright light whatever is kept concealed for good reasons. No, we have grown sick of this bad taste, this will to truth, to 'truth at any price', this youthful madness in the love of truth: we are too experienced, too serious, too jovial, too burned, too deep for that. . .We no longer believe that truth remains truth when one pulls off the veil; we have lived too much to believe this. Today we consider it a matter of decency not to wish to see everything naked, to be present everywhere, to understand and 'know' everything. 'Is it true that God is everywhere?' a little girl asked her mother; 'I find that indecent!' – a hint for philosophers! One should have more respect for the *bashfulness* with which nature has hidden behind riddles and iridescent uncertainties. Perhaps truth is a woman who has grounds for not showing her grounds? Perhaps her name is – to speak Greek – *Baubo*?[6]. . .Oh, those Greeks! They knew how to *live*: what is needed for that is to stop bravely at the surface, the fold, the skin; to worship appearance, to believe in shapes, tones, words – in the whole Olympus of appearance!

[5] Plutarch reports that in a temple in the Egyptian city of Sais, there was a veiled statue of the goddess Isis with the inscription: 'I am everything that is, that was, and that will be, and no mortal has <ever> raised my veil.' In his *Critique of Judgement* (1790, § 49) Kant says that this inscription is the 'perhaps most sublime thing ever said'. In a short historical essay 'Die Sendung Moses' the German poet and dramatist Friedrich Schiller (1759–1805) speculates on a possible influence of this cult on Moses and thus on the origin of monotheism. Schiller also wrote a poem entitled 'Das Verschleierte Bild zu Sais' which told of an Egyptian youth who was especially eager to know The Truth. One night he broke into the temple and violated the prohibition by lifting the veil, but when found the next morning, he could not report what he had seen and died an 'early death'. The Romantic poet Novalis (1772–1801) gives two further variants (1798–9). In the first the youth left the young woman he loved, Rosenblütchen, to go in search of wisdom, truth, etc. When he arrived at the temple he fell asleeep and dreamed that when he lifted the veil of the statue 'Rosenblütchen sank into his arms'. In the second variant, when he lifted the veil, he saw himself. See also below, § 57.

[6] When the goddess Demeter was grieving for the abduction of her daughter by Hades, god of the underworld, the witch Baubo made her laugh again for the first time by lifting her skirts and exposing herself.

Those Greeks were superficial – *out of profundity!* And is not this precisely what we are coming back to, we daredevils of the spirit who have climbed the highest and most dangerous peak of current thought and looked around from up there, looked *down* from up there? Are we not just in this respect – Greeks? Worshippers of shapes, tones, words? And therefore – artists?

Ruta near Genoa
Autumn, 1886

'Joke, Cunning, and Revenge'
Prelude in German Rhymes

1. Invitation

Dare to taste my fare, dear diner!
Come tomorrow it tastes finer
and day after even good!
If you still want more – I'll make it,
from past inspiration take it,
turning food for thought to food.

2. My Happiness

Since I grew weary of the search
I taught myself to find instead.
Since cross winds caused my ship to lurch
I sail with all winds straight ahead.

'Scherz, List, und Rache' is the title of a libretto written by Goethe and set to music by Peter Gast, Nietzsche's friend and disciple/secretary. The title itself, like the subtitle 'Prelude in German Rhymes', foreshadows the musical playfulness to be found both in the poems and in *The Gay Science*; it also voices the hope that readers will recognize in the German language a medium of grace and style, as seen for example in the writings of Goethe and Nietzsche. *Scherz, List und Rache* was not set to music in the 1780s, though Goethe had intended it for a composer, and he published it in 1790 with his other works. He had endeavoured in the 1780s, after his Italian journey, to reform the German comic opera in the direction of the Italian *opera buffa*.

3. Undaunted

Where you stand, there dig deep!
Below you lies the well!
Let obscurantists wail and weep:
'Below is always – hell!'

4. Dialogue

A. Was I ill? Have I recovered?
   Has my doctor been discovered?
   How have I forgotten all?
B. Now I know you have recovered:
   Healthy is who can't recall.

5. To the Virtuous

Our virtues too should step lively to and fro:
Like the verses of Homer, they have to come *and go*!

6. Worldly Wisdom

Stay not where the lowlands are!
Climb not into the sky!
The world looks best by far
when viewed from halfway high.

7. Vademecum – Vadetecum[1]

My way and language speak to you,
you follow me, pursue me too?
To thine own self and way be true:
Thus follow me, but gently do!

8. On the Third Shedding

Already cracks and breaks my skin,
my appetite unslaking
is fuelled by earth I've taken in:

---

[1] *Vademecum* is Latin for 'go with me', and refers to a book one carries all the time. *Vadetecum* is Nietzsche's improvement on the idea: 'go with yourself'.

This snake for earth is aching.
Among the stones and grass I wear
a path from fen to firth,
to eat what's always been my fare
you, my snake food, you my earth.

9. My Roses

Yes! My joy – it wants to gladden – ,
every joy wants so to gladden!
Would you pluck my rose and sadden?

You must crouch on narrow ledges,
prop yourself on ropes and wedges,
prick yourself on thorny hedges!

For my joy – it loves to madden!
For my joy – is malice laden!
Would you pluck my rose and sadden?

10. The Scornful One

Much do I let fall and spill,
thus I'm scornful, you malign.
One who drinks from cups too full will
often let much fall and spill – ,
yet never think to blame the wine.

11. The Proverb Speaks

Sharp and mild, dull and keen,
well known and strange, dirty and clean,
where both the fool and wise are seen:
All this am I, have ever been, –
in me dove, snake and swine convene!

12. To a Friend of Light

If you want to spare your eyes and your mind,
follow the sun from the shadows behind.

13. For Dancers

Slipp'ry ice
is paradise
as long as dancing will suffice.

14. The Good Man

Better an enmity cut from one block
than friendship held together by glue.

15. Rust

Rust must be added: sharpness goes unsung!
Else they will always say: 'He is too young!'

16. Upward

'How do I best get to the top of this hill?'
'Climb it, don't think it, and maybe you will.'

17. Motto of A Brute

Never beg! It's whining I dread!
Take, I beg you, just take instead!

18. Narrow Souls

It's narrow souls that I despise;
not good, not evil, not my size.

19. The Involuntary Seducer

He shot an empty word into the blue
to pass the time – and downed a woman too.

20. Consider This

A twofold pain is easier to bear
than one pain: care to take a dare?

21. *Against Arrogance*

Don't let your ego swell too much,
a bubble bursts with just a touch.

22. *Man and Female*

'Rob yourself the female, who to your heart appeals!' –
So thinks a man; but she won't rob, a woman only steals.

23. *Interpretation*

If I read me, then I read into me:
I can't construe myself objectively.
But he who climbs consuming his own might
bears me with him unto the brighter light.

24. *Medication for Pessimists*[2]

You whine that nothing pleases you?
Still pouting, friend, and must you mutter?
I hear you curse, and shout and sputter –
it breaks my heart and patience too!
Come with me, friend! A nice fat toad,
if swallowed voluntarily
with eyes closed and summarily –
might lessen your dyspeptic load.

25. *Request*

I know another person's thought
and who I am, I know that not.
My vision is too close to me –
I am not what I saw and see.
I'd use myself more perfectly
if I could move away from me.
Yet not so distant as my foe!
My closest friend's too far off, no –

---

[2] Nietzsche's inspiration for the toad as medicine derives from a maxim by Chamfort, to the effect that a toad ingested each morning will make the rest of the day taste better.

give me instead the middle ground!
Do you surmise what I propound?

26. *My Hardness*

I must leave by a hundred stairs,
I must ascend though I hear your cares:
'You are hard: Are we made of stone?'
I must leave by a hundred stairs,
And being a stair appeals to none.

27. *The Wanderer*

'The path ends! Abyss and deathly silence loom!'
You wanted this! Your will strayed to its doom!
Now wanderer, stand! Be keen and cool as frost!
Believe in danger now and you – are lost.

28. *Consolation for Beginners*

See the child, with pigs she's lying,
helpless, face as white as chalk!
Crying only, only crying –
will she ever learn to walk?
Don't give up! Stop your sighing,
soon she's dancing 'round the clock!
Once her own two legs are trying,
she'll stand on her head and mock.

29. *Stellar Egotism*

If I, round barrel that I am,
did not roll 'round me like a cam,
how could I bear, and not catch fire,
to the chase the sun as I desire?

30. *The Closest One*

The closest one from me I bar:
Away and up with him, and far!
How else could he become my star?

31. The Disguised Saint

Joy too great you are concealing,
you engage in dev'lish dealing,
devil's wit and devil's dress.
But no use! Your eye's revealing
piety and holiness!

32. The Bound Man

A. He stands and hears: what's wrong, he's thinking?
   What sound provokes his heart to sinking?
   What was it hurled him to the ground?
B. Like all who once in chains were bound,
   He hears around him – iron clinking.

33. The Solitary One

Despised by me are following and leading.
Commanding? Even worse to me than heeding!
Who does not scare *himself* can frighten no one:
The one who causes fear can lead another.
But just to lead myself is too much bother!
I love, as do the sea and forest creatures,
to lose myself a while in nature's features,
to hide away and brood in secret places
until, lured home at last from distant traces,
my self-seduction lets me see – my features.

34. Seneca et hoc genus omne[3]

They write and write their desiccat-
ing learned la-di-da-di,
as if *primum scribere*,
deinde philosophari.

35. Ice

Yes! At times I do make ice:
Useful is ice for digesting!

[3] Seneca (Roman philosopher) and his lot. The Latin: 'First write, then philosophize.'

If you had much for digesting,
oh how you would love my ice!

36. Juvenilia[4]

My old wisdom's A and O
sounded here: what did I hear?
Now it does not strike me so,
just the tired Ah! and Oh!
that youth inspired fills my ear.

37. Caution

Into that region trav'lers must not go:
And if you're smart, be cautious even so!
They lure and love you till you're torn apart:
They're halfwit zealots – : witless from the heart!

38. The Pious One Speaks

God loves us *because* he created us!
'Man created God!' – respond the jaded.
And yet should not love what he created?
Should even deny it *because* he made it?
Such cloven logic is limping and baited.

39. In Summer[5]

Beneath the sweat of our own brow
we have to eat our bread?
If you sweat, eat nothing now,
the wise physician said.
The Dog Star winks: what does it know?
What says its fiery winking?
Beneath the sweat of our own brow
our wine we should be drinking!

---

[4] Alpha and Omega are the first and last letters of the Greek alphabet, hence proverbially the 'alpha and omega' are said to comprise everything.
[5] Genesis 3:19: 'In the sweat of thy face shalt thou eat bread.'

40. *Without Envy*

His gaze is envyless: and him you praise?
No thirst for your esteem perturbs his gaze;
he has the eagle's vision for the long view,
it's stars he sees, just stars – he looks beyond you!

41. *Heracliteanism*

Happiness on earth, friends,
only stems from war!
Powder smoke, in fact, mends
friendship even more!
One in three all friends are:
Brothers in distress,
equals facing rivals,
free men – facing death!

42. *Principle of the All-Too-Refined*

Rather on your tiptoes stand
than crawling on all fours!
Rather through the keyhole scanned
than gazed through open doors!

43. *Admonition*

It's fame on which your mind is set?
Then heed what I say:
Before too long prepare to let
honor slip away.

44. *The Well-Grounded One*[6]

A scholar I? I've no such skill! –
I'm merely *grave* – just heavy set!
I fall and fall and fall until
I to the bottom get.

---

[6] *Gründlich* in German means thorough, based on *Grund* (ground).

45. *Forever*

'Today I come, I choose today' –
think all who come and mean to stay.
Though all the world may speculate:
'You come too early! Come too late!'

46. *Judgements of the Weary*

The sun is cursed by all men jaded;
to them the worth of trees is – shaded!

47. *Going Down*[7]

'He sinks, he falls now' – thus resumes your mocking;
in truth, look closely: Down to you he's walking!
His super-joy became too much to bear,
his super-light dispels your gloomy air.

48. *Against the Laws*

From now on time hangs by a hair
around my neck, suspended there:
from now on stars shine randomly,
sun, rooster crow, and shadow flee,
whatever brought time to my mind
that now is mute and deaf and blind: –
All nature's still in me, it balks
at ticking laws and ticking clocks.

49. *The Wise Man Speaks*

Unknown to folks, yet useful to the crowd,
I drift along my way, now sun, now cloud
and always I'm above this crowd!

---

[7] *Niedergang* means decline, but it is ambiguous because it is formed from *nieder* (down) and the past participle of *gehen* (to go). Compare Zarathustra's 'going under' in the prologue of *Thus Spoke Zarathustra*.

50. Lost His Head

Now she has wit – what led her to this find?
Because of her a man had lost his mind.
His head was rich before this misadventure:
His head went straight to hell – no! no! to her!

51. Pious Wishes[8]

'Keys should all just disappear,
lost from stem to stern,
and in keyholes far and near
skeletons should turn!'
Thus thinks when the day is done
each who is – a skeleton.

52. Writing With One's Foot

I do not write with hand alone:
My foot does writing of its own.
Firm, free, and bold my feet engage
in running over field and page.

53. 'Human, All Too Human.' A Book[9]

When looking back you're sad and not robust,
you trust the future when yourself you trust:
Oh bird, do you belong to eagle's brood?
Are you Minerva's favourite hoot hoot?

54. To My Reader

Strong teeth and good digestion too –
this I wish thee!
And once my book's agreed with you,
then surely you'll agree with me!

---

8 *Dietrich* in German is a skeleton key, or combination key capable of opening any lock. It is also a common given name for males.

9 Minerva, Roman goddess of wisdom, the arts and crafts, and medicine, was identified with the Greek goddess Athene, whose attribute was the sacred and wise owl. *Uhu* is the German word for eagle-owl, as well as the sound (hooting) made by owls.

55. The Realistic Painter

'To all of nature true!' – How does he plan?
Would nature fit an image *made by man*?
The smallest piece of world is infinite! –
He ends up painting that which he *sees fit*.
And what does he see fit? Paint what he *can*!

56. Poet's Vanity

I'll find wood, just give me substance
strong enough to bind like glue!
Cramming sense in rhyme is nonsense
worthy of a boast – or two!

57. Choosy Taste

Were it my choice to exercise,
I know that I would opt for
a cosy place in Paradise:
Better still – outside the door!

58. The Crooked Nose[10]

Your nose projects, so grand and plump,
into the land, its nostrils pump –
thus hornless rhino, lacking grace
you fall, proud mortal, on your face!
And that's the way it always goes:
Straight pride alongside crooked nose.

59. The Pen Scribbles

My pen, it scribbles: this is hell!
Have I been damned to have to scribble? –
I dip it boldly in the well
and write broad streams of inky drivel.
See how it flows, so full, so pure!
See how each thing I try succeeds!

---

[10] *Nashorn* means rhinoceros, from *Nase* (nose) and *Horn*.

The text's not lucid, to be sure –
So what? What I write no one reads.

60. Higher Men

He climbs on high – him we should praise!
But that one comes from high up always!
Immune to praise he lives his days,
he *is* the sun's rays!

61. The Sceptic Speaks

Your life is halfway spent,
the clock hand moves, your soul now quakes with fear!
Long roaming forth it went
and searched but nothing found – and wavers here?

Your life is halfway spent:
In pain and error how the hours did crawl!
Why can you not relent? –
Just this I seek – some reason for it all!

62. Ecce Homo

Yes! I know now whence I came!
Unsatiated like a flame
my glowing ember squanders me.
Light to all on which I seize,
ashen everything I leave:
Flame am I most certainly!

63. Stellar Morals

Ordained to move as planets do,
what matters, star, the dark to you?

Roll blithely through our human time!
Beyond its wretched mis'ry climb!

The furthest world deserves your shine:
For you compassion is a crime!

One law applies to you: be thine!

Book One

I

The teachers of the purpose of existence. – Whether I regard human beings with a good or with an evil eye, I always find them engaged in a single task, each and every one of them: to do what benefits the preservation of the human race. Not from a feeling of love for the race, but simply because within them nothing is older, stronger, more inexorable and invincible than this instinct – because this instinct constitutes *the essence* of our species and herd. One might quickly enough, with the usual myopia from five steps away, divide one's neighbours into useful and harmful, good and evil; but on a large-scale assessment, upon further reflection on the whole, one grows suspicious of this tidying and separating and finally abandons it. Even the most harmful person may actually be the most useful when it comes to the preservation of the species; for he nurtures in himself or through his effects on others drives without which humanity would long since have become feeble or rotten. Hatred, delight in the misfortunes of others, the lust to rob and rule, and whatever else is called evil: all belong to the amazing economy of the preservation of the species, an economy which is certainly costly, wasteful, and on the whole most foolish – but still *proven* to have preserved our race so far. I no longer know whether you, my dear fellow man and neighbour, are even *capable* of living in a way which is damaging to the species, i.e. 'unreasonably' and 'badly'. What *might* have harmed the species may have become extinct many thousands of years ago and may by now belong to the things that are no longer possible even for God. Pursue your best or your worst desires, and above all, perish! In both cases you are probably still in some way a promoter and benefactor of humanity and are thus entitled to your eulogists – as well as to your mockers! But you will never find someone who could completely mock you, the individual, even in your best qualities, someone who could bring home to you as far as truth allows your boundless, fly- and frog-like wretchedness! To laugh at oneself as one would have to laugh in order to laugh *from the whole truth* – for that, not even the best have had enough sense of truth, and the most gifted have had far too little genius! Perhaps even laughter still has a future – when the proposition 'The species is everything, an individual is always nothing' has become part of humanity and this ultimate liberation and irresponsibility is accessible to everyone at all times. Perhaps laughter will then have formed an alliance with wisdom; perhaps only 'gay science' will remain. At present, things are still quite different; at present, the comedy of existence has not yet 'become conscious' of itself; at present, we still live in the age of tragedy, in the age of moralities and religions. What is the meaning of the ever-new appearance of these founders of moralities and religions, of these instigators of fights about moral valuations, these teachers of pangs of conscience and religious wars? What is the meaning of these heroes on this stage? For these have been the heroes thus far; and everything else, even if at times it was all that we could see and was far too near, has always served only to set the stage for these heroes, whether as machinery and backdrop or in the role of confidant and servant. (The poets, for example, were always the servants of some kind of morality.) It is obvious that these tragedies, too, work in the interest of the *species*, even if they should believe that they are working in the interest of God, as God's emissaries. They, too, promote the life of the species *by promoting the faith in life*. 'Life is worth living', each of them shouts, 'there is something to life, there is something behind life, beneath it; beware!' This drive, which rules the highest as well as the basest of human beings – the drive for the preservation of the species – erupts from time to time as reason and passion of mind; it is then surrounded by a resplendent retinue of reasons and tries with all its might to make us forget that fundamentally it is drive, instinct, stupidity, lack of reasons. Life *ought to* be loved, *because* –! Man *ought to* advance himself and his neighbour, *because* –! What names all these Oughts and Becauses have been given and may yet be given in the future! The ethical teacher makes his appearance as the teacher of the purpose of existence in order that what happens necessarily and always, by itself and without a purpose, shall henceforth seem to be done for a purpose and strike man as reason and an ultimate commandment; to this end he invents a second, different existence and takes by means of his new mechanics the old, ordinary existence off its old, ordinary hinges. To be sure, in no way does he want us to *laugh* at existence, or at ourselves – or at him; for him, an individual is always an individual, something first and last and tremendous; for him there are no species, sums, or zeroes. Foolish and fanciful as his inventions and valuations may be, badly as he may misjudge the course of nature and deny its conditions – and all ethical systems hitherto have been so foolish and contrary to nature that humanity would have perished from every one had it gained power over humanity – all the same! Every time 'the hero' appeared on stage, something new was attained: the gruesome counterpart of laughter, that profound shock that many individuals feel at the thought: 'Yes, living is worth it! Yes, I am worthy of living!' Life and I and you and all of us became *interesting* to ourselves once again for a while. There is no denying that *in the long run* each of these great teachers of a purpose was vanquished by laughter, reason and nature: the brief tragedy always changed and returned into the eternal comedy of existence, and the 'waves of uncountable laughter' – to cite Aeschylus[1] – must in the end also come crashing down on the greatest of these tragedians. Despite all this corrective laughter, human nature on the whole has surely been altered by the recurring emergence of such teachers of the purpose of existence – *it has acquired one additional need*, the need for the repeated appearance of such teachers and such teachings of a 'purpose'. Man has gradually become a fantastic animal that must fulfil one condition of existence more than any other animal: man *must* from time to time believe he knows *why* he exists; his race cannot thrive without a periodic trust in life – without faith in the *reason in life*! And ever again the human race will from time to time decree: 'There is something one is absolutely forbidden henceforth to laugh at.' And the most cautious friend of man will add: 'Not only laughter and gay wisdom but also the tragic, with all its sublime unreason, belongs to the means and necessities of the preservation of the species.' And therefore! Therefore! Therefore! Oh, do you understand me, my brothers? Do you understand this new law of ebb and flood? We, too, have our time!

2

Intellectual conscience. – I keep having the same experience and keep resisting it anew each time; I do not want to believe it although I can grasp it as with my hands: *the great majority lacks an intellectual conscience* – indeed, it has often seemed to me as if someone requiring such a conscience would be as lonely in the most densely populated cities as he would be in the desert. Everyone looks at you with strange

---

[1] A mistranslation of lines 89–90 of *Prometheus Bound* formerly ascribed to the fifth-century (BC) Athenian dramatist Aeschylus. The lines actually read: 'countless laughter of the sea waves'.

eyes and goes on handling their scales, calling this good and that evil; nobody as much as blushes when you notice that their weights are underweight – nor do they become indignant with you; perhaps they laugh at your doubts. I mean: *to the great majority* it is not contemptible to believe this or that and to live accordingly *without* first becoming aware of the final and most certain reasons pro and con, and without even troubling themselves about such reasons afterwards: the most gifted men and the noblest women still belong to this 'great majority'. But what are goodheartedness, refinement, and genius to me when the person possessing these virtues tolerates slack feelings in his believing and judging and when he does not consider *the desire for certainty* to be his inmost craving and deepest need – as that which separates the higher human beings from the lower! I discovered in certain pious people a hatred of reason and I was well disposed towards them for that: at least this betrayed their bad intellectual conscience! But to stand in the midst of this *rerum concordia discors*[2] and the whole marvellous uncertainty and ambiguity of existence *without questioning*, without trembling with the craving and rapture of questioning, without at least hating the person who questions, perhaps even being faintly amused by him – that is what I feel to be *contemptible*, and this is the feeling I look for first in anyone. Some folly keeps persuading me that every person has this feeling, simply as human. That is my type of injustice.

3

Noble and common. – For common natures all noble, magnanimous feelings appear to be inexpedient and therefore initially incredible: they give a wink when they hear of such things and seem to want to say, 'Surely there must be some advantage involved; one cannot see through every wall' – they are suspicious of the noble person, as if he were furtively seeking his advantage. If they become all too clearly convinced of the absence of selfish intentions and gains, they view the noble person as a kind of fool: they despise him in his pleasure and laugh at the sparkle in his eye. 'How could one enjoy being at a disadvantage? How could one want with open eyes to be disadvantaged? Some disease of reason must be linked to the noble affection' – thus they think and look

---

[2] 'the discordant harmony of things'; from Horace, *Epistles* I.12.19

disparagingly, the way they disparage the pleasure that a madman derives from his fixed idea. What distinguishes the common nature is that it unflinchingly keeps sight of its advantage, and that this thought of purpose and advantage is even stronger than its strongest drives; not to allow these drives to lead it astray to perform inexpeditious acts – that is its wisdom and self-esteem. In comparison, the higher nature is more *unreasonable* – for the noble, magnanimous, and self-sacrificing person does in fact succumb to his drives; and in his best moments, his reason *pauses*. An animal that protects its young at the risk of its own life or during the mating period follows the female unto death does not think of danger and death; its reason likewise pauses because the pleasure in its brood or in the female and the fear of being deprived of this pleasure dominate it totally; the animal becomes stupider than it usually is – just like the person who is noble and magnanimous. Such persons have several feelings of pleasure and displeasure so strong that they reduce the intellect to silence or to servitude: at that point their heart displaces their head, and one speaks thenceforth of 'passion'. (Occasionally we also encounter the opposite, the 'reversal of passion', as it were; for example, somebody once laid his hand on Fontenelle's heart and said, 'What you have here, my dear sir, is also brains.'[3]) The unreason or odd reason (*Unvernunft oder Quervernunft*) of passion is what the common type despises in the noble, especially when this passion is directed at objects whose value seems quite fantastic and arbitrary. He is annoyed by the person who succumbs to the passion of the belly, but at least he comprehends the appeal that plays the tyrant in this case; but he cannot comprehend how anyone could, for example, risk health and honour for the sake of a passion for knowledge. The higher nature's taste is for exceptions, for things that leave most people cold and seem to lack sweetness; the higher nature has a singular value standard. Moreover, it usually believes that the idiosyncrasy of its taste is *not* a singular value standard; rather, it posits its values and disvalues as generally valid and so becomes incomprehensible and impractical. It is very rare that a higher nature has enough reason left over to understand and treat commonplace people as what they are; above all, it believes in its own passion as something that is present in everyone but

---

[3] French writer of fables (1657–1757); his most important work is the *Dialogues of the Dead* (1683) to which Nietzsche refers in § 94.

concealed, and in this belief it is full of ardour and eloquence. Now when such exceptional people do not themselves feel like exceptions, how can they ever understand the common natures and arrive at a proper estimate of the rule! – and so they, too, speak of the stupidity, inexpedience, and fancifulness of humanity, stunned that the world is taking such an insane course and that it will not commit itself to that which 'is needful'. – This is the eternal injustice of the noble.

4

What preserves the species. – The strongest and most evil spirits have so far done the most to advance humanity: time and again they rekindled the dozing passions – every ordered society puts the passions to sleep – , time and again they reawakened the sense of comparison, of contradiction, of delight in what is new, daring, unattempted; they forced men to pit opinion against opinion, ideal model against ideal model. Mostly by force of arms, by toppling boundary stones, by violating pieties – but also by means of new religions and moralities! In every teacher and preacher of what is new we find the same 'mischief' that makes conquerors infamous, even if its expression is subtler and does not instantly set the muscles in motion and for just that reason does not make one as infamous! What is new, however, is under all circumstances *evil*, being that which wants to conquer, to overthrow the old boundary stones and pieties; and only what is old is good! In every age the good men are those who bury the old thoughts deeply and make them bear fruit – the farmers of the spirit. But that land is eventually exhausted, and the ploughshare of evil must come time and again. Nowadays there is a thoroughly erroneous moral theory which is celebrated especially in England: it claims that judgements of 'good' and 'evil' sum up experiences of what is 'expedient' and 'inexpedient'; that what is called good preserves the species while what is called evil harms it. In truth, however, the evil drives are just as expedient, species-preserving, and indispensable as the good ones – they just have a different function.

5

Unconditional duties. – All persons who feel that they need the strongest words and sounds, the most eloquent gestures and postures, in order to be effective *at all* – revolutionary politicians, socialists, preachers of repentance with or without Christianity, all of whom refuse to accept semi-successes: they all speak of 'duties', and indeed always of duties with an unconditional character – without such duties they would have no right to their great pathos; they know that quite well! So they reach for moral philosophies that preach some categorical imperative, or they ingest a goodly piece of religion, as Mazzini[4] did, for example. Because they want the unconditional confidence of others, they first need unconditional confidence in themselves on the basis of some ultimate, indisputable and inherently sublime commandment, and they want to feel like and pass themselves off as its servants and instruments. Here we have the most natural and usually very influential opponents of moral enlightenment and scepticism; but they are rare. On the other hand, a very comprehensive class of these opponents can be found wherever self-interest teaches submission while reputation and honour seem to prohibit it. Whoever feels his dignity violated by the thought of being the *instrument* of a prince or party or sect or even a financial power – say, as the descendant of an old, proud family – but still wants to or must be this instrument before himself and before the public, needs poignant principles that can be mouthed any time, principles of an unconditional 'ought' to which one may openly submit and be seen to have submitted without shame. All refined servility clings to the categorical imperative and is the mortal enemy of those who want to deprive duty of its unconditional character: that is what decency demands of them, and not only decency.

6

Loss of dignity. – Reflection has lost all its dignity of form: we have made a laughing-stock of the ceremony and solemn gestures of reflection, and couldn't stand an old-style wise man. We think too fast, while on our way somewhere, while walking or in the midst of all sorts of business, even when thinking of the most serious things; we need little preparation, not even much silence: it is as if we carried around in our heads an unstoppable machine that keeps working even under the most unfavourable circumstances. Formerly, one could tell just by looking at a person

[4] Italian liberal (1805–72).

that he wanted to think – it was probably a rare occurrence! – , that he now wanted to become wiser and was preparing himself for a thought: one would set one's face as for prayer and stop walking; yes, one stood still for hours on the street once the thought 'arrived' – on one or two legs. The dignity of the matter required it!

7

Something for the industrious. – Anyone who now wishes to make a study of moral matters opens up for himself an immense field of work. All kinds of passions have to be thought through separately, pursued separately through ages, peoples, great and small individuals; their entire reason and all their evaluations and modes of illuminating things must be revealed! So far, all that has given colour to existence still lacks a history: where could you find a history of love, of avarice, of envy, of conscience, of piety, of cruelty? Even a comparative history of law or even of punishment is so far lacking entirely. Has anyone done research on the different ways of dividing up the day or of the consequences of a regular schedule of work, festivals, and the rest? Do we know the moral effects of foods? Is there a philosophy of nutrition? (The incessantly erupting clamour for and against vegetarianism proves that there is still no such philosophy!) Has anyone collected people's experiences of living together – in monasteries, for example? Has anyone depicted the dialectic of marriage and friendship? The customs of scholars, businessmen, artists, artisans – have they found their thinkers? There is so much in them to think about! Everything that humans have viewed until now as the 'conditions of their existence' and all the reason, passion, and superstition that such a view involves – has this been researched exhaustively? To observe how differently the human drives have grown and still could grow depending on the moral climate – that alone involves too much work for even the most industrious; it would require whole generations, and generations of scholars who would collaborate systematically, to exhaust the points of view and the material. The same applies to the demonstration of the reasons for the variety of moral climates (*'why* does the sun of one fundamental moral judgement and primary value-standard shine here – and another one there?'). Yet another new project would be to determine the erroneousness of all these reasons and the whole essence of moral judgements to date. If all these jobs were done, the most delicate question of all would emerge in the foreground: whether science is able to *furnish* goals of action after having proved that it can take such goals away and annihilate them; and then an experimenting would be in order, in which every kind of heroism could find satisfaction – an experimenting that might last for centuries and eclipse all the great projects and sacrifices of history to date. So far, science has not yet built its cyclops-buildings;[5] but the time for that will come, too.

8

Unconscious virtues. – All qualities of a person of which he is conscious – and especially those he supposes to be visible and plain to others also – are subject to laws of development entirely different from those qualities which are unknown or badly known to him, which conceal themselves by means of their subtlety even from the eye of a rather subtle observer and which know how to hide as if behind nothing at all. This might be compared to the subtle sculptures on the scales of reptiles: it would be a mistake to take them for ornaments or weapons, since one sees them only with a microscope, i.e. with an artificially sharpened eye, which similar animals for whom they might signify something like ornaments or weapons simply lack. Our visible moral qualities, and especially those that we *believe* to be visible, take their course; and the invisible ones, which have the same names but are neither ornaments nor weapons with regard to others, *also take their course*: probably a totally different one, with lines and subtleties and sculptures that might amuse a god with a divine microscope. For example, we have our diligence, our ambition, our acuteness – all the world knows about them – and in addition, we probably also have *our* industry, *our* ambition, *our* acuteness; but for these reptile scales, no microscope has yet been invented! At this point the friends of instinctive morality will say: 'Bravo! At least he considers unconscious virtues to be possible – and that's enough for us.' Oh, how little you are satisfied with!

---

[5] The Cyclopes, in ancient mythology, were one-eyed giants. Though represented in Homer as wild creatures, they elsewhere appear as workmen of superhuman power, and were credited with building massive ancient fortifications such as those of Tiryns.

9

Our eruptions. – Countless things that humanity acquired in earlier stages, but so feebly and embryonically that no one could tell that they had been acquired, suddenly emerge into the light much later, perhaps after centuries; meanwhile they have become strong and ripe. Some ages seem to lack completely some talent or virtue, just as some people do: but just wait for their children and grandchildren, if you have time to wait – they bring to light the inner qualities of their grandfathers, the qualities that their grandfathers themselves did not know about. Often it is already the son that betrays his father: the father understands himself better once he has a son. All of us harbour in ourselves hidden gardens and plantations; and, to use another metaphor, we are all growing volcanoes approaching their hour of eruption; how near or distant that is, of course, nobody knows, not even the good Lord.

10

A kind of atavism. – I prefer to understand the rare human beings of an age as suddenly appearing, late ghosts of past cultures and their powers: as atavisms of a people and its mores – that way one can really *understand* something about them! They now seem strange, rare, extraordinary; and whoever feels these powers in himself must nurse, defend, honor, and cultivate them against another world that resists them: and so he becomes either a great human being or a mad and eccentric one, unless he perishes too soon. Formerly, these same qualities were common and therefore considered ordinary: they weren't distinguishing. They were perhaps demanded, presupposed; it was impossible to become great through them, if only because there was also no danger of becoming mad and lonely through them. It is principally in the generations and castes that *conserve* a people that we find such recrudescences of old instincts, while such atavism is highly improbable where races, habits, and valuations change too rapidly. For tempo is as significant a power in the development of peoples as in music: in our case, what is absolutely necessary is an *andante* of development, as the tempo of a passionate and slow spirit – and that is after all what the spirit of conservative generations is like.

11

Consciousness (*Bewußtsein*)[6] – Consciousness (*Bewußtheit*) is the latest development of the organic, and hence also its most unfinished and unrobust feature. Consciousness gives rise to countless mistakes that lead an animal or human being to perish sooner than necessary, 'beyond destiny', as Homer puts it.[7] If the preserving alliance of the instincts were not so much more powerful, if it did not serve on the whole as a regulator, humanity would have to perish with open eyes of its misjudging and its fantasizing, of its lack of thoroughness and its incredulity – in short, of its consciousness; or rather, without the instincts, humanity would long have ceased to exist! Before a function is fully developed and mature, it constitutes a danger to the organism; it is a good thing for it to be properly tyrannized in the meantime! Thus, consciousness is properly tyrannized – and not least by one's pride in it! One thinks it constitutes the *kernel* of man, what is abiding, eternal, ultimate, most original in him! One takes consciousness to be a given determinate magnitude! One denies its growth and intermittences! Sees it as 'the unity of the organism'! This ridiculous overestimation and misapprehension of consciousness has the very useful consequence that an all-too-rapid development of consciousness was *prevented*. Since they thought they already possessed it, human beings did not take much trouble to acquire it – and things are no different today! The *task* of *assimilating knowledge* and making it instinctive is still quite new; it is only beginning to dawn on the human eye and is yet barely discernible – it is a task seen only by those who have understood that so far we have incorporated only our *errors* and that all of our consciousness refers to errors!

12

On the aim of science. – What? The final aim of science should be to give man as much pleasure and as little displeasure as possible? But what if

---

[6] The usual German word for 'consciousness' is *Bewußtsein* (literally 'being-in-a-state-of-aware-ness-of') and this is the term Nietzsche uses in the title of this paragraph. He then however shifts to the much more unusual word *Bewußtheit*, which has an ending (*heit*) that usually signifies an abstract property, and argues against the view that having such a property is something fundamental or especially important to humans.

[7] See *Iliad* 11.155 and XX.30, 336.

pleasure and displeasure are so intertwined that whoever *wants* as much as possible of one *must* also have as much as possible of the other – that whoever wants to learn to 'jubilate up to the heavens' must also be prepared for 'grief unto death'?[8] And that may well be the way things are! At least the Stoics believed that this is how things are, and they were consistent when they also desired as little pleasure as possible in order to derive as little pain as possible from life (by using the saying 'The virtuous man is the happiest man',[9] they had both a school slogan for the masses and a fine casuistic delicacy for the refined). Even today you still have the choice: either *as little displeasure as possible*, in short, lack of pain – and socialists and politicians of all parties fundamentally have no right to promise their people any more than that – or *as much displeasure as possible* as the price for the growth of a bounty of refined pleasures and joys that hitherto have seldom been tasted. Should you decide on the former, i.e. if you want to decrease and diminish people's susceptibility to pain, you also have to decrease and diminish their *capacity for joy*. With *science* one can actually promote either of these goals! So far it may still be better known for its power to deprive man of his joys and make him colder, more statue-like, more stoic. But it might yet be found to be the *great giver of pain*! – And then its counterforce might at the same time be found: its immense capacity for letting new galaxies of joy flare up!

13

On the doctrine of the feeling of power. – Benefiting and hurting others are ways of exercising one's power over them – that is all one wants in such cases! We *hurt* those to whom we need to make our power perceptible, for pain is a much more sensitive means to that end than pleasure: pain always asks for the cause, while pleasure is inclined to stop with itself and not look back. We *benefit* and show benevolence toward those who already depend on us in some way (that is, who are used to thinking of us as their causes); we want to increase their power because we thus increase our own, or we want to show them the advantage of being in our power – that way, they will be more satisfied with their situation and

---

[8] Quotation from Act III, Scene 2 of Goethe's *Egmont*, frequently cited in Germany as an archetypal description of the Romantic personality.

[9] This doctrine, originally defended by Socrates (see Xenophon, *Memorabilia* III.5), was a central part of Stoic ethics (see A. A. Long and D. Sedley, *The Hellenistic Philosophers* [Cambridge University Press, 1987], esp. vol. I, pp. 344–436, and esp. pp. 357–9).

more hostile towards and willing to fight against the enemies of *our* power. Whether in benefiting or hurting others we make sacrifices does not affect the ultimate value of our actions; even if we stake our lives, as martyrs do for their church, it is a sacrifice made for *our* desire for power or for the preservation of our feeling of power. He who feels 'I am in possession of the truth' – how many possessions does he not renounce in order to save this feeling! What would he not throw overboard in order to stay 'on top' – that is, *above* the others who lack 'the truth'! The state in which we hurt others is certainly seldom as agreeable, in an unadulterated way, as that in which we benefit others; it is a sign that we are still lacking power, or it betrays a frustration in the face of this poverty; it brings new dangers and uncertainties to the power we do possess and clouds our horizon with the prospect of revenge, scorn, punishment, failure. Only to the most irritable and covetous adherents of the feeling of power – to those for whom the sight of those who are already subjected (the objects of benevolence) is a burden and boredom – might it be more pleasurable to imprint the seal of power on the reluctant. It depends on how one is accustomed to *spice* one's life; it is a matter of taste whether one prefers the slow or the sudden, the safe or the dangerous and daring increase in power – one always seeks this or that spice according to one's temperament. An easy prey is something contemptible for proud natures; they take delight only at the sight of unbroken persons who could become their enemies and at the sight of all possessions that are hard to come by; they are often hard towards someone who is suffering, for he is not worthy of their contention and pride – but they are the more obliging toward their *equals*, against whom it would be honourable to fight and struggle *if* the occasion should arise. Spurred by the good feeling of *this* perspective, the members of the knightly caste became accustomed to treating each others with exquisite courtesy. Compassion is the most agreeable feeling for those who have little pride and no prospect of great conquests; for them, easy prey – and that is what those who suffer are – is something enchanting. Compassion is praised as the virtue of prostitutes.

14

The things people call love. – Greed and love: such different feelings these terms evoke! And yet it could be the same instinct, named twice:

once disparaged by those who already *have*, in whom the instinct has somewhat calmed down and who now fear for what they 'have'; the other time seen from the standpoint of the unsatisfied, the thirsty, and therefore glorified as 'good'. Our love of our neighbours – is it not a craving for new *property*? And likewise our love of knowledge, of truth, and altogether any craving for what is new? We slowly grow tired of the old, of what we safely possess, and we stretch out our hands again; even the most beautiful landscape is no longer sure of our love after we have lived in it for three months, and some more distant coast excites our greed: possession usually diminishes the possession. The pleasure we take in ourselves tries to preserve itself by time and again changing something new *into ourselves* – that is simply what possession means. To grow tired of a possession is to grow tired of ourselves. (One can also suffer from an excess – even the desire to throw away, to dole out, can take on the honorary name 'love'.) When we see someone suffering, we like to use this opportunity to take possession of him; that is for example what those who become his benefactors and those who have compassion for him do, and they call the lust for new possessions that is awakened in them 'love'; and their delight is like that aroused by the prospect of a new conquest. Sexual love, however, is what most clearly reveals itself as a craving for new property: the lover wants unconditional and sole possession of the longed-for person; he wants a power over her soul as unconditional as his power over her body; he wants to be the only beloved, to live and to rule in the other soul as that which is supreme and most desirable. If one considers that this means *excluding* the whole world from a precious good, from joy and enjoyment; if one considers that the lover aims at the impoverishment and deprivation of all the competitors and would like to become the dragon guarding his golden hoard as the most inconsiderate and selfish of all 'conquerors' and exploiters; if one considers, finally, that to the lover himself the rest of the world appears indifferent, pale, and worthless and that he is prepared to make any sacrifice, upset any order, subordinate any other interest; then one is indeed amazed that this wild greed and injustice of sexual love has been as glorified and deified as it has in all ages – yes, that this love has furnished the concept of love as the opposite of egoism when it may in fact be the most candid expression of egoism. Here is it evidently the have-nots and the yearning ones who have formed linguistic usage – there have probably always been too many of them.

Those who were granted much possession and satiety in this area must occasionally have made some casual remark about 'the raging demon', as did that most charming and beloved of all Athenians, Sophocles:[10] but Eros always laughed at such blasphemers; they were always precisely his greatest darlings. Here and there on earth there is probably a kind of continuation of love in which this greedy desire of two people for each other gives way to a new desire and greed, a *shared* higher thirst for an ideal above them. But who knows such love? Who has experienced it? Its true name is *friendship*.

15

From a distance. – This mountain makes the entire region it dominates attractive and significant in every way; having said this to ourselves for the hundredth time, we are so unreasonably and thankfully disposed toward it that we suppose that it, the bestower of such delight, must itself be the most delightful thing in the region – and so we climb it and are disappointed. Suddenly the mountain itself and the entire landscape around us, beneath us, seem to have lost their magic; we had forgotten that certain types of greatness, like certain types of goodness, want to be beheld only from a distance and always from below, not from above – only thus do they *have an effect.* Perhaps you know people near you who ought to view themselves only from a distance in order to find themselves at all tolerable or attractive and invigorating; self-knowledge is something they should be advised against.

16

Over the footbridge. – When dealing with people who are bashful about their feelings, one has to be able to dissimulate; they feel a sudden hatred towards anyone who catches them in a tender or enthusiastic or elevated feeling, as if he had seen their secrets. If one wants to do them good in such moments, one should make them laugh or utter some cold, jocular sarcasm: then their feeling freezes and they regain power over themselves. But I am giving the moral before the story. There was a time in our lives when we were so close that nothing seemed to obstruct

---

[10] See Plato, *Republic* 329c.

our friendship and brotherhood, and only a small footbridge separated us. Just as you were about to step on it, I asked you: 'Do you want to cross the footbridge to me?' – But then you didn't want to any more; and when I asked again, you were silent. Since then, mountains and torrential rivers, and everything which separates and alienates, have been cast between us, and even if we wanted to reach each other, we couldn't anymore! But when you think of that little footbridge now, you have no words anymore – only sobs and bewilderment.

17

Finding a motive for one's poverty. – There is clearly no trick that enables us to turn a poor virtue into a rich and overflowing one, but we can surely reinterpret its poverty nicely into a necessity, so that its sight no longer offends us and we no longer make reproachful faces at fate on its account. That is what the wise gardener does when he places the poor little stream in his garden in the arms of a nymph and thus finds a motive for its poverty: and who wouldn't need nymphs as he does?

18

Ancient pride. – The specific hue which nobility had in the ancient world is absent in ours because the ancient slave is absent from our sensibility. A Greek of noble descent found such immense intermediate stages and such a distance between his own height and that ultimate baseness that he could barely see the slave clearly any more: not even Plato could really see him. It is different with us, accustomed as we are to the *doctrine* of human equality, if not also to equality itself. A creature who is not at its own disposal and who lacks leisure is by no means something despicable to us on that account; perhaps each of us possesses too much of such slavishness in accordance with the conditions of our social order and activity, which are utterly different from those of the ancients. The Greek philosopher went through life feeling secretly that there were far more slaves than one might think – namely, that everyone who was not a philosopher was a slave;[11] his pride overflowed when he considered that even the mightiest men on earth might be his slaves. This pride, too, is

---

[11] Stoic doctrine; see e.g. Diogenes Laertius 7.121–2 (in Long and Sedley, *Philosophers*, vol. 1 p. 431) and Cicero, *De stoicorum paradoxiis, Paradoxon V*.

foreign and impossible for us; not even metaphorically does the word 'slave' possess for us its full force.

19

Evil. – Examine the lives of the best and the most fruitful people and peoples and ask yourselves whether a tree which is supposed to grow to a proud height could do without bad weather and storms: whether misfortune and exernal resistance, whether any kinds of hatred, jealousy, stubbornness, mistrust, hardness, greed, and violence do not belong to the *favourable* conditions without which any great growth even of virtue is scarcely possible? The poison from which the weaker nature perishes strengthens the strong man – and he does not call it poison.

20

The dignity of foolishness. – A few millennia further along the course set by the last century – and everything men do will display the highest prudence: but just that way prudence will lose all its dignity. Then it will, to be sure, be necessary to be prudent, but it will also be so commonplace and vulgar that even a moderately aristocratic taste will experience this necessity as a *vulgarity*. And just as a tyranny of truth and science could increase esteem for the lie, a tyranny of prudence could spur a new kind of nobility. To be noble might then come to mean: to entertain follies.

21

To the teachers of selflessness. – A person's virtues are called *good* with respect to their presumed effects not on him but on us and society – the praise of virtues has always been far from 'selfless', far from 'unegoistic'! For otherwise one would have had to recognize that the virtues (such as diligence, obedience, chastity, piety, justice) are mostly *harmful* to their possessors, being drives which dominate them all too violently and covetously and in no way let reason keep them in balance with the other drives. When you have a virtue – a real, complete virtue (and not just a small drive towards some virtue) – you are its *victim!* But the neighbour praises your virtue precisely on that account! One praises the diligent even if he should harm his vision or the originality and freshness of his spirit; one honours and feels sorry for the youth who has 'worked himself to death' because one thinks: 'For society as a whole the loss of even the best individual is merely a small sacrifice! Too bad that the sacrifice is necessary! It would surely be much worse though if the individual had thought otherwise and considered his own preservation and development more important than his work in the service of society!' And so one feels sorry for this youth, not for his own sake but because a devoted *tool*, ruthless towards itself – a so-called 'good man' – has been lost to society through his death. Perhaps one also asks whether it would not have been more useful to society if he had worked in a way that was less negligent towards himself and had preserved himself longer – yes, one admits that there would have been some advantage in that, but considers this other advantage to be greater and more last; that a *sacrifice* was made and the ethos of the sacrificial animal once again vindicated *for all to see*. What is, therefore, first really praised when virtues are praised is their instrumental nature and then the blind drive in every virtue that refuses to be held in check by the overall advantage of the individual – in short, the unreason in virtue that leads the individual to allow himself to be transformed into a mere function of the whole. The praise of virtues is the praise of something privately harmful – the praise of drives which deprive a human being of his noblest selfishness and of the strength for the highest form of self-protection. For the sake of inculcating and incorporating virtuous habits into people, to be sure, one emphasizes various effects of virtue that make virtue and private advantage appear as sisters – and there is in fact such a relationship! Blindly raging industriousness, for example – this typical virtue of an instrument – is represented as the road to riches and honour and as the best poison for curing boredom and the passions; but one keeps silent about its danger, its extreme dangerousness. That is how education always proceeds: it tries to condition the individual through various attractions and advantages to adopt a way of thinking and behaving that, when it has become habit, drive and passion, will rule in him and over him *against his ultimate advantage* but 'for the common good'. How often I see it: that blindly raging industriousness brings riches and honour but at the same time deprives the organs of refinement that make it possible to enjoy the riches and honour; also, that this chief antidote to boredom and to the passions at the same time dulls the senses and makes the spirit resistant to new attractions. (The most industrious age – our own – doesn't know how to make anything of all its industriousness and money except still more money and still more industriousness; for more genius is required to spend than to acquire! – Well, we'll still have our 'grandchildren'!) If education is successful, each virtue of the individual is a public utility and a private disadvantage with respect to the highest private end – probably involving some deterioration of the spirit and the senses or even a premature demise: consider from this standpoint the virtues of obedience, chastity, piety, and justice. The praise of the selfless, the self-sacrificing, the virtuous – that is, of the person who does not apply his entire strength and reason to *his own* preservation, development, elevation, promotion, and expansion of power, but rather lives, as regards himself, modestly and throughtlessly, maybe even with indifference and irony – this praise is certainly not born out of the spirit of selflessness! The 'neighbour' praises selflessness because *it brings him advantages*! If the neighbour himself thought 'selflessly', he would reject this decrease in strength, this harm for *his* benefit; he would work against the development of such inclinations, and above all he would affirm his selflessness by *not* calling it *good*! Hereby we hint at the fundamental contradiction in the morality that is very much honoured just now: the *motives* to this morality stand in opposition to its *principle*! What this morality wants to use as its proof, it refutes with its criterion of what is moral! In order not to contradict itself, the command 'You shall renounce yourself and sacrifice yourself' could be proclaimed only by a being which thereby renounced its own advantage and perhaps, through the demanded sacrifice of the individual, brought about its own destruction. But as soon as the neighbour (or society) recommends altruism *for the sake of its utility*, it is using the directly opposed principle, 'You shall seek your advantage even at the expense of everything else' – and thus one preaches, in the same breath, a 'Thou shalt' and a 'Thou shalt not'!

22

L'ordre du jour pour le roi.[12] – The day begins: let us begin to organize for this day the business and festivities of our most gracious master who

[12] 'The king's schedule for the day'

is still deigning to repose. His majesty has bad weather today: we shall be careful not to call it bad; we shall not speak of the weather – but we shall be a bit more ceremonious about the business than would otherwise be necessary and a bit more festive about the festivities. His majesty may even be ill: at breakfast we shall present the latest good news of last evening, the arrival of Mr Montaigne, who jokes so agreeably about his illness; he's suffering from a stone.[13] We shall receive a few persons (persons! What that puffed-up old frog who will be among them would say if he heard this word! 'I am not a person', he would say, 'but always the matter itself'[14]) – and this reception will take longer than anyone finds agreeable: that is reason enough to tell about the poet who wrote on his door, 'Whoever enters here will pay me an honour; whoever does not – a pleasure.'[15] Truly a polite way to express a rudeness! And perhaps this poet is for his part quite right in being rude: they say his poems are better than their maker. Well, then let him write many more and withdraw himself from the world as much as possible – that is after all the meaning of his civil incivility! Conversely, a prince is always worth more than his 'verse', even if – but what are we doing? We are gossiping and the whole court thinks we are already working and racking our brains – one sees no light earlier than the one burning in our window. Listen! Wasn't that the bell? Damn! The day and the dance are beginning and we don't know the programme! So we have to improvise – the whole world improvises its day. Let's just do today as the whole world does! And there my strange morning dream vanished, probably the victim of the hard strokes of the tower bell, which just announced the fifth hour with all of its customary importance. It seems to me that this time the god of dreams wanted to poke fun at my habit of starting the day by organizing it and making it tolerable *to myself*, and it may well be that I have often done this in too formal and princelike a manner.

---

[13] French moralist (1533–92) who discusses the pains (and pleasures) of his affliction in his essay 'Of Experience'

[14] Perhaps a reference to Montaigne's letter 'To the Reader', printed as introduction to his *Essays*

[15] In his notebook Nietzsche writes that this refers to 'Augier'; probably Emile Augier (1820–89), minor French dramatist who wrote on classical topics.

23

The signs of corruption. – Consider the following signs of those states of society that are necessary from time to time and that are designated by the word 'corruption'. As soon as corruption sets in anywhere, a colourful *superstition* takes over, and the previous common faith of a people becomes pale and powerless against it: for supersitition is free-spiritedness of the second rank – whoever succumbs to it selects certain forms and formulas that appeal to him and allows himself some freedom of choice. The superstitious person is always, compared to the religious person, much more of a 'person', and a superstitious society will be one in which there are many individuals and much delight in individuality. From this perspective, superstition always appears as *progress* against faith and as a sign that the intellect is becoming more independent and demanding its rights. Those who then complain about corruption are the devotees of the old religion and religiosity – until now they have also determined linguistic usage and given superstition a bad name even among the freest spirits. Let us realize that it is actually a symptom of *enlightenment.* Secondly, a society in which corruption spreads is accused of laxity; and it is obvious that the esteem of war and the pleasure in war diminish, while the comforts of life are now desired just as ardently as were warlike and athletic honours formerly. What is usually overlooked, however, is that the ancient civil energy and passion, which received a magnificent visibility through war and competitive games, has now transformed itself into countless private passions and has merely become less visible; indeed, in times of 'corruption' the power and force of a people's expended energies are probably greater than ever, and the individual spends them on a lavish scale which he could not previously have afforded – when he was not yet rich enough! And thus it is precisely in times of 'laxness' that tragedy runs through the houses and streets, that great love and great hatred are born and the flame of knowledge blazes up into the sky. Thirdly, it is usually said to the credit of such societies, as if one wanted to compensate for the reproaches of superstition and laxness, that they are milder and that cruelty declines drastically in comparison to the older, stronger, more devout age. But this praise I cannot endorse any more than the reproaches: I concede only that cruelty now *refines* itself and that its older forms henceforth offend taste; but wounding and torturing with word and eye reaches its highest cultivation in times of corruption – it is now alone that *malice* and the delight in malice are born. People who live in an age of corruption are witty and slanderous; they know that there are other kinds of murder than by dagger or assault; they also know that whatever is *well said* is believed. Fourthly, when 'morals decay', those beings emerge for the first time who are called tyrants: they are the precursors and as it were the precocious *firstling instances of individuals*. Just a little bit longer and this fruit of fruits hangs ripe and yellow on the tree of a people – and this tree existed only for the sake of this fruit! Once decay has reached its peak along with the struggle of all sorts of tyrants, the Caesar always appears, the final tyrant who puts an end to the weary wrestling for sole rule by putting weariness to work for himself. In his age the individual is usually ripest and culture is therefore at its highest and most fruitful stage, but not for the sake of him and not through him, though those of the highest culture like to flatter their Caesar by claiming to be *his* work. In truth they need peace from without because they have enough unrest and work within. In these times, bribery and treason are at their peak, for the love of the newly discovered ego is now much mightier than the love of the old, used-up, touted-to-death 'fatherland', and the need to secure oneself from the terrible ups and downs of luck opens even noble hands as soon as someone who is mighty and wealthy shows himself willing to pour gold into them. There is now so very little secure future; one lives for today: a state of soul that makes an easy game for all seducers, for one allows oneself to be seduced and bribed only 'for today' and reserves the future and virtue for oneself! As is well known the individuals, these true 'in-and-for-themselves', care more about the moment than do their opposites, the herd people, for they consider themselves just as unpredictable as the future. They also like to join up with people of violence because they think themselves capable of actions and information which the common people would neither understand nor forgive, while the tyrant or Caesar would understand the rights of the individual even in his excesses and has an interest in advocating and even abetting a bolder private morality. For he thinks of himself and wants his self to be thought of as Napoleon once expressed it in his classic manner : 'I have the right to answer all charges against me with an eternal "That is me." I am apart from all the world and accept conditions from no one. I want people to submit even to my fantasies and to find it natural when I yield to this or that distraction.' That is what Napoleon once replied to his wife when she had reasons to question her husband's marital fidelity.[16] Times of corruption are those in which the apples fall from the tree: I mean the individuals, the seed-bearers of the future, the spiritual colonizers and shapers of new states and communities. Corruption is just a rude word for the *autumn* of a people.

24

Different forms of dissatisfaction. – The weak and, as it were, feminine discontented types are those who are innovative at making life more beautiful and profound; the strong discontents – the men among them, to stick with the metaphor – are innovative at making it better and safer. The former show their weakness and femininity by gladly letting themselves be deceived from time to time and occasionally resting content with a bit of intoxication and gushing enthusiasm, though they can never be satisfied entirely and suffer from the incurability of their dissatisfaction; they are also the promoters of all who know how to procure opiates and narcotic consolations, and consequently they resent those who esteem physicians above priests – thus they assure the *continuance* of real distress! Had there not been a surplus of these discontents in Europe since the middle ages, the celebrated European capacity for constant *transformation* might never have developed, for the demands of the strong discontents are too crude and basically too undemanding not eventually to be brought to a final rest. China, for example, is a country where large-scale discontentment and the capacity for *change* became extinct centuries ago; and in Europe too the socialists and state idolaters, with their measures for making life better and safer, might easily establish Chinese conditions and a Chinese 'happiness', provided they are first able to extirpate that sicklier, more tender, more feminine discontentment and romanticism that is for the moment still superabundant here. Europe is a patient who owes the utmost gratitude to his incurability and to the perpetual changes in his affliction: these incessantly new conditions, these no less incessantly new dangers, pains, and modes of information have finally generated an intellectual

---

[16] Reported in *Mémoires de Madame de Rémusat* (3 vols., Paris, 1879–80), vol. I, pp. 114f., a copy of which Nietzsche had in his library

irritability that approximates genius and that is in any case the mother of all genius.

25

Not predestined for knowledge. – There is a stupid humility that is by no means rare, and those afflicted with it are altogether unfit to become votaries of knowledge. For as soon as a person of this type perceives something striking, he turns on his heel, as it were, and says to himself, 'You have made a mistake! Where were your senses? This cannot be the truth!' And then, instead of looking and listening more keenly again, he runs away, as if intimidated, from the striking thing and tries to shake it from his mind as fast as possible. For his inner canon says: 'I want to see nothing that contradicts the prevalent opinion. Am *I* made to discover new truths? There are already too many old ones.'

26

What is life? – Life – that is: continually shedding something that wants to die; Life – that is: being cruel and inexorable against anything that is growing weak and old in us, and not just in us. Life – therefore means: being devoid of respect for the dying, the wretched, the aged? Always being a murderer? And yet old Moses said: 'Thou shalt not kill.'[17]

27

The renouncer. – What does the renouncer do? He strives for a higher world, he wants to fly further and higher than all affirmers – *he throws away much* that would encumber his flight, including some things that are not valueless, not disagreeable to him: he sacrifices it to his desire for the heights. This sacrificing, this throwing away, is now precisely what alone becomes visible in him and leads people to call him the renouncer, and thus he stands before us, shrouded in his hood as if he were the soul of a hairshirt. But he is quite satisfied with the impression that he makes on us: he wants to conceal from us his desire, his pride, his intention to soar *beyond* us. Yes, he is cleverer than we thought, and so polite

---

[17] Moses was the supposed author of the Pentateuch, the first five books of the Bible which include, in Exodus, 20, the Ten Commandments.

towards us – this affirmer! For he is just as we are even in his renunciation.

28

Harming with what is best in oneself. – At times our strengths propel us so far ahead that we can no longer stand our weaknesses and perish from them. We may even foresee this outcome and still will have it no other way. Thus we become hard against that within us that wants to be spared, and our greatness is also our mercilessness. Such an experience, for which we must in the end pay with our lives, is a parable for the whole effect of great human beings on others and on their age: precisely with what is best in them, with what only they can do, they destroy many who are weak, insecure, in the process of becoming, of willing, and thus they are harmful. It can even happen that, all in all, they are harmful only because what is best in them is accepted and as it were imbibed only by those whom it affects like an overly potent drink: they lose their mind and their selfishness; they become so intoxicated that they are bound to break their limbs on all the wrong paths down which their intoxication drives them.

29

The add-on-liars. – When people in France started to fight the Aristotelian unities[18] and others consequently also started to defend them, one could see again something that is so often apparent but that people are loath to see: *one lied to oneself*, inventing reasons for these laws, simply to avoid admitting that one had become *used* to them and would no longer have it any other way. And that is what one does, and has always done, within every prevailing morality and religion: the reasons and intents behind habits are invented only when some people start attacking the habits and *asking* for reasons and intents. Here we have the great dishonesty of conservatives of all times – they are the add-on-liars.

---

[18] In seventeenth-century France aestheticians (mis)read Aristotle (see his *Poetics*, esp. chapter 8 [1451a.16–35]) as requiring that a tragedy exhibit unity of time, place, and plot.

30

The comedy of the famous. – Famous men who *need* their fame, e.g. all politicians, never choose allies and friends without ulterior motives: from one they want a piece of the splendour and reflected splendour of his virtue; from another the fear-inspiring aspects of certain dubious qualities that everyone knows him to have; from another they steal the reputation of his idleness, his lying in the sun, because it serves their own ends to appear inattentive and sluggish at times – it conceals the fact that they actually lie in wait; now they need a visionary around; now an expert; now a thinker; now a pedant, as if he were their present self; but just as quickly they don't need them any more! And so the surroundings and exteriors of famous men die off continually, even while everything seems to be pushing to get into these surroundings and lend them their character; in this, they are like big cities. Their reputation is continually changing, like their character, for their changing methods demand these changes and push forward now this, now that real or fictitious characteristic onto the stage. Their friends and allies belong, as I said, to these stage properties. What they want, however, must stand all the much more firmly and unshakeably and be splendidly seen from afar; and this, too, sometimes requires its comedy and its theatrics.

31

Trade and nobility. – Buying and selling are common by now, like the art of reading and writing; everyone has practised it, even if he is not a tradesman, and gets more practice at this technique every day – just as formerly, in the age of a more savage humanity, everyone was a hunter and practised the technique of hunting every day. In that age, hunting was common; but eventually it became a privilege and thereby lost its everyday and common character – because it stopped being necessary and became a thing of moods and luxury. The same thing could happen to buying and selling one day. One can imagine social conditions in which there is no buying and selling and in which this technique gradually becomes unnecessary. Perhaps some individuals who are not as subject to the laws of the general condition will then give themselves permission to buy and sell as a *luxury of sentiment*. Only then would trade become something exquisite, and the noble might enjoy trade as much as they hitherto enjoyed war and politics, while conversely the assessment of politics could have changed completely. Even now it is ceasing to be the art of the nobleman, and it is quite possible that some day one will find it so base that, along with all political literature and journalism, one classifies it as a 'prostitution of the spirit'.

32

Undesired disciples. – 'What can I do with these two young men!' cried an irritated philosopher who 'corrupted' the youth as Socrates once had done;[19] they are unwelcome students. This one can't say 'no' and the other one says 'half and half' about everything. If they adopted my doctrine, the first would *suffer* too much, for my way of thinking requires a warlike soul, a desire to hurt, a delight in saying no, a hard skin; he would languish from open and internal wounds. And the other would strike a compromise with everything he represents and thereby make it into a mediocrity – such a disciple I wish on my enemies.

33

Outside the lecture-room. – 'In order to prove to you that man is fundamentally a good-natured animal, I would remind you of how credulous he has been for so long. Only now, quite late and after tremendous self-conquest, has he become a *distrustful* animal. Yes, man is now more evil than ever.' I do not understand this: why should man be more distrustful and evil now? 'Because he now has a science – needs a science.'

34

Historia abscondita.[20] – Every great human being exerts a retroactive force: for his sake all of history is put on the scale again, and a thousand secrets of the past crawl out of their hiding places – into *his* sunshine. There is no telling what may yet become a part of history. Maybe the

---

[19] One of the charges on which Socrates was condemned to death was that of 'corrupting the youth'; see Plato, *Apology* 24 b–c.

[20] 'hidden history'

past is still essentially undiscovered! So many retroactive forces are still needed!

35

Heresy and witchcraft. – To think otherwise than is customary is much less the effect of a superior intellect than of strong, evil inclinations – detaching, isolating, defiant, gloating, and malicious inclinations. Heresy is the adjunct of witchcraft and surely no more harmless and least of all anything venerable. Heretics and witches are two species of evil people; what they have in common is that they also feel evil but are impelled by an unconquerable lust to harm what is prevailing (people or opinions). The Reformation, which was a kind of redoubling of the medieval spirit at a time when it was no longer accompanied by a good conscience, produced both in the greatest abundance.

36

Last words. – One will recall that the emperor Augustus, that frightful man who had as much self-control and who could be as silent as any wise Socrates, became indiscreet against himself with his last words: he let his mask fall for the first time when he made it clear that he had worn a mask and acted a comedy – he had played the father of the fatherland and the wisdom on the throne well enough to create the proper illusion! *Plaudite amici, comoedia finita est!*[21] The thought of the dying Nero – *qualis artifex pereo!*[22] – was also the thought of the dying Augustus: actor's vanity! Actor's prolixity! And truly the opposite of the dying Socrates![23] But Tiberius died silently, this most tormented of all self-tormentors – *he* was genuine and no actor! What might have passed through his mind at the end? Maybe this: 'Life – that is a long death. What a fool I was to shorten so many lives! Was *I* made to be a benefactor? I should have given them eternal *life*: that way, I could have *seen them die* forever. *That's* why I had such good eyes: *qualis spectator*

---

[21] 'Father of the Fatherland' was an honorary title bestowed by the Roman Senate on the emperor Augustus. In his biography (chapter 99) Suetonius reports that these Latin words (= 'Applaud, my friends, the comedy is over!') were among the last Augustus spoke on his deathbed.

[22] 'I die, what a loss to art!' (as reported by Suetonius, *Life of Nero*, chapter 49)

[23] Socrates insisted that a decorous silence be preserved while he was being executed; see Plato, *Phaedo* 117c–e, but see below, § 340, p. 193.

pereo![24] When after a long death-struggle he seemed to recover his strength, it was considered advisable to smother him with pillows – he died a double death.[25]

37

Because of three errors. – One has promoted science during the last centuries partly because it was through science that one hoped best to understand God's goodness and wisdom – the main motive in the soul of the great Englishmen (such as Newton);[26] partly because one believed in the absolute usefulness of knowledge, especially in the most intimate affiliation between morality, knowledge, and happiness – the main motive in the soul of the French (such as Voltaire);[27] and partly because one believed that in science one had and loved something selfless, harmless, self-sufficient, and truly innocent in which the evil drives of humanity had no part at all – the main motive in the soul of Spinoza,[28] who felt divine in attaining knowledge – in sum, because of three errors.

38

The explosive ones. – When one considers how the energy of young men needs to explode, one is not surprised to see them decide so unsubtly and so unselectively for this or that cause: what thrills them is the sight of the zeal surrounding a cause and, so to speak, the sight of the burning match – not the cause itself. The subtler seducers therefore know how to create in them the expectation of an explosion and to disregard justifying their cause: reasons are not the way to win over these powder kegs!

39

Changed taste. – Change in common taste is more important than that in opinions; opinions along with proofs, refutations, and the whole

[24] 'I die, but what a good observer I was!'
[25] Tiberius' end is described in Suetonius, *Life of Tiberius* (chapter 73) and in Tacitus, *Annals* VI.50.
[26] English physicist and mathematician (1643–1727)
[27] Paradigmatic French rationalist of the Enlightenment (1694–1778)
[28] Jewish philosopher who lived most of his life in Amsterdam (1632–77)

intellectual masquerade are only symptoms of a changed taste and most certainly *not* what they are so often taken to be, its causes. How does common taste change? Through individuals – powerful, influential, and without any sense of shame – who announce and tyrannically enforce *their hoc est ridiculum, hoc est absurdum*,[29] i.e. the judgement of their taste and disgust: thus they put many under pressure, which gradually turns into a habit among even more and finally becomes a *need of everyone*. The reason why these individuals sense and 'taste' differently is usually found in a peculiarity of their lifestyle, nutrition, digestion, maybe a deficit or excess of inorganic salts in their blood and brains – in short, in their *physis*:[30] they have the courage to own up to their *physis* and to heed its demands down to its subtlest tones. Their aesthetic and moral judgements are such 'subtlest tones' of the *physis*.

40

On the lack of noble style. – Soldiers and leaders still have a far higher relation to one another than do workers and employers. So far at least, all cultures with a military basis are still high above so-called industrial culture: the latter in its present form is altogether the most vulgar form of existence that has ever been. Here it is simply the law of need operating: one wants to live and has to sell oneself, but one despises those who exploit this need and *buy* the worker. It is strange that submission to powerful, frightening, yes, terrifying persons, to tyrants and generals, is experienced to be not nearly as distressing as this submission to unknown and uninteresting persons, which is what all the greats of industry are: the worker usually sees in the employer only a cunning, bloodsucking dog of a man who speculates on all distress and whose name, figure, manner, and reputation are completely indifferent to him. So far the manufacturers and large-scale commercial entrepreneurs have apparently been much too lacking in all the manners and signs of *higher race* that alone enable a person to become *interesting*; if they had the refinement of noble breeding in their eye and gesture, there might not be any socialism of the masses. For the masses are basically prepared to submit to any kind of *slavery* provided that the superiors constantly legitimize themselves as higher, as *born* to command –

---

[29] 'This is ridiculous, this is absurd.'
[30] Greek for 'nature'

through refined demeanour! The commonest man senses that refinement cannot be improvised and that one has to honour in it the fruit of long ages – but the absence of the higher demeanour and the notorious manufacturer's vulgarity with ruddy, plump hands give him the idea that it is only accident and luck that elevated one above the other in this case: well, then, he infers, let *us* try accident and luck! Let *us* throw the dice! – and socialism begins.

41

Against remorse. – The thinker sees his own actions as experiments and questions, as seeking explanations of something: to him, success and failure are primarily *answers*. To be vexed or even to feel remorse because something goes wrong – he leaves that to those who act because they were ordered to do so and who expect a beating when his gracious lordship is not pleased with the result.

42

Work and boredom. – Seeking work for the sake of wages – in this, nearly all people in civilized countries are alike; to all of them, work is just a means and not itself the end, which is why they are unrefined in their choice of work, provided it yields an ample reward. Now there are rare individuals who would rather perish than work without taking *pleasure* in their work: they are choosy, hard to please, and have no use for ample rewards if the work is not itself the reward of rewards. To this rare breed belong artists and contemplative men of all kinds, but also men of leisure who spend their lives hunting, travelling, in love affairs, or on adventures. All of them want work and misery as long as it is joined with pleasure, and the heaviest, hardest work, if need be. Otherwise they are resolutely idle, even if it spells impoverishment, dishonour, and danger to life and limb. They do not fear boredom as much as work without pleasure; indeed, they need a lot of boredom if *their* work is to succeed. For the thinker and for all inventive spirits, boredom is that disagreeable 'lull' of the soul that precedes a happy voyage and cheerful winds; he has to endure it, must *await* its effect on him – precisely *that* is what lesser natures are totally unable to achieve! To fend off boredom at any price is vulgar, just as work without pleasure is vulgar. Perhaps

Asians are distinguished as above Europeans by their capacity for a longer, deeper calm; even their narcotics work slowly and require patience, in contrast to the revolting suddenness of the European poison, alcohol.

43

What the laws betray. – It is a grave error to study a people's penal code as if it were an expression of its character; the laws do not betray what a people is but rather what appears to it as foreign, strange, uncanny, outlandish. The laws concern the exceptions to the morality of custom (*Sittlichkeit der Sitte*)[31], and the severest punishments are for things that accord with the customs of the neighbouring people. Thus the Wahanabis[32] have only two mortal sins: having a god other than the Wahanabi god and – smoking (which they call 'the disgraceful way of drinking'). 'And what about murder and adultery?' asked the Englishman, amazed, who found this out. 'God is gracious and merciful', the old chief replied. Thus the old Romans had the notion that a woman could commit only two mortal sins: adultery and – drinking wine. Old Cato thought that kissing among relatives had been made into a custom only in order to keep the women under control in this regard; a kiss meant, 'Does she smell of wine?'[33] Women caught with wine were actually put to death; and certainly not just because sometimes women under the influence of wine completely forgot how to say no; above all, the Romans feared the orgiastic and Dionysian cult which afflicted the women of southern Europe from time to time when wine was still new in Europe – feared it as a foreign monster that overthrew the basis of Roman sensibility; to them it seemed like a betrayal of Rome, like the embodiment of the foreign.

---

[31] Nietzsche here uses the expression *Sittlichkeit der Sitte*, and similar phrases occur elsewhere (e.g. in § 46, *die Sitte der Sittlichkeit*). Hegel had distinguished between *Sittlichkeit*, the ethical outlook embodied in a society's customary practice, and *Moralität*, an abstract, reflective, code such as that insisted upon in Kant's philosophy. It is unclear, but unlikely, that Nietzsche was aware of Hegel's own particular version of this distinction, but Nietzsche's formulations emphasize strongly the customary aspect of traditional ethical life.

[32] Islamic sect in central Arabia. The anecdote which follows is taken from William Gifford Palgrave's *A Narrative of a Year's Journey through Central and Eastern Arabia 1862–1863* (translated into German in 1867–8).

[33] Reported in Plutarch's *Quaestiones romanae*, 6.

44

The supposed motives. – Important as it may be to know the motives from which humanity has acted so far, it might be even more essential to know the *belief* people had in this or that motive, i.e. what humanity has imagined and told itself to be the real lever of its conduct so far. For people's inner happiness and misery has come to them depending on their belief in this or that motive – *not* through the actual motives. The latter are of second-order interest.

45

Epicurus.[34] – Yes, I am proud to experience Epicurus' character in a way unlike perhaps anyone else and to enjoy, in everything I hear and read of him, the happiness of the afternoon of antiquity: I see his eye gaze at a wide whitish sea, across shoreline rocks bathed in the sun, as large and small creatures play in its light, secure and calm like the light and his eye itself. Only someone who is continually suffering could invent such happiness – the happiness of an eye before which the sea of existence has grown still and which now cannot get enough of seeing the surface and this colourful, tender, quivering skin of the sea: never before has voluptuousness been so modest.

46

Our amazement. – It is a deep and fundamental stroke of luck that science discovers things that *stand up* under examination and that furnish the basis, again and again, for further discoveries – after all, it could be otherwise! Indeed, we are so convinced of the uncertainty and the fantastical quality of our judgements and of the eternal change of human laws and concepts that it actually amazes us *how well* the results of science stand up! Formerly, one knew nothing of the changeableness of everything human; the habit of attachment to customary morality (*Sitte der Sittlichkeit*) sustained the faith that the entire inner life of

---

[34] Late fourth-century BC Athenian philosopher who held that pleasure (correctly understood) was the goal of human life. This paragraph is probably influenced by Lucretius, *On the Nature of Things*, Bk. II, 1–61, which describes the effects to be expected from following the Epicurean doctrine.

humanity was fastened to iron necessity with eternal clamps; perhaps people then experienced a similarly voluptuous amazement when they told each other stories and fairy tales. The miraculous did a lot of good to those who at times grew weary of the rule and of eternity. To lose firm ground for once! To float! To err! To be mad! – that was part of the paradise and debauchery of former ages, whereas our bliss is like that of the shipwrecked man who has climbed ashore and is standing with both feet on the firm old earth – marvelling because it does not bob up and down.

47

On the suppression of the passions. – If one constantly forbids oneself the expression of the passions, as if that were something to be left for the 'common', coarser, middle-class, peasant types – i.e. if one wants to suppress not the passions themselves but only their language and gesture – one still attains *in addition* what one did not desire: the suppression of the passions themselves, at least their weakening and alteration – the most instructive example being furnished by the court of Louis XIV and everything that depended on it. The age that *followed*, brought up in the suppression of expression, no longer had the passions themselves and had in their place a graceful, shallow, playful manner – an age marked by an incapacity for bad manners, so that even an insult was accepted and returned with obliging words. Perhaps the present age supplies the most notable counterpart: everywhere, in life and on the stage, and not the least in everything written, I see the delight in all the *coarser* outbursts and gestures of passion: what is demanded these days is a certain convention of the passionate – but not passion itself! Nevertheless, eventually passion *itself* will be reached this way, and our progeny will be *genuinely savage* and not just savage and unruly in demeanour.

48

Knowledge of distress. – Perhaps nothing separates human beings or ages from each other more than the different degrees of their knowledge of distress – distress of the soul as well as of the body. Regarding the latter we moderns may well, in spite of our frailties and fragilities, be bunglers and dreamers owing to lack of ample first-hand experience, compared with an age of fear, the longest of all ages, when individuals had to protect themselves against violence and to that end had themselves to become men of violence. In those days, a man received ample training in bodily torments and deprivations and understood that even a certain cruelty towards himself, as a voluntary exercise in pain, was a necessary means of his preservation; in those days, one trained one's surroundings to endure pain; in those days, one gladly inflicted pain and saw the most terrible things of this kind happen to others without any other feeling than that of one's own safety. As regards the distress of the soul, however, I look at each person today to see whether he knows it through experience or description; whether he still considers it necessary to fake this knowledge, say, as a sign of refined cultivation, or whether at the bottom of his soul he no longer believes in great pains of the soul and reacts to its mention in much the same way as to the mention of great bodily sufferings, which make him think of his toothaches and stomachaches. But that is how most people seem to me to be these days. The general inexperience with both sorts of pain and the relative rarity of the sight of suffering individuals have an important consequence: pain is hated much more now than formerly; one speaks much worse of it; indeed, one can hardly endure the presence of pain *as a thought* and makes it a matter of conscience and a reproach against the whole of existence. The emergence of pessimistic philosophers is in no way the sign of great, terrible states of distress; rather, these question marks about the value of all life are made in times when the refinement and ease of existence make even the inevitable mosquito bites of the soul and the body seem much too bloody and malicious, and the poverty of real experiences of pain makes one tend to consider *painful general ideas* as already suffering of the highest rank. There is a recipe against pessimistic philosophies and excessive sensitivity, things which seem to me to be the real 'distress of the present' – but this recipe may sound too cruel and would itself be counted among the signs that lead people to judge, 'existence is something evil'. Well, the recipe against this 'distress' is: *distress*.

49

Magnanimity and related things. – Those paradoxical phenomena, like the sudden coldness in the behaviour of the emotional person, or the humour of the melancholy person, or above all *magnanimity* as a sudden renunciation of revenge or a satisfaction of envy, appear in people who have a powerful inner centrifugal force, in people of sudden satiety and sudden nausea. Their satisfactions are so quick and strong that they are immediately followed by weariness and aversion and a flight into the opposite taste: in this opposite, the cramp of feeling is resolved – in one person by sudden cold, in another by laughter, in a third by tears and self-sacrifice. The magnanimous person – at least the type of magnanimous person who has always made the strongest impression – strikes me as a person with a most extreme thirst for vengeance, who sees satisfaction nearby and drinks it down *already in imagination* so fully, thoroughly and to the last drop that a tremendous, quick nausea follows this quick excess and he now rises 'above himself', as they say, and forgives his enemy, indeed blesses and honours him. With this rape of himself, with this mockery of his drive for revenge he only gives in to the new drive which just now has become powerful in him (disgust), and he does so just as impatiently and excessively as just a moment ago he imaginatively *anticipated* and, as it were, exhausted his delight in revenge. Magnanimity has the same degree of egoism as revenge, only egoism of a different quality.

50

The argument from growing solitary. – The reproach of conscience is weak in even the most conscientious people compared to the feeling: 'This or that is against the morals (*die gute Sitte*) of *your* society.' Even the strongest person still *fears* a cold look or a sneer on the face of those among whom and for whom he has been brought up. What is he really afraid of? Growing solitary! This is the argument that refutes even the best arguments for a person or a cause. – Thus the herd instinct speaks out in us.

51

The sense of truth. – I approve of any form of scepticism to which I can reply, 'Let's try it!' But I want to hear nothing more about all the things and questions that don't admit of experiment. This is the limit of my 'sense of truth'; for there, courage has lost its right.

52

What others know about us. – What we know about ourselves and remember is not as decisive to our life's happiness as it is believed to be. One day, what *others* know (or think they know) about us assails us – and then we realize that that is more powerful. It is easier to deal with a bad conscience than a bad reputation.

53

Where the good begins. – At the point where the poor power of the eye is no longer able to see the evil drive as such, owing to its increasing subtlety, man posits the realm of goodness; and the feeling of now having stepped into the land of goodness excites all those impulses that had been threatened and limited by the evil drive, such as the feeling of security, of comfort, of benevolence. So: the duller the eye, the more extensive the good! Hence the eternal cheerfulness of the common people and of children! Hence the gloominess and grief – akin to a bad conscience – of the great thinkers!

54

The consciousness of appearance. – How wonderful and new and yet how fearful and ironic my new insight makes me feel towards all of existence! I have *discovered* for myself that the ancient humanity and animality, indeed the whole prehistory and past of all sentient being, continues within me to fabulate, to love, to hate, and to infer – I suddenly awoke in the middle of this dream, but only to the consciousness that I am dreaming and that I *must* go on dreaming lest I perish – as the sleepwalker has to go on dreaming in order to avoid falling down. What is 'appearance' to me now! Certainly not the opposite of some essence – what could I say about any essence except name the predicates of its appearance! Certainly not a dead mask that one could put on an unknown x and probably also take off x! To me, appearance is the active and living itself, which goes so far in its self-mockery that it makes me feel that here there is appearance and a will-o'-the-wisp and a dance of spirits and nothing else – that among all these dreamers, even I, the 'knower', am dancing my dance; that the one who comes to know is a means of prolonging the earthly dance and thus is one of the masters of ceremony of existence, and that the sublime consistency and interrelatedness of all knowledge may be and will be the highest means to *sustain* the universality of dreaming, the mutual comprehension of all dreamers, and thereby also *the duration of the dream.*

55

The ultimate noblemindedness. – So what makes a person 'noble'? Certainly not making sacrifices; even those burning with lust make sacrifices. Certainly not following some passion, for there are contemptible passions. Certainly not that one does something for others without selfishness: perhaps no one is more consistently selfish than the noble one. – Rather, the passion that overcomes the noble one is a singularity, and he fails to realize this: the use of a rare and singular standard and almost a madness; the feeling of heat in things that feel cold to everyone else; a hitting upon values for which the scale has not yet been invented; a sacrifice on altars made for an unknown god; a courage without any desire for honours; a self-sufficiency that overflows and communicates to men and things. Hitherto, then, it was rarity and the unawareness of this rarity that made noble. Note, however, that by means of this standard everything usual, near, and indispensable, in short, that which most preserved the species, and in general the *rule* of humanity hitherto, was inequitably judged and on the whole slandered in favour of the exceptions. To become the advocate of the rule – that might be the ultimate form and refinement in which noblemindedness manifests itself on earth.

56

The desire for suffering. – When I think of the desire to do something, how it continually tickles and goads the millions of young Europeans who cannot endure boredom and themselves, I realize that they must have a yearning to suffer something in order to make their suffering a likely reason for action, for deeds. Neediness is needed! Hence the clamour of the politicians; hence the many false, fictitious, exaggerated 'emergencies' of all kinds and the blind readiness to believe in them. This young world demands that not happiness, but unhappiness should approach or become visible *from outside*; and its imagination is already busy turning this unhappiness into a monster ahead of time so that afterwards it can fight a monster. Were these distress-addicts to feel within themselves the power to do themselves good from within, to do something for themselves, they would know how to create their very own distress. Their inventions could then become more refined and their satisfactions sound like good music, while they now fill the world with their clamour about distress, and consequently, all too often with the *feeling of distress*! They do not know what to do with themselves – and so they paint the unhappiness of others on the wall; they always need others! And continually other others! – Pardon me, my friends, I have ventured to paint my *happiness* on the wall.[35]

---

[35] A reversal of the German expression 'Don't paint the devil on the wall' (because by doing so you will cause him to appear).

Book Two

57

To the realists. – You sober people who feel armed against passion and phantastical conceptions and would like to make your emptiness a matter of pride and an ornament – you call yourself realists and insinuate that the world really is the way it appears to you: before you alone reality stands unveiled, and you yourselves are perhaps the best part of it – oh, you beloved images of Sais![1] But aren't you too in your unveiled condition still most passionate and dark creatures, compared to fish, and still all too similar to an artist in love? And what is 'reality' to an artist in love! You still carry around the valuations of things that originate in the passions and loves of former centuries! Your sobriety still contains a secret and inextirpable drunkenness! Your love of 'reality', for example – oh, that is an old, ancient 'love'! In every experience, in every sense impression there is a piece of this old love; and some fantasy, some prejudice, some irrationality, some ignorance, some fear, and whatever else, has worked on and contributed to it. That mountain over there! That cloud over there! What is 'real' about that? Subtract just once the phantasm and the whole human *contribution* from it, you sober ones! Yes, if you could do *that*! If you could forget your background, your past, your nursery school – all of your humanity and animality! There is no 'reality' for us – and not for you either, you sober ones – we are not nearly as strange to one another as you think, and perhaps our good will to transcend drunkenness is just as respectable as your belief that you are altogether *incapable* of drunkenness.

58

Only as creators! – This has caused me the greatest trouble and still does always cause me the greatest trouble: to realize that *what things are called* is unspeakably more important than what they are. The reputation, name, and appearance, the worth, the usual measure and weight of a thing – originally almost always something mistaken and arbitrary, thrown over things like a dress and quite foreign to their nature and even to their skin – has, through the belief in it and its growth from generation to generation, slowly grown onto and into the thing and has

---

[1] See above, 'Preface', footnote 5, p. 8.

become its very body: what started as appearance in the end nearly always becomes essence and *effectively acts* as its essence! What kind of a fool would believe that it is enough to point to this origin and this misty shroud of delusion in order to *destroy* the world that counts as 'real', so-called 'reality'! Only as creators can we destroy! – But let us also not forget that in the long run it is enough to create new names and valuations and appearances of truth in order to create new 'things'.

59

We artists. – When we love a woman, we easily come to hate nature because of all the repulsive natural functions to which every woman is subject; we prefer not to think about it at all, but when our soul for once brushes against these matters, it shrugs impatiently and, as just said, casts a contemptuous look at nature: we feel insulted; nature seems to intrude on our property and with the most profane hands at that. In cases like this one refuses to hear anything about physiology and decrees secretly to oneself, 'I will hear nothing of the idea that the human being is anything other than soul and form!' 'The human being under the skin' is an abomination and unthinkable to all lovers, a blasphemy against God and love. Now, the way lovers still feel about nature and naturalness is how every worshipper of God and his 'holy omnipotence' formerly felt: in everything that was said about nature by astronomers, geologists, physiologists, and doctors, he saw an intrusion on his choicest property and thus an attack – and a shameless one at that! Even the 'law of nature' sounded to him like a slander against God; he would basically much rather have seen all of mechanics traced back to moral acts of will and choice – but since no one could do him that service, he *concealed* nature and mechanics from himself as best he could and lived in a dream. Oh, these people of former times knew how to *dream* and didn't even need to fall asleep first! – and we men of today also still know it all too well, despite all our good will towards waking and the day! We need only to love, to hate, to desire, simply to feel – *at once* the spirit and power of the dream comes over us, and we climb with open eyes, impervious to all danger, up the most dangerous paths, onto the roofs and towers of fantasy, and without any vertigo, as though born to climb – we sleepwalkers of the day! We artists! We who conceal naturalness! We who are moon- and God-struck! We untiring wanderers, silent as death, on heights that we see not as heights but as our plains, as our safety.

60

Women and their action at a distance. – Do I still have ears? Am I all ear and nothing else? Here I stand amidst the fire of the surf, whose white flames are licking at my feet: from all sides it is howling, threatening, screaming, shrieking at me, while the old earth-rattler[2] sings his aria in the lowest of depths, deep as a roaring bull, while pounding such an earth-rattling beat that the hearts of even these weather-beaten monsters of the rocks are trembling in their bodies. Suddenly, as if born out of nothingness, there appears before the gate of this hellish labyrinth only a few fathoms away a large sailing ship, gliding along as silently as a ghost. Oh, this ghostly beauty! How magically it touches me! What? Has all the calm and silence of the world embarked here? Is my happiness itself sitting in this quiet place – my happier self, my second, immortalized self?[3] Not yet to be dead, but also no longer alive? As a spiritlike, silent, watching, gliding, hovering intermediate being? As though I were that ship that moves over the dark sea with its white sails like an enormous butterfly! Yes! To move *over* existence! That's it! That would be it! – It seems as though the noise here has made me into a dreamer? All great noise makes us place happiness in silence and distance. When a man stands in the midst of *his own* noise, in the midst of his own surf of projects and plans, he is also likely to see gliding past him silent, magical creatures whose happiness and seclusion he yearns for – *women*. He almost believes that his better self lives there amongst the women: in these quiet regions even the loudest surf turns into deathly silence and life itself into a dream about life. Yet! Yet! My noble enthusiast, even on the most beautiful sailing ship there is so much sound and noise, and unfortunately so much small, petty noise! The magic and the most powerful effect of women is, to speak the language of the philosophers, action at a distance, *actio in distans*:[4] but that requires, first and foremost – *distance*!

---

[2] The standard epithet of the Greek god Poseidon, who was thought to rule the seas and be responsible for earthquakes, is 'earth-shaker' (see *Iliad* VII.445, VIII.201, IX.362, etc.).
[3] The German term Nietzsche uses here means both 'dead' and 'made immortal'.
[4] 'action at a distance'

61

In honour of friendship. – That the feeling of friendship was in antiquity considered the highest feeling, even higher than the most celebrated pride of the self-sufficient sage, indeed, as it were, as its sole and even holier sibling: this is very well expressed in the story of the Macedonian king who gave a world-despising Athenian philosopher a talent and got it back. 'What?' said the king, 'Has he then no friend?'[5] He meant: 'I honour this pride of the wise and independent man, but I would honour his humanity even more highly if the friend in him had won over his pride. The philosopher has lowered himself before me by showing that he doesn't know one of the two highest feelings – and the higher one at that.'

62

Love. – Love forgives the beloved even his lust.

63

The woman in music. – Why do warm and rainy winds also bring on a musical mood and the inventive pleasure of melody? Are they not the same winds that fill the churches and give women thoughts of love?

64

Sceptics. – I am afraid that old women in their most secret heart of hearts are more sceptical than all men: they believe the superficiality of existence to be its essence, and all virtue and depth is to them merely a veil over this 'truth', the very desirable veil over a pudendum – in other words, a matter of decency and shame, and no more!

65

Devotion. – There are noble women with a certain poverty of spirit who know no other way to *express* their deepest devotion than to offer their

---

[5] A talent is a large sum of money. I have been unable to discover the origin of this story.

virtue and sense of shame: it is what they hold as their highest possession. And often this gift is accepted without incurring as profound an obligation as the donors suppose – a very melancholy story!

66

The strength of the weak. – All women are subtle at exaggerating their weaknesses; indeed they are inventive at weaknesses in order to appear as utterly fragile ornaments that are harmed by even a speck of dust: their way of living is supposed to remind men of their clumsiness and burden their conscience with this. Thus they defend themselves against the strong and 'the law of the jungle'.

67

Feigning oneself. – She loves him now and gazes ahead with such calm confidence, like a cow. But alas! What bewitched him was precisely that she seemed utterly changeable and unfathomable! He already had too much steady weather in himself! Wouldn't she do well to feign her old character? To feign lovelessness? Isn't that the counsel of – love? *Vivat comoedia!*[6]

68

Will and willingness. – Someone took a youth to a wise man and said: 'Look, he is being corrupted by women!' The wise man shook his head and smiled. 'It is men who corrupt women', he exclaimed, 'and the failings of women should be atoned for and set right in men – for man makes for himself the image (*Bild*) of woman, and woman shapes herself (*bildet sich*) according to this image (*Bild*)'. 'You are too gentle towards women', said one in the company; 'you do not know them!' The wise man replied, 'The way of men is will; the way of women is willingness – that is the law of the sexes; truly a hard law for women! All human beings are innocent of their existence; women, however, are doubly innocent. Who could have oil and mercy enough for them?' 'Forget oil! Forget gentleness!' shouted someone else from the crowd; 'one has to

---

[6] 'Long live comedy!'

raise women better!' 'One has to raise men better', said the wise man and beckoned to the youth to follow him. – But the youth did not follow him.

69

Capacity for revenge. – That someone cannot defend himself and therefore also does not want to – this is not enough to disgrace him in our eyes; but we have a low regard for anyone who has neither the capacity nor the good will for revenge – regardless of whether it is a man or a woman. Would a woman be able to hold us (or 'enthrall' us, as they say) if we did not consider her able under certain circumstances to wield a dagger deftly (any kind of dagger) *against* us? Or against herself – which in certain cases would be the more severe revenge (Chinese revenge).

70

The women who master the masters. – A deep and powerful alto voice, such as one sometimes hears in the theatre, suddenly raises the curtain upon possibilities that we usually do not believe in. All at once we believe that somewhere in the world there could be women with lofty, heroic, royal souls, capable of and ready for grandiose retorts, resolutions, and sacrifices, capable of and ready for mastery over men, because in them the best of man aside from his sex has become an incarnate ideal. To be sure, the intention of the theatre is *not* at all that such voices convey this concept of women; normally they are supposed to represent the ideal male lover, for example a Romeo; but to judge from my experience, the theatre quite regularly miscalculates on this point, as does the composer who expects such effects from such a voice. One does not believe in *these* lovers: such voices always retain a motherly and housewifely colouring, and most of all when love is in their tone.

71

On female chastity. – There is something quite amazing and monstrous in the upbringing of upper-class women; indeed, maybe there is nothing more paradoxical. The whole world agrees that they should be brought up as ignorant as possible about matters erotic, and that one has to impart in their souls a deep shame in the face of such things and the most extreme impatience and flight at the merest suggestion of them. Really, in this matter alone the 'honour' of a woman in its entirety is at risk: what else would one not forgive them? But here they are supposed to remain ignorant deep in their hearts: they are supposed to have neither eyes, nor ears, nor words, nor thoughts for this their 'evil'; yes, even knowledge is here an evil. And then to be hurled as if by a gruesome lightning bolt into reality and knowledge, with marriage – and precisely by the man they love and esteem the most: to catch love and shame in a contradiction and to have to experience all at once delight, surrender, duty, pity, terror at the unexpected proximity of god and beast, and who knows what else! There one has tied a psychic knot that may have no equal. Even the compassionate curiosity of the wisest connoisseur of human psychology (*Menschenkenner*) is insufficient for guessing how this or that woman manages to accommodate herself to this solution of the riddle and to this riddle of a solution, and what dreadful, far-reaching suspicions must stir in her poor, unhinged soul; indeed, how the ultimate philosophy and scepticism of woman casts anchor at this point! Afterwards, the same deep silence as before, and often a silence directed at herself; she closes her eyes to herself. Young women try very hard to appear superficial and thoughtless; the most refined among them simulate a kind of impertinence. Women easily experience their men as a question-mark regarding their honour and their children as an apology or atonement – they need children and wish for them in an altogether different way from that in which a man wishes for children. In sum, one cannot be too gentle towards women!

72

Mothers. – Animals think differently about females than humans do; they consider the female to be the productive being. There is no paternal love among them, only something like love for the children of a beloved and a getting used to them. In their children females have a satisfaction of their desire to dominate, a possession, an occupation, something that is totally intelligible to them and can be prattled with: all this taken together is motherly love – it is to be compared to the love of an artist for his work. Pregnancy has made women gentler, more patient, more timid, more pleased to submit; and just so does spiritual pregnancy produce the character of the contemplative type, to which the female character is related: these are male mothers. – Among animals the male sex is considered the beautiful one.

73

Holy cruelty. – A man holding a newborn in his hand approached a holy man. 'What should I do with this child?' he asked; 'it is wretched, misshapen, and doesn't have life enough to die'. 'Kill it!' shouted the holy man with a terrible voice; 'kill it and hold it in your arms for three days and three nights to create a memory for yourself: thus you will never again beget a child when it is not time for you to beget'. When the man had heard this, he walked away disappointed; and many people reproached the holy man because he had advised a cruelty; for he had advised killing the child. 'But is it not crueller to let it live?' said the holy man.

74

The unsuccessful. – Those poor women are always unsuccessful who, in the presence of the one they love, become restless and insecure and talk too much: for men are most surely seduced by a certain secret and phlegmatic tenderness.

75

The third sex. – 'A small man is a paradox, but still a man; but small women seem to me, when compared to tall women, to belong to another sex', said an old dancing master. A small woman is never beautiful – said old Aristotle.[7]

76

The greatest danger. – Had there not always been a majority of men who felt the discipline of their heads – their 'rationality' – to be their pride, their obligation, their virtue, and who were embarrassed or ashamed by all fantasizing and debauchery of thought, being the friends of 'healthy common sense', humanity would have perished long ago! The greatest

---

[7] Aristotle doesn't actually say exactly this, but see his *Nichomachean Ethics* 1123b.6–8 and *Rhetoric* 1361a. 6–7.

danger that hovered and still hovers over humanity is the outbreak of *madness* – that is, the outbreak of arbitrariness in feeling, seeing, and hearing; the enjoyment in the lack of discipline of the head, the joy in human unreason. The opposite of the world of the madman is not truth and certainty but the generality and universal bindingness of a faith; in short, the non-arbitrary in judgement. And man's greatest labour so far has been to reach agreement about very many things and to lay down a *law of agreement* – regardless of whether these things are true or false. This is the discipline of the head which has preserved humanity – but the counter-drives are still so powerful that it is basically with little confidence that one may speak of the future of humanity. The picture of things still moves and shifts continually, and perhaps more and faster from now on than ever before; continually, the most select minds bristle at this universal bindingness – the explorers of *truth* above all! Continually this faith, as a commonplace belief shared by everyone, breeds nausea and a new lust in subtler minds; and the slow tempo for all spiritual processes which this faith makes necessary, this imitation of the tortoise that is recognized as the norm here, would by itself be sufficient to turn artists and poets into deserters: it is these impatient minds in whom a veritable delight in madness breaks out, because madness has such a cheerful tempo! What is needed, then, are virtuous intellects – oh, I'll use the most unambiguous word – what is needed is *virtuous stupidity*; what is needed are unwavering beat-keepers of the *slow* spirit, so that the believers of the great common faith stay together and go on dancing their dance: it is an exigency of the first order which commands and demands. *We others are the exception and the danger* – we stand eternally in need of defence! – Now there is certainly something to be said for the exception, *provided it never wants to become the rule.*

77

The animal with a good conscience. – The vulgar element in everything that pleases in Southern Europe – be it Italian opera (e.g. Rossini and Bellini)[8] or the Spanish adventure novel (most readily accessible to us in

---

8 Gioachino Rossini (1792–1868) wrote thirty-six operas in the years between 1810 and 1829, then retired, devoting the remaining forty years of his life to culinary pleasures in Paris. Vincenzo Bellini's (1801–35) most famous opera is *Norma*. The music of Rossini and Bellini was very highly regarded by Arthur Schopenhauer (1788–1860), the modern philosopher who influenced the young Nietzsche most deeply.

the French disguise of Gil Blas)[9] – does not escape me; but it does not offend me, just as little as does the vulgarity that one encounters on a walk through Pompeii and basically even when reading any ancient book.[10] Why is this? Is it because there is no shame and everything vulgar acts as confidently and self-assuredly as anything noble, lovely, and passionate in the same kind of music or novel? 'The animal has its own right, just like the human being; let it run about freely – and you too, my dear fellow man, are still an animal despite everything!' – That seems to me to be the moral of the story and the peculiarity of Southern humanity. Bad taste has its right just as good taste does – and even a prior right if it answers to a great need, provides guaranteed satisfaction and as it were a universal language, an unconditionally intelligible mask and gesture; good, refined taste, on the contrary, is always somewhat searching, deliberate, not altogether sure how it is to be understood: it is not and never was popular! What is and remains popular is the *mask*! So let them all continue to go their way, all those masklike elements in the melodies and cadenzas, in the leaps and gaieties of the rhythm of these operas! Ancient life, too! What can one understand about it when one does not understand the delight in the mask, the good conscience in everything mask-like! Here is the bath and the recreation of the ancient spirit – and maybe the rare and sublime natures of the old world needed this bath more than the vulgar. A vulgar turn in Northern works, for example in German music, on the other hand, offends me unspeakably. Here there is *shame*; the artist has lowered himself in his own eyes and could not even help blushing: we are ashamed with him and are so offended because we suspect that he believed he had to lower himself for our sakes.

78

What we should be grateful for. – Only artists, and especially those of the theatre, have given men eyes and ears to see and hear with some pleasure what each himself is, himself experiences, himself wants; only they have

---

[9] *Histoire de Gil Blas de Santillane* (4 vols., 1715–35) by Alain-René Lesage is one of the original picaresque novels.

[10] The Roman city of Pompeii, near present-day Naples, was preserved by being covered in ash by an eruption of the volcano Vesuvius in AD 79. Excavation of the site began in the mid-nineteenth century. Nietzsche visited Naples and its environs several times. The 'vulgarity' of which he speaks is probably the prominent display of a variety of forms of erotic art.

taught us to value the hero that is hidden in each of these everyday characters and taught the art of regarding oneself as a hero, from a distance and as it were simplified and transfigured – the art of 'putting oneself on stage' before oneself. Only thus can we get over certain lowly details in ourselves. Without this art we would be nothing but fore-ground, and would live entirely under the spell of that perspective which makes the nearest and most vulgar appear tremendously big and as reality itself. Maybe there is a similar sort of merit in that religion which bade one to see the sinfulness of every individual through a magnifying glass and turned the sinner into a great, immortal criminal: by describing eternal perspectives around him, it taught man to view himself from a distance and as something past and whole.

79

The attraction of imperfection. – I see here a poet who, like some people, exerts a greater attraction through his imperfections than through all that reaches completion and perfection under his hand – indeed, his advantage and fame are due much more to his ultimate incapacity than to his ample strength. His work never wholly expresses what he really would like to express, what he *would like to have seen*: it seems as if he has had the foretaste of a vision, but never the vision itself – yet a tremendous lust for this vision remains in his soul, and it is from this that he derives his equally tremendous eloquence of desire and craving. With it he lifts his listener above his work and all 'works' and lends him wings to rise to heights which listeners otherwise never reach; and so, having themselves become poets and seers, they give the creator of their happiness their due admiration, as if he had led them immediately to the vision of what was for him holiest and most ultimate; as if he had really attained his goal and really *seen* and communicated his vision. The fact that he never reached his goal benefits his fame.

80

Art and nature. – The Greeks (or at least the Athenians) liked to hear good speech; indeed, they had a greedy craving for it which distin-guishes them more than anything else from the non-Greeks. And so they demanded even of passion on stage that it speak well, and submitted with delight to the unnaturalness of dramatic verse – after all, in nature, passion is so taciturn! So mute and bashful! Or when it finds words, so confused and irrational and a shame to itself! Now thanks to the Greeks, we have all grown accustomed to this unnaturalness on stage, just as we endure and gladly endure that other unnaturalness, *singing* passion, thanks to the Italians. We have developed a need that we cannot satisfy in reality: to hear people in the most difficult situations speak well and at length; it delights us now when the tragic hero still finds words, reasons, eloquent gestures, and altogether a radiant spirit where life approaches the abyss and a real human being would usually lose his head and certainly his fine language. This kind of *deviation from nature* is perhaps the most pleasant meal for human pride; for its sake man loves art as the expression of a lofty, heroic unnaturalness and convention. We rightly reproach a dramatic poet if he does not transform everything into reason and words but always retains in his hand a residue of *silence* – just as one is dissatisfied with the musician at the opera who cannot find a melody for the highest affect but only a sentimental 'natural' stammering and screaming. For here nature is *supposed* to be contradicted! Here the vulgar charm of illusion is *supposed* to give way to a higher charm! The Greeks go far, far on this road – terrifyingly far! Just as they make the stage as narrow as possible and forbid themselves all effects through deep backgrounds; just as they make facial expressions and easy movement impossible for the actor and transform him into a solemn, stiff, masked puppet, so they also have deprived passion itself of any deep background and dictated to it a law of beautiful speech; yes, on the whole they have done everything to counteract the elemental effect of images that arouse fear and compassion – *for fear and compassion were precisely what they did not want*. With all due respect to Aristotle, he certainly didn't hit the nail, let alone on the head, when he discussed the final purpose of Greek tragedy.[11] Just consider the Greek tragic poets and what most stimulated their industriousness, their sensitivity, their competitiveness – certainly not the aim of overwhelming the spectator with emotions. The Athenian went to the theatre *to hear pleasing speech*! Pleasing speeches were what preoccupied Sophocles[12] – pardon the heresy! It is quite different with

[11] In his *Poetics* (chapter 6, 1449b.24ff.) Aristotle says that tragedy has its effect by producing 'pity/compassion' and 'fear' in the audience.
[12] Athenian dramatist of the fifth century BC

serious opera. All of its masters try to keep the audience from understanding the characters. Occasionally catching a word might help the
inattentive listener, but on the whole the situation must explain itself –
the speeches don't matter! This is how they all think and have pulled
their pranks with words. Maybe they only lacked the courage to express
fully their ultimate disregard for words: with just a little more impu-
dence, Rossini[13] would have had everyone sing nothing but la-la-la-la –
and that would have made good sense. One shouldn't believe the words
of characters in opera, but rather their sound! That is the difference,
that is the beautiful *unnaturalness* for the sake of which one goes to the
opera. Even the *recitativo secco*[14] is not really meant to be heard as word
and text: this kind of half-music is rather supposed initially to give the
musical ear a short rest (rest from the *melody* as the most sublime and
therefore also the most challenging pleasure of this art) – but very soon
also something else, namely, a growing impatience, a growing aversion,
a new desire for *whole* music, for melody. How are things with Richard
Wagner's art,[15] considered from this perspective? Is it the same,
perhaps? Perhaps different? Often it has seemed to me as if one had to
memorize the words *and* music of his creations before the performance,
for otherwise – so it appeared to me – one *would hear* neither the words
nor even the music.

81

Greek taste. – 'What is beautiful about that?' said the surveyor after a
performance of *Iphigenia*. 'Nothing is proved in it!'[16] Were the Greeks

[13] See above, Book II footnote 8, p. 77. In *Opera and Drama* Wagner claims that Rossini had
reduced opera to absolute melody, destroying its dramatic content and so opera itself.

[14] 'dry recitative'. 'Recitative' is a style of composing vocal music that tries to keep the musical
form as close as possible to the cadences of normal speech. 'Dry' recitative is one in which the
musical texture is sparse and the voice or voices are accompanied only by a minimal number of
instruments (e.g. keyboard and violoncello).

[15] Richard Wagner (1813–83) in his theoretical writings returned again and again to the question
of the proper relation between words and music in opera.

[16] Nietzsche takes this anecdote from Schopenhauer's *World as Will and Representation* (vol. I,
Book 3, § 36) where it is used to illustrate the complete discrepancy between, on the one hand,
the kind of intelligence used in everyday experience, science, and mathematics (ability, according
to Schopenhauer, to subsume things under the 'principle of sufficient reason') and, on the other,
aesthetic contemplation. The *Iphigenia* in question is the play by the French dramatist Jean
Racine (1639–99).

that far away from this taste? In Sophocles, at least, 'everything is proved'.

82

Esprit[17] *as un-Greek.* – The Greeks are indescribably logical and simple in all their thought; at least in their long good age they never wearied of this, as so often do the French, who all too gladly take a little leap into the opposite and actually only endure the spirit of logic when, through a series of such small leaps into the opposite, it betrays its *sociable* civility, its sociable self-denial. Logic strikes them as necessary, like bread and water, but also, like these, as a kind of prisoners' food as soon as it is enjoyed pure and plain. In good company one must never want to be entirely and solely right, which is what all pure logic wants; hence the small dose of unreason in all French *esprit*. The Greeks' sense of sociability was far less developed than that of the French is and was; that is why there is so little *esprit* in even their most spirited men; that is why there is so little humour in even their humorists; that is why – oh! One will not even believe these sentences of mine, and how many more of the same sort are yet on my mind! – *Est res magna tacere*[18] – says Martial along with all garrulous people.

83

Translations. – One can estimate the degree of an age's historical sense from the way it makes *translations* and seeks to absorb past ages and books. The French of Corneille's age[19] as well as those of the Revolution seized Roman antiquity in a way we no longer dare to – thanks to our higher historical sense. And Roman antiquity itself: how violently and yet naively it laid its hand on everything good and lofty in the older Greek antiquity! How they translated things into the Roman present! How deliberately and insouciantly they brushed the dust off the wings of that butterfly called 'The-Twinkling-of-an-Eye'! In this way Horace

---

[17] 'Spirit'; the word often refers to a lively imagination.
[18] 'It is a great thing to keep silent' (Martial IV.80.6). Martial was a Roman epigrammatist who lived in the first century AD.
[19] French dramatist (1606–84) who wrote a number of tragedies on ancient subjects

translated Alcaeus or Archilochus[20] now and then, as did Propertius with Callimachus and Philetas (poets of the same rank as Theocritus,[21] if we *may* judge): what did they care that the real creator had experienced this and that and written the signs of it into his poem! As poets they were averse to the antiquarian inquisitiveness that precedes the sense for history; as poets, they did not accept these utterly personal things and names and all those things that serve as the mask and costume of a city, coast, century. Rather they quickly replaced them with what was contemporary and Roman. They seem to ask us: 'Should we not make new for ourselves what is old and put *ourselves* into it? Should we not be allowed to breathe our soul into their dead body? For it is dead, after all: how ugly everything dead is!' They did not know the pleasure of a sense for history; what was past and alien was embarrassing to them; and as Romans, they saw it as an incentive for a Roman conquest. In fact at that time one conquered by translating – not merely by leaving out the historical, but also by adding allusions to the present and, above all, crossing out the name of the poet and replacing it with one's own – not with any sense of theft but with the very best conscience of the *imperium Romanum*.[22]

84

On the origin of poetry. – The lovers of what is fantastic in humans, who also advocate the view that morality is instinctive, reason as follows: 'Supposing that usefulness has always been venerated as the supreme deity, then where in all the world does poetry come from? This act of making speech rhythm counteracts rather than contributes to the clarity of communication, and yet it has shot up and is still shooting up all over the earth like a mockery of all useful expediency! The wildly beautiful irrationality of poetry refutes you, you utilitarians! Precisely to want to *get away* from usefulness for once – that is what has elevated humanity; that is what has inspired it to morality and art!' Now, in this case I must

---

[20] Archilochus (seventh century BC) and his slightly younger contemporary Alcaeus were early Greek poets who became models for the writing of poetry in Latin, for instance by Horace (first century BC).

[21] The Roman poet Sextus Propertius (first century BC) cites the Greek poets Callimachus and Philetas (both fourth/third century BC) as models (2.34.31–2; 3.1.1; 3.9.42–3). The Sicilian bucolic poet Theocritus (early third century BC) also revered Philetas.

[22] 'Roman empire'

side with the utilitarians for once – after all, they are so seldom right, it is pitiful! In those ancient times that called poetry into being, one really did aim at utility, and a very great utility at that; back then, when one let rhythm penetrate speech – that rhythmic force that reorganizes all the atoms of a sentence, bids one to select one's words and gives thoughts a new colour and makes them darker, stranger, more distant: a *superstitious utility*, of course! Rhythm was supposed to make a human request impress the gods more deeply after it was noticed that humans remember a verse better than ordinary speech; one also thought one could make oneself audible over greater distances with the rhythmic tick-tock; the rhythmic prayer seemed to get closer to the ears of the gods. Above all, one wanted to take advantage of that elemental over-powering force that humans experience in themselves when listening to music: rhythm is a compulsion; it engenders an unconquerable desire to yield, to join in; not only the stride of the feet but also the soul itself gives in to the beat – probably also, one inferred, the souls of the gods! By means of rhythm one thus tried to *compel* them and to exercise a power over them: one cast poetry around them like a magical snare. There was another, stranger notion, and it may be precisely what contributed most powerfully to the origin of poetry. Among the Pythagoreans[23] it appears as a philosophical doctrine and as an educational contrivance; but even long before there were philosophers, one acknowledged music to have the power to discharge the emotions, to cleanse the soul, to soothe the *ferocia animi*[24] – and indeed precisely through its rhythmic quality. When one had lost the proper tension and harmony of the soul, one had to *dance* to the beat of the singer – that was the prescription of this healing art. With it, Terpander quelled an uprising; with it, Empedocles pacified a lunatic; with it, Damon purged a youth who was languishing from love; with it, one also sought to appease the ferocious, vindictive gods.[25] One began by driving the

---

[23] A group of philosophers centred in Southern Italy who claimed to be followers of Pythagoras (sixth century BC). They led a life of ritual purity and were especially devoted to the study of mathematics and harmonics.

[24] 'ferocity of the soul'

[25] This anecdote about Terpander (seventh century BC), one of the earliest Greek musicians who can be identified as a historical figure, is reported in chapter 42 of *On Music*, a short treatise (almost certainly incorrectly) attributed to Plutarch. The fifth-century (BC) Sicilian politician, philosopher, and shaman Empedocles had a keen interest in all sorts of purgatives. Damon was a fifth-century (BC) Athenian politician and theorist of music who was particularly interested in the effects of music on the soul. Plato's discussion of this topic in Book III of *Republic* is probably

giddiness and exuberance of their passions to their peak, that is, one drove the madman wild, made the vindictive person drunk with lust for revenge. All orgiastic cults wanted to discharge the *ferocia*[26] of some deity all at once and turn it into an orgy so that the deity would feel freer and calmer afterwards and leave man in peace. Etymologically, *melos*[27] means a tranquillizer, not because it is itself tranquil, but because its effect makes one tranquil. And not only in the cult song, but also in the mundane song of the most ancient times there is the presumption that rhythmic quality exercises a magical force; when bailing water, for instance, or rowing, the song is a bewitchment of the demons believed to be at work here; it makes them compliant, unfree, and a tool of humans. And whenever one acts, one has an occasion to sing – *every* action is tied to the assistance of spirits: incantation and conjuration seem to be the primordial form of poetry. When verse was used in oracles – the Greeks said that the hexameter was invented at Delphi – rhythm was also supposed to exercise a compulsion.[28] To ask for a prophecy – that meant originally (according to the derivation of the Greek word that seems most probable to me) to have something determined: one thought one could force the future by gaining Apollo's favour – he who according to the oldest views is much more than a god of foresight. The way the formula is pronounced, with literal and rhythmic precision, is how it binds the future; the formula, however, is the invention of Apollo, who as god of rhythm can also bind the goddesses of fate. In short: was there anything more *useful* than rhythm to the old superstitious type of human being? One could do everything with it: promote some work magically; compel a god to appear, to be near, to listen; mould the future according to one's own will; discharge some excess (of fear, of mania, of pity, of vengefulness) from one's soul, and not only one's own soul but also that of the most evil demon. Without verse one was nothing; through verse one almost became a god. Such a basic feeling cannot be completely eradicated – and still today, after millennia of work at fighting such superstition, even the wisest of us occasionally becomes a fool for rhythm, if only insofar as he *feels* a

influenced by his views, and Plato actually mentions him at 400B. This anecdote is recounted in Martianus Capella (probably fifth century AD), *De nuptiis Philologiae et Mercurii* IX.926.

[26] 'ferocity'

[27] 'musical phrase, tune, melody'. It is unclear on what Nietzsche is basing this etymological speculation.

[28] Pausanias X.5.7

thought to be *truer* when it has a metric form and presents itself with a divine hop, skip, and jump. Is it not amusing that the most serious philosophers, strict as they otherwise are in all matters of certainty, still appeal to *the sayings of poets* to lend their thoughts force and credibility? And yet it is more dangerous for a truth when a poet agrees with it than when he contradicts it! For as Homer says: 'The bards tell many a lie'.[29]

85

The good and the beautiful. – Artists constantly *glorify* – they do nothing else – and in particular all those states and things reputed to give man the occasion for once to feel good, or great, or drunk, or merry, or well and wise. These *select* things and states, whose value for human *happiness* is considered certain and well-defined, are the artists' objects: artists always lie in wait to discover such things and to draw them into the realm of art. I want to say: they are not themselves the appraisers of happiness and of the happy man, but they always crowd around these appraisers with the greatest curiosity and the urge to make immediate use of their appraisals. They become like this because in addition to their impatience they also have the big lungs of heralds and the feet of runners, and are always among the first to glorify the *new* good, and often *appear* to be the first to name it good and to appraise it as good. This, however, as I already said, is a mistake: they are only quicker and louder than the real appraisers. – But who *are* the real appraisers? – The rich and the idle.

86

On theatre. – This day I had strong and elevated feelings again, and if on its eve I could have music and art, I know very well what music and art I would *not* like to have, namely, the kind that tries to intoxicate its audience and *drive it to the height* of a moment of strong and elevated feelings – an art for those everyday souls who in the evening look not like victors on triumphal chariots but rather like tired mules who have been whipped somewhat too often by life. What would those people know of 'higher moods' were there no intoxicating substances and

---

[29] Not actually to be found in Homer, but a proverbial Greek saying. See Aristotle, *Metaphysics* 983a.3 and Solon, *Fragment 21* (Diels).

whip-lashes of ideals! – and so they have their inspirers as they have their wines. But what is their drink and their drunkenness *to me*! What is wine to the inspired! He looks instead with a sort of disgust at the means and the mediators that are supposed to produce an effect without sufficient reason – aping the high tide of the soul! What? One gives the mole wings and proud conceits – before bedtime, before he crawls into his hole? One sends him to the theatre and puts big glasses before his blind and tired eyes? People whose lives are not a 'dramatic action' but a business sit before the stage and look at strange creatures for whom life is more than a business? 'It's proper that way', you say; 'it's entertaining that way; it's culture!' Well then! In that case I all too often lack culture, for this sight is all too often disgusting to me. Whoever has enough tragedy and comedy in himself probably does best to stay away from the theatre; or, should there be an exception, the entire event – including theatre and audience and poet – becomes the actual tragic and comic spectacle to him, so that the piece that is performed means little to him by comparison. What do the Fausts and Manfreds[30] of the theatre matter to someone who is himself somewhat like Faust and Manfred? – whereas the fact *that* such figures are brought on stage is certainly something for him to think about. The *strongest* thoughts and passions are there presented before those who are capable not of thought and passion – but of *intoxication!* And the *former* as a means to the latter! And theatre and music as the hashish-smoking and betel-chewing of the European! Oh, who will tell us the entire history of narcotics? – It is nearly the history of 'culture', our so-called higher culture!

87

On the vanity of artists. – I believe that artists often do not know what they can do best because they are too vain and have set their minds on something prouder than these small plants seem to be that are new, strange, and beautiful and really capable of growing to perfection on their soil. That which in the last instance is good in their own garden and vineyard is not fully appreciated by them, and their love and insight are not of the same order. Here is a musician who, more than any other musician, is master at finding the tones from the realm of suffering,

---

[30] In Byron's tragedy *Manfred* (1817) the hero is burdened with excessive knowledge and tries in vain to attain forgetfulness.

dejected, tormented souls and at giving speech even to the mute animals. Nobody equals him at the colours of late autumn, at the indescribably moving happiness of a last, very last, very briefest enjoyment; he knows a tone for those secret, uncanny midnights of the soul, where cause and effect seem to have gone awry and something can come to be 'from nothing' at any moment; more happily than anyone else, he draws from the very bottom of human happiness and so to speak from its drained cup, where the most bitter and repulsive drops have merged, for better or for worse, with the sweetest ones; he knows how the soul wearily drags itself along when it can no longer leap and fly, nor even walk; he has the shy glance of concealed pain, of understanding without solace, of taking farewell without confession; yes, as the Orpheus[31] of all secret misery he is greater than anyone, and he has incorporated into art some things that seemed inexpressible and even unworthy of art, and which could only be scared away and not be grasped by words in particular – some very small and microscopic features of the soul: yes, he is master at the very small. But he doesn't *want* to be! His *character* likes great walls and bold frescoes much better! It escapes him that his *spirit* has a different taste and disposition and likes best of all to sit quietly in the corners of collapsed houses – there, hidden, hidden from himself, he paints his real masterpieces, which are all very short, often only a bar long – only there does he become wholly good, great, and perfect; perhaps only there. – But he doesn't know it! He is too vain to know it.

88

Being serious about truth. – Being serious about truth! How differently people understand these words! The very same opinions and types of proof and scrutiny that a thinker may consider a frivolity in himself to which he has, to his shame, succumbed on this or that occasion – these very same views may give an artist who encounters them and lives with them for a while the feeling that he has now become deeply serious about truth and that it is admirable that he, as an artist, has at the same time the most serious desire for the opposite of appearance. So it can happen that it is precisely with his ardent seriousness that someone

---

[31] The legendary Orpheus was supposed to be able to do extraordinary things, such as bringing his wife back to life from the dead, through the power of his music.

betrays how shallow and undemanding his mind has been in playing the field of knowledge so far. – And does not everything that we take to be *important* betray us? It shows us what sort of thing has weight for us and for what sort of thing we have no weights.

89

Now and formerly. – What do all our art of artworks matter if we lose that higher art, the art of festivals! Formerly, all artworks were displayed on the great festival road of humanity, as commemorations and memorials of high and happy moments. Now one uses artworks to lure poor, exhausted, and sick human beings to the side of humanity's road of suffering for a short lascivious moment; one offers them a little intoxication and madness.

90

Lights and shadows. – Books and drafts mean different things to different thinkers: one has collected in a book the lights that he was able swiftly to steal and carry home from the rays of some insight that dawned on him; another is able to convey only the shadows, the after-images in grey and black, of that which built itself up in his soul the day before.

91

Caution. – As is well known, Alfieri[32] lied very much when he told his amazed contemporaries his life story. He lied from that despotism against himself which he also revealed in the way he created his own language and tyrannized himself into becoming a poet – he had finally found a severe form of sublimity into which he *pressed* his life and his memory: no doubt there was much agony in all this. – I also would not believe a life story of Plato, written by himself – any more than that of Rousseau[33] or the *vita nuova*[34] of Dante.

[32] an important Italian dramatist (1749–1803)
[33] In addition to his political writings (e.g. *The Social Contract*) Jean-Jacques Rousseau (1712–78) wrote an important autobiography, the *Confessions* (1781).
[34] *Vita Nuova* ('New Life') is a collection of Dante Alighieri's (1265–1321) poems connected by prose commentaries of a semi-autobiographical kind.

92

Prose and poetry. – It is remarkable that the great masters of prose have almost always also been poets, be it publicly or only in secret, in the 'closet'; and verily, one writes good prose only *face to face with poetry*! For this is an uninterrupted, courteous war with poetry: all its attractions depend on the fact that poetry is constantly evaded and contradicted; everything abstract wants to be presented as a prank against poetry and as if with a mocking voice; everything dry and cool is supposed to drive the lovely goddess into lovely despair; often there are *rapprochements*, reconciliations for a moment, and then a sudden leap back and derisive laugh; often the curtain is raised and a harsh light is let in just as the goddess is enjoying her dusks and muted colours; often the word is taken out of her mouth and sung according to a melody that makes her cover her refined ears with her refined hands – and so there are a thousand delights of this war, including defeat, of which the unpoetic, the so-called men of prose, know nothing at all – which is why they write and speak only bad prose! *War is the father of all good things;*[35] war is also the father of good prose! In this century, four very strange and truly poetic persons attained a mastery of prose, for which this century is otherwise not made – out of a lack of poetry, as I have suggested. Excluding Goethe, who may fairly be claimed by the century that produced him, I see Giacomo Leopardi, Prosper Mérimée, Ralph Waldo Emerson, and Walter Savage Landor, the author of *Imaginary Conversations,*[36] as worthy of being called masters of prose.

93

But then why do you write? – A: I am not one of those who *think* with a wet quill in hand; much less one of those who abandon themselves to their passions right before the open inkwell, sitting on their chair and staring at the paper. I am annoyed or ashamed by all writing; to me,

[35] Variant of the famous saying by the pre-Socratic philosopher Heraclitus of Ephesus (late sixth century BC): 'War is the father of all things.' This is number 53 in the standard collections (Diels-Kranz).

[36] Giacomo Leopardi (1798–1837); Italian lyric poet, also admired for his prose writings, notably *Operette Morali* (1827). The French writer Prosper Mérimée (1803–70) is now perhaps best known as the author of a 'Carmen' on which the libretto of the opera of that name by Bizet is based. Ralph Waldo Emerson (1803–82) was an American 'Transcendentalist' writer highly regarded by Nietzsche. Walter Savage Landor (1775–1864) was an English prose writer.

writing is nature's call – to speak of it even in simile is repugnant to me. B: But why, then, do you write? – A: Well, my friend, I say this in confidence: until now I have found no other means of getting *rid* of my thoughts. – B: And why do you want to get rid of them? – A: Why do I want to? Do I want to? I have to. – B: Enough! Enough!

94

Growth after death. – Those audacious little words about moral matters that Fontenelle threw out in his immortal *Dialogues of the Dead*[37] were considered in his time to be paradoxes and games of a not wholly innocent wit; even the highest judges of taste and of the mind saw nothing more in it – indeed, maybe not even Fontenelle himself. Now something incredible transpires: these thoughts become truths! Science proves them! The game gets serious! And we read these dialogues with a different feeling than Voltaire[38] and Helvétius[39] read them, and involuntarily we promote their creators to a different and *much higher* rank of mind than they did. Rightly? Wrongly?

95

Chamfort.[40] – That someone who knew humanity and the masses as well as Chamfort still joined the masses and did not stand aside in philosophical renunciation and defence, I can only explain as follows: one instinct in him was stronger than his wisdom and was never satisfied: his hatred of all nobility of blood; perhaps his mother's old hatred, which was only too easy to explain and which he had sanctified through love of his mother – an instinct for revenge harking back to his boyhood, waiting for the hour to avenge his mother. And now his life and his genius – and alas! no doubt mostly the paternal blood in his veins – had seduced him to join the ranks of this nobility as an equal, for many, many years! But eventually he could no longer stand the sight of

---

[37] See above, Book I, footnote 3, p. 31.
[38] See above, Book I, footnote 27, p. 55.
[39] French Encyclopedist who defended a form of hedonistic materialism in his major work *On the Spirit* (1758)
[40] French politician and writer (1741–94). Nietzsche's source for most of the material in this section is *Histoire de Chamfort, sa vie et ses œuvres* by P.-J. Stahl (Paris, no date of publication given), a book which Nietzsche had in his library.

himself, the sight of the 'old type of man' under the old regime; he was gripped with a violent passion of repentance which led him to put on the clothes of the mob, as *his* kind of hairshirt! His bad conscience was his failure to take revenge. If Chamfort had remained just a little bit more a philosopher, the Revolution would not have had its tragic wit and sharpest sting: it would be considered a much stupider event and would not seduce so many minds. But Chamfort's hatred and revenge educated a whole generation, and the most illustrious human beings passed through this school. Note that Mirabeau[41] looked up to Chamfort as to his higher and older self from which he expected and endured impulses, warnings, and verdicts – Mirabeau, who as a human being belongs to a quite different order of greatness than even the foremost statesmen of yesterday and today. It is peculiar that despite such a friend and advocate – after all, we have Mirabeau's letters to Chamfort – this wittiest of all moralists has remained a stranger to the French, no less than Stendhal,[42] who has perhaps had the most thoughtful eyes and ears of all Frenchmen of *this* century. Is it that the latter basically had too much of the Dutchman or Englishman within himself to be tolerable to the Parisians? Whereas Chamfort, a man who was rich in depths and backgrounds of the soul – gloomy, suffering, ardent – a thinker who found laughter necessary as a remedy against life and who nearly considered himself lost on those days when he had not laughed – seems much more like an Italian, related to Dante and Leopardi, than a Frenchman! We know Chamfort's last words: 'Ah! mon ami', he said to Sieyès,[43] 'je m'en vais enfin de ce monde, où il faut que le cœur se brise ou se bronze –'.[44] Those are surely not the words of a dying Frenchman.

96

Two speakers. – Of these two speakers, the one can show the full rationality of his cause only when he abandons himself to passion: this

---

[41] An important political figure in the early stages of the French Revolution, admired by Nietzsche: see *The Genealogy of Morality* I.10.

[42] French novelist (1783–1842). He was born Marie Henri Beyle, 'Stendhal' being a pseudonym.

[43] French politician and theorist whose *What is the Third Estate?* (1789) had great influence on the early course of the French Revolution.

[44] 'Ah, my friend, I am finally about to leave this world in which the heart must either break or plate itself with steel.'

alone pumps enough blood and heat into his brain to force his lofty intellect to reveal itself. The other attempts the same thing now and then – to present his cause with the help of passion, sonorously, violently, and captivatingly – but usually with little success. He then quite soon starts speaking obscurely and confusedly; he exaggerates, makes omissions, and arouses mistrust about the rationality of his cause; indeed, he himself comes to feel this mistrust, and this explains sudden leaps into the coldest and most repugnant tones which make the audience doubt whether his whole passion was genuine. In his case, passion inundates the mind every time – maybe because it is stronger than in the first speaker. But he is at the peak of his strength when he resists the pressing storm of his feeling and virtually derides it: only then does his mind completely step out of its hiding place – a logical, mocking, playful, and yet terrifying mind.

97

On the garrulousness of writers. – There is a garrulousness of rage – frequent in Luther, also in Schopenhauer. A garrulousness due to an exceedingly large supply of conceptual formulations, as in Kant. A garrulousness due to a delight in ever-new twists of the same thing: one finds this in Montaigne. A garrulousness of spiteful natures: whoever reads the publications of our time will recall two writers here. A garrulousness from a delight in good words and forms of language: not rare in Goethe's prose. A garrulousness from an inner pleasure in noise and confusion of feelings: for example in Carlyle.[45]

98

In praise of Shakespeare. – The most beautiful thing I can say in praise of Shakespeare *as a human being* is this: he believed in Brutus and didn't cast a speck of suspicion on this type of virtue! To him he devoted his best tragedy – it is still called by the wrong name[46] – to him and to the most dreadful epitome of lofty morality. Independence of soul! That's what's at stake here! No sacrifice can be too great for that: one has to be capable of sacrificing even one's dearest friend for it, even if he should

---

[45] British writer on history and politics (1795–1881).
[46] Shakespeare's *The Tragedy of Julius Caesar*

be the most marvellous human being, the ornament of the world, the genius without peer – if one loves freedom as the freedom of great souls and *this* freedom is endangered because of him: that is what Shakespeare must have felt! The height at which he places Caesar is the finest honour he could bestow on Brutus: only thus does he raise Brutus' inner problem to immense proportions as well as the strength of mind that was able to cut *this* knot! And was it really political freedom that drove this poet to sympathize with Brutus – and turned him into Brutus' accomplice? Or was political freedom only a symbolism for something inexpressible? Could it be that we confront some unknown dark event and adventure from the poet's own soul about which he wanted to speak only in signs? What is all of Hamlet's melancholy compared to that of Brutus! And perhaps Shakespeare knew the latter as he knew the former – through first-hand experience! Maybe he also had his dark hour and his evil angel, like Brutus! But whatever such similarities and secret references there may have been: before the whole figure and virtue of Brutus, Shakespeare threw himself to the ground and felt unworthy and distant – he wrote the evidence for this into his tragedy. Twice in the tragedy he introduced a poet,[47] and twice he poured such impatient and ultimate contempt upon him that it sounds like a cry – like the cry of self-contempt. Brutus, even Brutus loses patience when the poet enters – conceited, pathetic, obtrusive, as poets usually are – as a being who appears to be bursting with possibilities of greatness, even moral greatness, although in the philosophy of deed and life he rarely attains even a passable integrity. 'When he knows his time, *I'll know his humour. /* What should the wars do with these jiggling fools? / Companion, hence!'[48] shouts Brutus. This should be translated back into the soul of the poet who wrote it.

99

Schopenhauer's followers. – What happens when people of a higher culture and barbarians come into contact: the lower culture usually takes on the vices, weaknesses, and excesses of the higher culture, on which basis it feels a certain attraction to that culture and finally, by way

---

[47] Act III, Scene 3 and Act IV, Scene 3
[48] Nietzsche read and cited Shakespeare in the translation by Schlegel and Tieck. The text gives the English original. The italics are Nietzsche's own.

of the acquired vices and weaknesses, accepts some overflow of the valuable force of the higher culture – one can also observe this nearby and without travelling to barbarian peoples, to be sure in a form that is somewhat over-refined and intellectualized and not so easily palpable. And what do *Schopenhauer's* German followers usually take over at first from their master? In relation to his higher culture, they must feel barbarous enough to be at first barbarously fascinated and seduced by him. Is it his sense for hard facts, his good will to clarity and reason, that so often makes him appear so English and so un-German? Or is it the strength of his intellectual conscience, which *endured* a life-long contradiction between being and willing and forced him to contradict himself continually and on almost every point in his writings? Or is it his cleanliness in matters of the church and of the Christian god? – for here his cleanliness was unprecedented among German philosophers, so that he lived and died 'as a Voltairean'.[49] Or was it his immortal doctrine of the intellectuality of intuition, of the a priori nature of the causal law, of the instrumental nature of the intellect and the unfreedom of the will?[50] No, all this does not enchant and is not felt to be enchanting; but Schopenhauer's mystical embarrassments and evasions in those places where the factual thinker let himself be seduced and corrupted by the vain urge to be the unriddler of the world; the indemonstrable doctrine of *One Will* ('all causes are merely occasional causes of the appearance of the will at this time and this place'; 'the will to life is present wholly and undividedly in every being, even the least, as completely as in all beings that have ever been, are, and shall be, taken together'),[51] the *denial of the individual* ('all lions are at bottom only one lion'; 'the plurality of individuals is an illusion',[52] just as *development* is only an illusion – he calls Lamarck's thoughts 'an ingenious, absurd error'),[53] his ecstatic reveries on *genius* ('in aesthetic intuition the individual is no longer individual but pure, will-less, painless, timeless subject of knowledge'; 'the subject, in being wholly taken up in the object it intuits, has become the object itself'),[54] the nonsense about *compassion* and how, as the

---

[49] The outspoken anti-clericalism of Voltaire (see above, Book I, footnote 27, p. 55) gave him the reputation of being an atheist.

[50] See *World as Will and Representation*, vol. I, Book 4, § 54, and vol. II, Book 2, §§ 19, 4.

[51] Ibid., vol. I, Book 4, § 60 and vol. II, Book 2, § 25

[52] Ibid., vol. I, Book 2, § 28; vol. II, Book 3, § 38, and vol. II, Book 4, § 41

[53] French naturalist (1744–1829) who believed that acquired characteristics could be biologically inherited

[54] See *World as Will and Representation*, vol. I, Book 3, § 38.

source of all morality, it enables one to make the break through the *principium individuationis*;[55] and also such claims as 'death is actually the purpose of existence',[56] 'one cannot deny *a priori* the possibility that a magical effect cannot also emanate from someone who has already died' – these and other such *excesses* and vices of the philosopher are always what is accepted first of all and made into a matter of faith – for vices and excesses are the easiest to imitate and require no extensive preparatory practice. But let us discuss the most famous of living Schopenhauerians, Richard Wagner. What happened to him has happened to other artists: he misinterpreted the characters he created and misunderstood the philosophy that was implicit in his own art. Until the middle of his life, Richard Wagner let himself be misled by Hegel; he repeated this mistake when he started reading Schopenhauer's doctrine into his characters and began expressing himself in terms of 'will', 'genius', and 'compassion'. Nevertheless it will remain true that nothing goes so directly against the spirit of Schopenhauer as what is genuinely Wagnerian in Wagner's heroes: I mean the innocence of the utmost selfishness; the faith in great passion as the good in itself, in a word, what is Siegfried-like[57] in the countenances of his heroes. 'All of this smells even more like Spinoza than like me', Schopenhauer might say. Although Wagner would have good reason to look for some other philosopher than Schopenhauer, the enchantment to which he succumbed with regard to this thinker has blinded him not only to other philosophers but also to science; his entire art increasingly wants to present itself as a companion piece and supplement to Schopenhauer's philosophy, and with increasing explicitness it renounces the loftier ambition of becoming a companion piece and supplement to human knowledge and science. And not only is it the whole secretive splendour of this philosophy – which would also have attracted a Cagliostro[58] – that draws him to this, but the particular gestures and affects of the philosophers were always seducers as well! Wagner is Schopenhauerian, for example, in his exasperation over the corruption of the German

---

[55] 'The principle of individuation'. Schopenhauer believed that the reality of the universe was an undifferentiated Will which however appeared to us as a world of distinct things subject to the 'principle of individuation'. Ibid., vol. I, Book 2, § 23, and vol. I, Book 4, § 68

[56] Ibid., vol. II, Book 4, § 49

[57] The third opera in Wagner's four-part cycle *Der Ring des Nibelungen* tells the story of the hero Siegfried, who can be taken to represent an energetic, unspoiled humanity of the future.

[58] Notorious eighteenth-century charlatan

language;[59] even, however, if one should approve of Wagner's imitation of Schopenhauer in this point, one must not conceal the fact that Wagner's style itself suffers rather seriously from all those ulcers and tumours whose sight so enraged Schopenhauer. Regarding the Wagnerians who write German, Wagnerianism is starting to prove as dangerous as any Hegelianism ever has. Wagner is Schopenhauerian in his hatred of the Jews, to whom he is unable to do justice even in their greatest deed; after all, the Jews are the inventors of Christianity.[60] Wagner is Schopenhauerian in his attempt to conceive of Christianity as a seed of Buddhism that has drifted far and to prepare a Buddhistic age for Europe, with an occasional reconciliation with Catholic-Christian formulas and sentiments.[61] Wagner is Schopenhauerian when he preaches mercy in our relations with animals; as we know, Schopenhauer's predecessor in this was Voltaire, who may also, like his successors, have known to disguise his hatred of certain things and persons as mercy towards animals.[62] At least Wagner's hatred of science, which finds expression in his preaching, certainly does not come from a spirit of mercy and goodness – any more, obviously, than it does from any *spirit* at all. In the end, the philosophy of an artist is of little significance if it is merely an afterthought (*eine nachträgliche Philosophie*) and does not harm the art itself. One cannot be too careful to avoid bearing ill will against an artist for an occasional, perhaps very unfortunate and presumptuous masquerade; let us not forget that, without exception, our dear artists are to some extent actors and have to be, and that

---

[59] Wagner: 'Bericht an Seine Majestät den König Ludwig II. von Bayern über eine in München zu errichtende deutsche Musikschule'; Schopenhauer: 'Über Schriftstellerei und Stil' in his *Parerga und Paralipomena* (vol. II, chapter 23)

[60] Wagner: *Das Judentum in der Musik* (1850); Schopenhauer: 'Zur Rechtslehre und Politik' in *Parerga und Paralipomena* (vol. II, chapter 9, § 132) (Jews should have civil rights, but it is 'absurd' to grant them rights of political participation), 'Über die Universitäts-Philosophie' in *Parerga und Paralipomena* (vol. I) (One of the major defects of 'modern' philosophy, especially that of Hegel, is that it has imposed on itself the task of arguing for the truth of a 'Jewish mythology') etc.

[61] Wagner: *Religion und Kunst* (1880); Schopenhauer: *World as Will and Representation*, vol. II, Book 4, § 41

[62] Wagner, *Religion und Kunst* (1880). In Act I of *Parsifal* Gurnemanz lectures the young Parsifal on the evils of killing animals. Schopenhauer, 'Preisschrift über die Grundlage der Moral' § 19. In this essay, as generally, Schopenhauer connects proto-animal-liberation views with anti-Semitism (see above, Book II, footnote 60), arguing that Europeans treat animals badly because the Old Testament posits an absolute distinction between animals and humans, and claiming that anyone not 'chloroformed by the *foetor Iudaicus* [Jewish stench]' would see that animals and humans were essentially the same and thus should be treated with similar compassion.

without acting they would hardly be able to hold out very long. Let us remain faithful to Wagner in what is *true* and original in him – and especially, as his disciples, by remaining faithful to ourselves in what is true and original in us. Let us leave him his intellectual tempers and cramps; let us, in all fairness, ask what strange kinds of nourishment and needs an art like his may *require* in order to be able to live and grow! It doesn't matter that as a thinker he is so often wrong; justice and patience are not for *him*. Enough that his life is justified before itself and remains justified – this life which shouts at every one of us: 'Be a man and do not follow me – but yourself! Yourself!'[63] *Our* life, too, shall be justified before ourselves! We too shall freely and fearlessly, in innocent selfishness, grow and blossom from ourselves! And as I contemplate such a person, the following sentences still come to mind today as they did before: 'That passion is better than Stoicism and hypocrisy; that being honest even in evil is better than losing oneself to the morality of tradition; that the free man can be good as well as evil, but the unfree man is a disgrace to nature and has no share in heavenly or earthly comfort; finally that *everyone who wants to be free must become so through himself*, and that freedom does not fall into anyone's lap as a wondrous gift' (*Richard Wagner in Bayreuth*, p. 94).[64]

100

Learning how to pay homage. – Men have to learn to pay homage just as they have to learn to feel contempt. Anyone who breaks new paths and has led many people onto new paths discovers with amazement how clumsy and poor those many are at expressing their gratitude; indeed, how seldom gratitude *is able* to express itself at all. It is as though whenever gratitude wants to speak, something gets caught in her throat so that she just clears her throat and falls silent clearing her throat. The way in which a thinker comes to sense the effects of his thoughts and their reorganizing and unsettling power is almost a comedy; it seems at times as if those who have been affected basically feel insulted and can

---

[63] Goethe's highly overwrought novel *The Sufferings of Young Werther* tells the story of a young man who is unhappy in love and shoots himself. When real young men began dressing and acting like Werther, and a few actually shot themselves, citing his example, Goethe decided he needed to intervene and had these words placed as a motto before the second edition of the text (1775).

[64] Nietzsche quotes from his own essay orginally published as part of *Untimely Meditations* (1876).

only express what they take to be their threatened independence through a welter of incivilities. Entire generations are needed to invent merely a polite convention for thanks; and only very late comes that time when even gratitude has acquired a kind of spirit and genius; by then, someone is usually also around to be the great recipient of the gratitude, not only for what good he himself has done, but mostly for what his predecessors have slowly heaped up as a treasure of the highest and best.

101

Voltaire.[65] – Wherever there was a court, there were laws of good speech and thus also laws of style for all who wrote. The language of the court, however, is the language of the courtier, *who has no area of expertise* and who forbids himself convenient technical expressions even in conversation about scientific matters because they smack of areas of expertise; that is why, in countries with a courtly culture, technical expressions and everything that betrays a specialist is considered a *stylistic blemish*. Now that all courts have become caricatures of past and present, one is amazed to find even Voltaire unspeakably inflexible and punctilious on this point (for example in his judgement of such stylists as Fontenelle[66] and Montesquieu[67]) – for we are all emancipated from courtly taste, while Voltaire *perfected* it!

102

A word to the philologists. – That there are books so valuable and regal that entire generations of scholars are well employed when, through their efforts, these books are preserved in a pure and intelligible state – philology exists to reinforce this faith again and again. It presupposes that there is no dearth of those rare human beings (even if one doesn't see them right away) who really know how to use such valuable books – probably those who themselves write or could write such books. I mean that philology presupposes a noble faith – that for the sake of a few who always 'will come' but are not there, a very great deal of painstaking,

---

[65] See above, Book I, footnote 27, p. 55 and Book II, footnote 49, p. 95.
[66] See above, Book I, footnote 3, p. 31.
[67] French political theorist (1689–1755)

even unclean work first needs to be done: it is all work *in usum Delphinorum*.[68]

103

On German music. – Today German music is, more than any other, the music of Europe only because it alone has given expression to the transformation that Europe underwent through the Revolution: only German composers know how to lend expression to animated masses of people; how to create that enormous artificial noise that doesn't even have to be very loud – whereas for example Italian opera knows only choruses of servants or soldiers, but not 'people'.[69] Moreover, in all German music one can hear a deep bourgeois envy of nobility, especially of *esprit* and *élégance* as expressions of a courtly, knightly, old, self-assured society. This music is not like that of Goethe's singer before the gate, which also pleases 'in the great hall' and actually pleases the king; the idea is not 'The knights looked bravely thither, and the fair down at their laps'.[70] Even grace (*Grazie*) does not appear in German music without pangs of conscience; only in the presence of native charm (*Anmut*), the rustic sister of grace, does the German begin to feel wholly moral – and from that point on increasingly so, all the way up to his rapturous, erudite, often gruff 'sublimity', the sublimity of Beethoven. If you want to picture the human being for *this* music, well, just imagine Beethoven as he appears beside Goethe – say, at their encounter at Teplitz:[71] as semi-barbarism beside culture, as the people beside nobility, as the good-natured human being next to the good and more than merely 'good' human being, as the visionary beside the artist, as

---

[68] The eldest son of the King of France and heir apparent to the throne was called 'the Dauphin'. In order to ensure that his son received the best education possible the French king Louis XIV had a special edition of Greek and Latin authors made 'in usum Delphini' (i.e. 'for the use of the Dauphin'). This edition deleted passages from the works that were considered objectionable for one reason or another. *In usum Delphinorum* means 'for the use of Dauphins'.

[69] This is an extraordinary statement, which must reflect Nietzsche's selective view of Italian opera. In particular, the chorus of Hebrew slaves from Verdi's *Nabucco* (1842), 'Va pensiero', became one of the most famous patriotic songs of the Italian Risorgimento.

[70] Poem by Goethe from his novel *Wilhelm Meister*, Book ii, chapter 11.

[71] Goethe and Beethoven, walking together in the spa town of Teplitz, encountered the Empress and her entourage. The staunch republican Beethoven tried to get Goethe to follow his example of not making way for the Imperial Suite, but Goethe, who was for decades an official at the small German court of Weimar, politely stepped aside and removed his hat as the Empress passed.

the man in need of comfort next to the man who is comforted, as the exaggerating and suspicious man next to the fair-minded, as the moody self-tormentor, the foolishly ecstatic, the blissfully unhappy, the guilelessly immoderate, as the presumptuous and crude – and all in all, the 'untamed human being':[72] that is how Goethe himself experienced and characterized him – Goethe, the exception among Germans for whom no music of equal rank has yet been found! Consider finally whether the ever more widely reaching contempt for melody and the atrophy of the melodic sense among Germans can be understood as a democratic boorishness and after-effect of the Revolution. For melody has such an open joy in lawfulness and such a revulsion towards everything that is inchoate, unformed, and arbitrary that it sounds like a strain from the *old* order of things European and like a seduction and return to it.

104

On the sound of the German language. – We know where the German comes from that for a few centuries has been accepted as literary German. The Germans, with their reverence for everything that came from *the court*, have deliberately taken the chanceries as their model in everything they had to *write*, such as letters, documents, wills, and so forth. To write in the style of the chanceries was to write like the courts and the government – that was something distinguished compared to the German spoken in the city in which one happened to live. Eventually one drew the consequences and started to speak the way one wrote – thus one became even more discriminating in word formations, in the choice of words and phrases, and finally also in sound: one affected a courtly tone when speaking, and in the end the affectation became natural. Perhaps nothing like this has happened anywhere else: the triumph of written style over speech and the affectation and pomposity of a whole people as the foundation of a common language that is no longer a mere conjunction of dialects. I believe that the sound of the German language in the middle ages, and especially in the time after the middle ages, was deeply rustic and vulgar; in the last few centuries it has become a bit more refined, primarily because one felt compelled to imitate so many French, Italian, and Spanish sounds –

---

[72] Goethe describes Beethoven thus in a letter to the former's friend Zelter of 2 September 1812.

particularly on the part of the German (and Austrian) nobility, which could in no way be content with the mother tongue. But despite this exercise, German must have sounded unbearably vulgar to Montaigne or even Racine; and to this day, in the mouth of travellers even in the midst of an Italian rabble, it sounds very coarse and hoarse, as if it originated in the back woods in smoky cabins and rude regions. I note today that among the former admirers of the chanceries a similar yearning for refinement of sound is spreading, and that the Germans are starting to obey a most peculiar 'acoustic spell' which could, in the long run, become a real danger to the German language – for one would seek in vain to find more abhorrent sounds in Europe. Something scornful, cold, indifferent, careless in one's voice: that is what sounds 'refined' to Germans today – and I hear the good will to this refinement in the voices of young officials, teachers, women, merchants; even little girls are starting to imitate this officers' German. For the officer – specifically the Prussian officer – is the inventor of these sounds: this same officer who as military man and specialist possesses that admirable tact of modesty which all Germans could stand to learn (including German professors and musicians!). But as soon as he speaks and moves, the German officer is the most immodest and distasteful figure in old Europe – quite unselfconsciously, without any doubt! Nor are the good Germans conscious of this when they admire him as the man of the foremost and most distinguished society and gladly let him 'set the tone'. And so he does! First it is the sergeants and the non-commissioned officers who imitate and coarsen his tone. Just listen to the shouted commands that positively surround German cities with a roar now that they drill outside all the gates: what presumptuousness, what raging sense of authority, what scornful coldness reverberates from this roar! Are the Germans really supposed to be a musical people? It is certain that the Germans are becoming militarized in the sound of their language; it is probable that once they have got used to speaking in a military tone, they will eventually also start writing that way. For being used to certain sounds has a profound effect on character – one soon has the words and phrases, and finally also the thoughts that fit this sound! Maybe the Germans already write like officers; maybe I just read too little of what is written in Germany. But one thing I know more certainly: the public German proclamations that also reach other countries are inspired not by German music but by this new sound of a distasteful presumptuousness. In almost every speech of the foremost German statesman, and even when he lets himself be heard only through his imperial mouthpiece,[73] is an accent that repels with revulsion the ear of a foreigner. But the Germans endure it – they endure themselves.

105

The Germans as artists. – When the German really works up a passion (and not merely the usual good will to passion!), he behaves as he must, and thinks no further about his behaviour. But the truth is that his behaviour is then very clumsy and ugly, as if lacking in tact and melody, so that the spectators merely have their own feelings of embarrassment or pathos and nothing more – *unless* he elevates himself into that state of sublimity and rapture, of which many passions are capable. Then even the German becomes *beautiful!* An idea of *the height at which* beauty first begins to pour its magic even over Germans drives the German artists into the heights and superheights and excesses of passion: in other words, a genuinely deep desire to rise beyond, at least look beyond, the ugliness and clumsiness – to a better, lighter, more southern, sunnier world. And so their cramps are often just indications that they would like to *dance*: these poor bears in which hidden nymphs and sylvan gods are at work – and at times still higher deities!

106

Music as advocate – 'I am thirsting for a master composer', said an innovator to his disciple, 'who can learn my thoughts from me and hereafter speak them in his language: that way I will better penetrate into people's ears and hearts. With tones one can seduce people into every error and every truth: who could *refute* a tone?' – 'So you would like to be considered irrefutable?' said his disciple. The innovator replied: 'I wish for the sprout to become a tree. For a teaching to become a tree, it has to be believed for a good while; for it to be believed, it has to be considered irrefutable. The tree needs storms, doubts,

---

[73] This probably refers to Chancellor Bismarck ('foremost statesman') and Emperor Wilhelm I ('imperial mouthpiece').

worms, and malice in order to reveal the nature and strength of its sprout; may it break if it is not strong enough! But a sprout can only be destroyed – not refuted!' When he had said that, his disciple cried impetuously: 'But I believe in your cause and consider it so strong that I will say everything, everything that I still have on my mind against it'. The innovator laughed to himself and wagged a finger at him. 'This kind of discipleship', he said, 'is the best, but it is dangerous and not every kind of teaching can withstand it'.

107

Our ultimate gratitude to art. – Had we not approved of the arts and invented this type of cult of the untrue, the insight into general untruth and mendacity that is now given to us by science – the insight into delusion and error as a condition of cognitive and sensate existence – would be utterly unbearable. *Honesty* would lead to nausea and suicide. But now our honesty has a counterforce that helps us avoid such consequences: art, as the *good* will to appearance. We do not always keep our eyes from rounding off, from finishing off the poem; and then it is no longer eternal imperfection that we carry across the river of becoming – we then feel that we are carrying a *goddess*, and are proud and childish in performing this service. As an aesthetic phenomenon existence is still *bearable* to us, and art furnishes us with the eye and hand and above all the good conscience to be *able* to make such a phenomenon of ourselves. At times we need to have a rest from ourselves by looking at and down at ourselves and, from an artistic distance, laughing *at* ourselves or crying *at* ourselves; we have to discover the *hero* no less than the *fool* in our passion for knowledge; we must now and then be pleased about our folly in order to be able to stay pleased about our wisdom! And precisely because we are at bottom grave and serious human beings and more weights than human beings, nothing does us as much good as the *fool's cap*: we need it against ourselves – we need all exuberant, floating, dancing, mocking, childish, and blissful art lest we lose that *freedom over things* that our ideal demands of us. It would be a *relapse* for us, with our irritable honesty, to get completely caught up in morality and, for the sake of the overly severe demands that we there make on ourselves, to become virtuous monsters and scarecrows. We have also to *be able* to stand *above* morality

– and not just to stand with the anxious stiffness of someone who is afraid of slipping and falling at any moment, but also to float and play above it! How then could we possibly do without art and with the fool? – And as long as you are in any way *ashamed* of yourselves, you do not yet belong amongst us!

Book Three

108

New battles. – After Buddha was dead, they still showed his shadow in a cave for centuries – a tremendous, gruesome shadow. God is dead; but given the way people are, there may still for millennia be caves in which they show his shadow. – And we – we must still defeat his shadow as well!

109

Let us beware. – Let us beware of thinking that the world is a living being. Where would it stretch? What would it feed on? How could it grow and procreate? After all, we know roughly what the organic is; are we then supposed to reinterpret what is inexpressibly derivative, late, rare, accidental, which we perceive only on the crust of the earth, as something essential, common, and eternal, as those people do who call the universe an organism? This nauseates me. Let us beware even of believing that the universe is a machine; it is certainly not constructed to one end, and the word 'machine' pays it far too high an honour. Let us beware of assuming in general and everywhere anything as elegant as the cyclical movements of our neighbouring stars; even a glance at the Milky Way raises doubts whether there are not much coarser and more contradictory movements there, as well as stars with eternally linear paths, etc. The astral order in which we live is an exception; this order and the considerable duration that is conditioned by it have again made possible the exception of exceptions: the development of the organic. The total character of the world, by contrast, is for all eternity chaos, not in the sense of a lack of necessity but of a lack of order, organization, form, beauty, wisdom, and whatever else our aesthetic anthropomorphisms are called. Judged from the vantage point of our reason, the unsuccessful attempts are by far the rule; the exceptions are not the secret aim, and the whole musical mechanism repeats eternally its tune, which must never be called a melody – and ultimately even the phrase 'unsuccessful attempt' is already an anthropomorphism bearing a reproach. But how could we reproach or praise the universe! Let us beware of attributing to it heartlessness or unreason or their opposites: it is neither perfect, nor beautiful, nor noble, nor does it want to become any of these things; in no way does it strive to imitate man! In no way do our aesthetic and moral judgements apply to it! It also has no drive to self-preservation or any other drives; nor does it observe any laws. Let us beware of saying that there are laws in nature. There are only necessities: there is no one who commands, no one who obeys, no one who transgresses. Once you know that there are no purposes, you also know that there is no accident; for only against a world of purposes does the word 'accident' have a meaning. Let us beware of saying that death is opposed to life. The living is only a form of what is dead, and a very rare form. Let us beware of thinking that the world eternally creates new things. There are no eternally enduring substances; matter is as much of an error as the god of the Eleatics.[1] But when will we be done with our caution and care? When will all these shadows of god no longer darken us? When will we have completely de-deified nature? When may we begin to *naturalize* humanity with a pure, newly discovered, newly redeemed nature?

110

Origin of knowledge. – Through immense periods of time, the intellect produced nothing but errors; some of them turned out to be useful and species-preserving; those who hit upon or inherited them fought their fight for themselves and their progeny with greater luck. Such erroneous articles of faith, which were passed on by inheritance further and further, and finally almost became part of the basic endowment of the species, are for example: that there are enduring things; that there are identical things; that there are things, kinds of material, bodies; that a thing is what it appears to be; that our will is free; that what is good for me is also good in and for itself. Only very late did the deniers and doubters of such propositions emerge; only very late did truth emerge as the weakest form of knowledge. It seemed that one was unable to live with it; that our organism was geared for its opposite: all its higher functions, the perceptions of sense and generally every kind of sensation, worked with those basic errors that had been incorporated since time immemorial. Further, even in the realm of knowledge those propositions became the norms according to which one determined 'true' and 'untrue' – down to the most remote areas of pure logic. Thus

---

[1] Group of philosophers in the early fifth century BC who argued that the world of change was a mere appearance of an underlying unchanging being

the *strength* of knowledge lies not in its degree of truth, but in its age, its embeddedness, its character as a condition of life. Where life and knowledge seem to contradict each other, there was never any serious fight to begin with; denial and doubt were simply considered madness. Those exceptional thinkers, like the Eleatics, who still posited and clung to the opposites of the natural errors, believed in the possibility of also *living* this opposite: they invented the sage as the man of unchangeability, impersonality, universality of intuition, as one and all at the same time, with a special capacity for that inverted knowledge; they had the faith that their knowledge was at the same time the principle of *life*. But in order to be able to claim all this, they had to *deceive* themselves about their own state: they had fictitiously to attribute to themselves impersonality and duration without change; they had to misconstrue the nature of the knower, deny the force of impulses in knowledge, and generally conceive reason as a completely free, self-originated activity. They closed their eyes to the fact that they, too, had arrived at their propositions in opposition to what was considered valid or from a desire for tranquillity or sole possession or sovereignty. The subtler development of honesty and scepticism finally made also these people impossible; even their life and judgements proved dependent on the ancient drives and fundamental errors of all sentient existence. This subtler honesty and scepticism arose wherever two conflicting propositions seemed to be *applicable* to life because both were compatible with the basic errors, and thus where it was possible to argue about the greater or lesser degree of *usefulness* for life; also wherever new propositions showed themselves to be not directly useful, but at least also not harmful, as expressions of an intellectual play impulse, and innocent and happy like all play. Gradually the human brain filled itself with such judgements and convictions; and ferment, struggle, and lust for power developed in this tangle. Not only utility and delight, but also every kind of drive took part in the fight about the 'truths'; the intellectual fight became an occupation, attraction, profession, duty, dignity – knowledge and the striving for the true finally took their place as a need among the other needs. Henceforth, not only faith and conviction, but also scrutiny, denial, suspicion, and contradiction were a *power*; all 'evil' instincts were subordinated to knowledge and put in its service and took on the lustre of the permitted, honoured, useful and finally the eye and the innocence of the *good*. Thus knowledge became a part of life and, as life, a continually growing power, until finally knowledge and the ancient basic errors struck against each other, both as life, both as power, both in the same person. The thinker – that is now the being in whom the drive to truth and those life-preserving errors are fighting their first battle, after the drive to truth has *proven* itself to be a life-preserving power, too. In relation to the significance of this battle, everything else is a matter of indifference: the ultimate question about the condition of life is posed here, and the first attempt is made here to answer the question through experiment. To what extent can truth stand to be incorporated? – that is the question; that is the experiment.

I I I

The origin of the logical. – What is the origin of logic in man's head? Surely it arose out of the illogical, the realm of which must originally have been immense. But innumerable beings drew inferences in a way different from that in which we do now perished; nonetheless, they might have been closer to the truth! He, for instance, who did not know how to find 'identity' often enough, both with regard to nourishment and to hostile animals – that is, he who subsumed too slowly and was too cautious in subsumption – had a slighter probability of survival than he who in all cases of similarity immediately guessed that they were identical. The predominant disposition, however, to treat the similar as identical – an illogical disposition, for there is nothing identical as such – is what first supplied all the foundations for logic. Similarly, in order for the concept of substance to originate, which is indispensable to logic though nothing real corresponds to it in the strictest sense, it was necessary that for a long time changes in things not be seen, not be perceived; the beings who did not see things exactly had a head start over those who saw everything 'in a flux'. As such, every great degree of caution in inferring, every sceptical disposition, is a great danger to life. No living being would be preserved had not the opposite disposition – to affirm rather than suspend judgement, to err and make things up rather than wait, to agree rather than deny, to pass judgement rather than be just – been bred to become extraordinarily strong. The course of logical thoughts and inferences in our brains today corresponds to a process and battle of drives that taken separately are all very illogical and unjust; we usually experience only the outcome of the battle: that is how quickly and covertly this ancient mechanism runs its course in us.

112

Cause and effect. – We call it 'explanation', but 'description' is what distinguishes us from older stages of knowledge and science. We are better at describing – we explain just as little as all our predecessors. We have uncovered a diverse succession where the naive man and investigator of older cultures saw only two different things, 'cause' and 'effect', as they said; we have perfected the picture of becoming but haven't got over, got behind the picture. The series of 'causes' faces us much more completely in each case; we reason, 'this and that must precede for that to follow' – but we haven't thereby *understood* anything. The specifically qualitative aspect for example of every chemical process, still appears to be a 'miracle', as does every locomotion; no one has 'explained' the push. And how could we explain! We are operating only with things that do not exist – with lines, surfaces, bodies, atoms, divisible times, divisible spaces. How is explanation to be at all possible when we first turn everything into a *picture* – our picture! It is enough to view science as an attempt to humanize things as faithfully as possible; we learn to describe ourselves more and more precisely as we describe things and their succession. Cause and effect: there is probably never such a duality; in truth a continuum faces us, from which we isolate a few pieces, just as we always perceive a movement only as isolated points, i.e. do not really see, but infer. The suddenness with which many effects stand out misleads us; it is a suddenness only for us. There is an infinite number of processes that elude us in this second of suddenness. An intellect that saw cause and effect as a continuum, not, as we do, as arbitrary division and dismemberment – that saw the stream of the event – would reject the concept of cause and effect and deny all determinedness.

113

On the doctrine of poisons. – So much has to come together in order for scientific thought to originate, and all these necessary forces have had to be separately invented, practised, cultivated! In their separateness they have, however, very often had a totally different effect from that which they have today when in the realm of scientific thought they mutually limit and keep each other in check: they have worked as poisons, e.g. the doubting drive, the denying drive, the waiting drive, the collecting drive, the dissolving drive. Many hecatombs of human beings had to be sacrificed before these drives learned to grasp their coexistence and feel like functions of one organizing force in one human being! And how far we still are from the time when artistic energies and the practical wisdom of life join with scientific thought so that a higher organic system will develop in relation to which the scholar, the physician, the artist, and the lawmaker, as we now know them, would have to appear as paltry antiquities!

114

The scope of the moral. – As soon as we see a new picture, we immediately construct it with the help of all the old experiences we have had *depending on the degree* of our honesty and justice. There are no experiences other than moral ones, not even in the realm of sense perception.

115

The four errors. – Man has been educated by his errors: first, he saw himself only incompletely; secondly, he endowed himself with fictitious attributes; thirdly, he placed himself in a false rank order in relation to animals and nature; fourthly, he invented ever new tables of goods and for a time took them to be eternal and unconditioned – so that now this, now that human drive and condition occupied first place and was ennobled as a result of this valuation. If one discounts the effect of these four errors, one has also discounted humanity, humaneness, and 'human dignity'.

116

Herd instinct. – Wherever we encounter a morality, we find an evaluation and ranking of human drives and actions. These evaluations and rankings are always the expression of the needs of a community and herd: that which benefits *it* the most – and second most, and third most

– is also the highest standard of value for all individuals. With morality the individual is instructed to be a function of the herd and to ascribe value to himself only as a function. Since the conditions for preserving one community have been very different from those of another community, there have been very different moralities; and in view of essential changes in herds and communities, states and societies that are yet to come, one can prophesy that there will yet be very divergent moralities. Morality is herd-instinct in the individual.

117

Herd pangs of conscience. – During the longest and most remote periods of time there was a kind of pang of conscience completely different from that which exists now. Today one feels responsible only for what one wants and does, and finds one's pride in oneself: all our teachers of justice start from this feeling of self and pleasure in the individual (*des Einzelnen*), as if the spring of justice (*des Rechts*)[2] had always arisen here. But for the longest period of humanity's existence there was nothing more frightful than feeling alone (*einzeln*). To be alone (*allein*), to experience things by oneself (*einzeln*), to neither obey nor rule, to represent an individual (*ein Individuum bedeuten*) – that was no pleasure back then, but a punishment; one was sentenced 'to be an individual (*Individuum*)'. Freedom of thought was considered discomfort itself. While we experience law and conformity as compulsion and loss, one formerly experienced egoism as a painful thing, as an actual affliction. To be a self, to estimate oneself according to one's own measure and weight – that was contrary to taste in those days. The inclination to this would have been considered madness, for every misery and every fear were associated with being alone (*Alleinsein*). Back then, 'free will' had bad conscience as its closest neighbour. The more unfreely one acted, the more the herd instinct and not the sense of self spoke through the action, the more moral one considered oneself. In those days, everything that hurt the herd, whether the individual had willed it or not, gave the individual pangs of conscience – and his neighbour as well; indeed, the whole herd! On this point we have relearned most of all.

---

[2] The German word 'Recht' is usually ambiguous, meaning both 'right' and 'law'. In this case it seems best to render it as 'justice'.

N. DOES KNOW THAT THE HERD IS DYING.

118

Benevolence. – Is it virtuous when a cell transforms itself into a function of a stronger cell? It has to. And is it evil when the stronger cell assimilates the weaker? It also has to; this is necessary for it, since it strives for superabundant replenishment and wants to regenerate itself. Accordingly one should make a distinction in benevolence between the drive to appropriate and the drive to submit, depending on whether it is the stronger or the weaker who experiences it. Joy and desire go together in the stronger, who wants to transform something into a function of himself; joy and the wish to be desired go together in the weaker, who wants to become a function. Compassion is essentially the former, a pleasant stirring of the drive to appropriate at the sight of the weaker; however, we must still keep in mind that 'strong' and 'weak' are relative concepts.

119

No altruism! – In many people I see a surplus strength and pleasure in wanting to become a function; they press towards and have the most delicate sense for all places where precisely *they* can be a function. Here belong those women who turn themselves into some function of a man that is especially weakly developed in him, and to that extent become his purse or his politics or his sociability. Such beings preserve themselves best when they insert themselves into another organism; if they do not succeed at this, they become cranky, irritated, and devour themselves.

120

Health of the soul. – The popular medical formulation of morality (the originator of which is Ariston of Chios), 'virtue is the health of the soul',[3] would, in order to be useful, have to be changed at least to read, 'your virtue is the health of your soul'. For there is no health as such, and all attempts to define such a thing have failed miserably. Deciding what is health even for your *body* depends on your goal, your horizon, your powers, your impulses, your mistakes and above all on the ideals

---

[3] Ariston lived in the third century BC. This is fragment number 359 in *Stoicorum veterum fragmenta*, ed. von Arnim.

and phantasms of your soul. Thus there are innumerable healths of the body; and the more one allows the particular and incomparable to rear its head again, the more one unlearns the dogma of the 'equality of men', the more the concept of a normal health, along with those of a normal diet and normal course of an illness, must be abandoned by our medical men. Only then would it be timely to reflect on the health and illness of the *soul* and to locate the virtue peculiar to each man in its health – which of course could look in one person like the opposite of health in another. Finally, the great question would still remain whether we can *do without* illness, even for the development of our virtue; and whether especially our thirst for knowledge and self-knowledge do not need the sick soul as much as the healthy; in brief, whether the will to health alone is not a prejudice, a cowardice and a piece of most refined barbarism and backwardness.

121

Life not an argument. – We have arranged for ourselves a world in which we are able to live – by positing bodies, lines, planes, causes and effects, motion and rest, form and content; without these articles of faith no one could endure living! But that does not prove them. Life is not an argument; the conditions of life might include error.

122

Moral scepticism in Christianity. – Christianity, too, has made a great contribution to enlightenment: it taught moral scepticism in an extremely trenchant and effective way – accusing, embittering, but with untiring patience and refinement; it annihilated in every single man the faith in his 'virtues'. It caused those great virtuous men, of whom there was no dearth in antiquity, to disappear forever from the face of the earth – those popular men who with a faith in their own perfection went about with the dignity of a toreador. When we now, educated in this Christian school of scepticism, read the moral books of antiquity, e.g. those of Seneca or Epictetus,[4] we feel an amusing superiority and are full of secret insights and overviews, as if a child were speaking before

---

[4] Two stoic philosophers: Seneca (first century AD) was a wealthy member of the Roman ruling class. Epictetus (late first/early second century) was a freed Greek slave.

an old man or an overenthusiastic young beauty were speaking before La Rochefoucauld;[5] we know better what virtue is! In the end, however, we have applied this same scepticism also to all *religious* states and procedures, such as sin, repentance, grace, sanctification; and we have all allowed the worm to dig so deeply that even when reading Christian books we now have the same feeling of refined superiority and insight: we also know the religious feelings better! And it is time to know them well and to describe them well, for even the pious of the old faith are dying out: let us save their image and their type at least for knowledge!

123

Knowledge more than a means. – Even *without* this new passion – I mean the passion for knowledge – science would be promoted: up to now science has grown and matured without it. The good faith in science, the prejudice in its favour that rules our modern states (and formerly even the Church), is essentially based on the fact that this unconditional tendency and urge has manifested itself in science so rarely and that science is specifically regarded *not* as a passion but as a condition and 'ethos'. Indeed, often mere *amour-plaisir*[6] of knowledge (curiosity) is sufficient, or *amour-vanité*,[7] being accustomed to it with the ulterior motive of honour and bread; it is even enough for many that they have a surplus of leisure and do not know what to do with it except read, collect, arrange, observe, recount – their 'scientific drive' is their boredom. Pope Leo X[8] once (in his brief to Beroaldus)[9] sang the praise of science: he designated it the most beautiful ornament and the greatest pride of our life, a noble occupation in happiness and unhappiness; 'without it', he says finally, 'all human undertakings would lack a firm hold – indeed, even with it they are changeable and unstable enough!' But this fairly sceptical pope keeps silent, like all other churchly eulogists of science, his final judgement on science. Although one might

---

5 The *Reflections* of La Rochefoucauld (1613–80) contain a wealth of exceptionally astute and disillusioned observations about human action and motivation.

6 'the love which is pleasure'

7 'the love which is vanity'. Nietzsche takes the distinction between *amour-plaisir* and *amour-vanité* from Stendhal (see above, Book II, footnote 42, p. 92) who actually distinguishes four kinds of love; see his *De l'amour*, chapter 1.

8 Originally Giovanni de' Medici (1475–1521), elected to the Papacy in 1513; very active patron of the arts

9 Minor Italian humanist (1472–1518)

infer from his words that he places science above art – strange as this may be for such a friend of the arts – in the end it is nothing but politeness when he does not speak of what he, too, places high above all science: 'revealed truth' and the 'eternal salvation of the soul'. Compared to that, what are ornaments, pride, entertainment, and the security of life to him! 'Science is something second-class; nothing ultimate, unconditional; not an object of passion' – this judgement was held back in Leo's soul: the truly Christian judgement about science! In antiquity the dignity and recognition of science were diminished by the fact that even among her most zealous disciples the striving for *virtue* took first place, and that one thought one had given knowledge one's highest praise when one celebrated it as the best means to virtue. It is something new in history that knowledge wants to be more than a means.

124

In the horizon of the infinite. – We have forsaken the land and gone to sea! We have destroyed the bridge behind us – more so, we have demolished the land behind us! Now, little ship, look out! Beside you is the ocean; it is true, it does not always roar, and at times it lies there like silk and gold and dreams of goodness. But there will be hours when you realize that it is infinite and that there is nothing more awesome than infinity. Oh, the poor bird that has felt free and now strikes against the walls of this cage! Woe, when homesickness for the land overcomes you, as if there had been more *freedom* there – and there is no more 'land'!

125

The madman. – Haven't you heard of that madman who in the bright morning lit a lantern and ran around the marketplace crying incessantly, 'I'm looking for God! I'm looking for God!' Since many of those who did not believe in God were standing around together just then, he caused great laughter. Has he been lost, then? asked one. Did he lose his way like a child? asked another. Or is he hiding? Is he afraid of us? Has he gone to sea? Emigrated? – Thus they shouted and laughed, one interrupting the other. The madman jumped into their midst and pierced them with his eyes. 'Where is God?' he cried; 'I'll tell you! *We have killed him* – you and I! We are all his murderers. But how did we do this? How were we able to drink up the sea? Who gave us the sponge to wipe away the entire horizon? What were we doing when we unchained this earth from its sun? Where is it moving to now? Where are we moving to? Away from all suns? Are we not continually falling? And backwards, sidewards, forwards, in all directions? Is there still an up and a down? Aren't we straying as though through an infinite nothing? Isn't empty space breathing at us? Hasn't it got colder? Isn't night and more night coming again and again? Don't lanterns have to be lit in the morning? Do we still hear nothing of the noise of the grave-diggers who are burying God? Do we still smell nothing of the divine decomposition? – Gods, too, decompose! God is dead! God remains dead! And we have killed him! How can we console ourselves, the murderers of all murderers! The holiest and the mightiest thing the world has ever possessed has bled to death under our knives: who will wipe this blood from us? With what water could we clean ourselves? What festivals of atonement, what holy games will we have to invent for ourselves? Is the magnitude of this deed not too great for us? Do we not ourselves have to become gods merely to appear worthy of it? There was never a greater deed – and whoever is born after us will on account of this deed belong to a higher history than all history up to now!' Here the madman fell silent and looked again at his listeners; they too were silent and looked at him disconcertedly. Finally he threw his lantern on the ground so that it broke into pieces and went out. 'I come too early', he then said; 'my time is not yet. This tremendous event is still on its way, wandering; it has not yet reached the ears of men. Lightning and thunder need time; the light of the stars needs time; deeds need time, even after they are done, in order to be seen and heard. This deed is still more remote to them than the remotest stars – *and yet they have done it themselves!*' It is still recounted how on the same day the madman forced his way into several churches and there started singing his *requiem aeternam deo*.[10] Led out and called to account, he is said always to have replied nothing but, 'What then are these churches now if not the tombs and sepulchres of God?'

---

[10] 'Grant God eternal rest.' A transformation of that part of the service for the dead which reads 'Requiem aeternam dona eis [scilicet, mortuis], Domine' ('Lord, grant them [the dead] eternal rest')

ACC TO KAUS More

THIS IS ONE OF THE MOST

FAMOUS PASSAGE OF THE BOOK

126

Mystical explanations – Mystical explanations are considered deep; the truth is, they are not even shallow.

127

Aftereffects of the oldest religiosity. – Every thoughtless person believes that the will alone is effective; that willing is something simple, absolutely given, underivable, and intelligible in itself. When he does something, e.g. strikes something, he is convinced that it is *he* who is striking, and that he did the striking because he *wanted* to strike. He does not even notice a problem here; the feeling of *will* suffices for him to assume cause and effect, but also to believe that he *understands* their relation. He knows nothing of the mechanism of what happened and the hundredfold delicate work that has to be done to bring about the strike, or of the incapacity of the will as such to do even the slightest part of this work. The will is to him a force that works by magic: the belief in the will as the cause of effects is the belief in forces that work by magic. Now, originally man believed, wherever he saw something happen, that a will had to be the cause and that beings with a personal will had to be operating in the background – the concept of mechanics was quite foreign to him. But since man believed for immense periods of time only in persons (and not in substances, forces, things, etc.), the faith in cause and effect has become for him the fundamental faith that he uses everywhere something happens – still today instinctively and as an atavism of the oldest origin. The propositions, 'no effect without a cause', 'every effect again a cause', appear as generalizations of much narrower propositions: 'no effecting without willing'; 'it is possible to have an effect only on willing beings'; 'no suffering of an effect is ever pure and without consequences, but all suffering is an agitation of the will' (towards action, defence, revenge, retribution) – but in the prehistory of humanity the former and latter propositions were identical: the former were not generalizations of the latter, but the latter were elucidations of the former.[11] With his assumption that only that which wills exists, Schopenhauer enthroned a primordial mythology; he

---

[11] See Schopenhauer, 'Über die vierfache Wurzel des Satzes vom zureichenden Grunde' (1813).

seems never to have attempted an analysis of the will because like everyone else he *believed* in the simplicity and immediacy of all willing – whereas willing is actually such a well-practised mechanism that it almost escapes the observing eye. Against him I offer these propositions: first, in order for willing to come about, a representation of pleasure or displeasure is needed. Secondly, that a violent stimulus is experienced as pleasure or pain is a matter of the *interpreting* intellect, which, to be sure, generally works without our being conscious of it (*uns unbewußt*); and one and the same stimulus *can* be interpreted as pleasure or pain. Thirdly, only in intellectual beings do pleasure, pain, and will exist; the vast majority of organisms has nothing like it.

128

The value of prayer. – Prayer has been invented for people who never really have thoughts of their own and who know no elevation of the soul or do not notice it if it occurs: what are such people to do in sacred places or in all important situations in life that demand calm and a kind of dignity? In order that they at least do not *disturb*, the wisdom of all founders of religions, small as well as great, has prescribed to them the formulas of prayer as a long mechanical work of the lips, combined with exertion of the memory and a same fixed posture of hands and feet and eyes! So they may, like the Tibetans, go ahead regurgitating their 'om mane padme hum'[12] countless times or, as in Benares, count the name of the god off their fingers, Ram-Ram-Ram[13] (and so on, with or without charm), or honour Vishnu with his thousand names,[14] or Allah with his ninety-nine; or they may use prayer-mills and rosaries – the main point is that this work keeps them still for a time and makes them a tolerable sight: their type of prayer has been invented for the benefit of the pious who know thoughts and elevations of their own. And even they have their tired hours, when a string of venerable words and sounds and a mechanical piety do them good. But supposing these rare human beings – in every religion the religious person is an exception – can figure out what to do; those who are poor in spirit cannot figure out

[12] This is a formula which adepts repeat in certain forms of Buddhist meditation as a help to attaining spiritual enlightenment. The literal meaning seems to be something like: 'You [Buddha] the centre of the lotus-flower'.
[13] The god of a monotheistic Hindu cult centred in Benares
[14] One of the major gods of the Hindu pantheon

what to do, and to forbid them their prayer-rattling is to deprive them of their religion – as Protestantism increasingly shows us more and more. From such people religion wants only that they *keep still* with their eyes, hands, legs, and other organs; thus they are made beautiful for a time and – more like human beings!

129

The conditions for God. – 'God himself cannot exist without wise people', said Luther,[15] and with good reason; but 'God can exist even less without unwise people' – that our good Luther did not say!

130

A dangerous decision. – The Christian decision to find the world ugly and bad has made the world ugly and bad.

131

Christianity and suicide. – When Christianity came into existence the inclination to suicide was very strong – Christianity turned it into a lever of its power: it allowed only two kinds of suicide, dressed them up with the highest dignity and the highest hopes and forbade all others in a terrible manner. But martyrdom and the ascetic's slow suicide were permitted.

132

Against Christianity. – What decides against Christianity now is our taste, not our reasons.

133

Principle. – An inescapable hypothesis to which humanity must have recourse again and again is still *more powerful* in the long run than the

---

[15] This passage in Luther's work has not been located.

best believed faith in something untrue (such as the Christian faith). In the long run: that means here a hundred thousand years.

134

Pessimists as victims. – Wherever a deep dissatisfaction with existence comes to prevail, it is the aftereffects of some great dietary mistake made by a people over a long time that are coming to light. Thus the spread of Buddhism (*not* its origin) depended greatly on the Indians' excessive and almost exclusive diet of rice and the general enervation resulting from it. Perhaps the modern European discontent is due to the fact that our prehistory, the entire middle ages, was given to drinking thanks to the influence of Germanic tastes on Europe: the middle ages means the alcohol poisoning of Europe. – The German dissatisfaction with life is essentially a winter sickness exacerbated by the effects of cellar air and the noxious stove fumes in German living rooms.

135

Origin of sin. – Sin, as it is now experienced wherever Christianity reigns or once reigned: sin is a Jewish feeling and a Jewish invention; and given that this is the background of all Christian morality, Christianity can be said to have aimed at 'Judaizing' the whole world. The extent to which this has succeeded in Europe is best brought out by how alien Greek antiquity – a world without feelings of sin – strikes our sensibility as being, despite all the good will expended by entire generations and many excellent individuals to approach and incorporate this world. 'Only when you *repent* does God have mercy on you' – to a Greek, that is an object of ridicule and an annoyance; he would say, 'Maybe slaves feel that way.' What is here being presupposed is a being who is powerful, supremely powerful and yet enjoys revenge: his power is so great that no harm whatsoever can be done unto him except in matters of honour. Every sin is an injury of respect, a *crimen laesae majestatis divinae*[16] – and nothing further! Feeling spiritually crushed, degraded, wallowing in the dust – that is the first and last condition of

---

[16] The Roman legal code contained a provision for punishing a crime called *crimen laesae maiestatis* which originally seems to have meant denigrating or insulting the honour and dignity of the Roman people. The phrase Nietzsche uses would mean: 'crime of insulting the dignity of god'.

his grace; in sum, restoration of his divine honour! Whether the sin has done any other harm; whether it has planted some deep, growing calamity that seizes and strangles one person after another like a disease; this honour-craving Oriental couldn't care less: sin is an assault on him, not on humanity! He gives those to whom he grants his grace also this same nonchalance about the natural consequences of sin. God and humanity are here conceived as so separate and opposite that there can basically be no sin against humanity – every deed is supposed to be considered *only with respect to its supernatural consequences*, not with respect to its natural consequences; that is what Jewish feeling, to which everything natural is indignity itself, demands. The Greeks, by contrast, were closer to the thought that even sacrilege can have dignity – even theft, as in the case of Prometheus;[17] even the slaughter of cattle as the expression of an insane envy, as in the case of Ajax:[18] in their need to incorporate into and devise some dignity for sacrilege, they invented *tragedy* – an art form and a pleasure that has remained utterly and profoundly foreign to the Jew, despite all his poetic talent and inclination towards the sublime.

136

The chosen people. – The Jews, who feel they are the chosen people of all peoples precisely because they are the moral genius of all peoples (owing to their ability *more profoundly to despise* the human being in themselves than any other people) – the Jews take a pleasure in their divine monarch and the holy which is similar to that which the French nobility took in Louis XIV. This nobility had surrendered all its power and sovereignty and had become contemptible: in order not to feel this, in order to be able to forget this, there was a need for a royal splendour, a royal authority and plenitude of power *without equal* to which only the nobility had access. In rising to the height of the court by virtue of this privilege and seeing from there everything as beneath oneself, as

---

[17] Demi-god who is said to have stolen fire from the gods and to have given it to humans, thereby initiating the process of civilization. An extant tragedy ascribed to Aeschylus treats the punishment of Prometheus for this crime: he was fettered to a rock in the Caucasus while an eagle fed on his liver. See above, Book I, footnote 1, p. 29 and also below, § 300, p. 170.

[18] Because of a slight to his standing as a warrior, Ajax went mad and killed a large number of cattle, deludedly thinking they were the Greek leaders who had wronged him. Sophocles treats this subject in his tragedy *Ajax*.

contemptible, one got over an irritable conscience. Thus one deliberately built the tower of royal power ever higher into the clouds and staked on it the ultimate building stones of one's own power.

137

Speaking in a parable. – A Jesus Christ was possible only in a Jewish landscape – I mean one over which the gloomy and sublime thunder clouds of the wrathful Jehovah hovered continually. Here alone was the rare and sudden piercing of a single sunbeam through the gruesome general and perpetual day-night experienced as a miracle of 'love', as the ray of the most undeserved 'grace'. Only here could Christ dream of his rainbow and his heavenly ladder on which God descended to man; everywhere else good weather and sunshine were too much of a rule and everyday occurrence.

138

Christ's error. – The founder of Christianity thought that there was nothing from which men suffered more than their sins. That was his error – the error of one who felt himself free of sin and who lacked experience of it! Thus his soul filled itself with that wonderful fantastic compassion for a torment that was rarely a very great torment even among his people, who invented sin! But the Christians have found a way of retroactively vindicating their master and of sanctifying his error into 'truth'.

139

The colour of the passions. – People like St Paul have an 'evil eye' for the passions: they come to know only what is dirty, disfiguring, and heartbreaking about them; hence their ideal impulse seeks the annihilation of the passions, which they see totally purified in the divine. Quite unlike St Paul and the Jews, the Greeks turned their ideal impulse precisely towards the passions and loved, elevated, gilded and deified them; evidently passion made them feel not only happier but also purer and more divine than usual. And the Christians? Did they want to become Jews in this respect? Did they perhaps succeed?

140

Too Jewish. – If God wanted to become an object of love, he should first of all have had to give up judging and justice: a judge, even a merciful one, is no object of love. The founder of Christianity lacked delicacy of feeling in this regard, being a Jew.

141

Too oriental. – What? A god who loves men provided that they believe in him and who casts evil gazes and threats at anyone who does not believe in this love? What? A love hemmed in by conditions as the feeling of an almighty god? A love that has not even mastered the feeling of honour and roused vengefulness? How oriental this all is! 'If I love you, what does that concern you?'[19] is surely a sufficient critique of all of Christianity.

142

Incense. – Buddha says: 'Don't flatter your benefactors!' Repeat this saying in a Christian church and it will instantly clear the air of everything Christian.

143

The greatest advantage of polytheism. – For an individual to posit his *own* ideal and to derive from it his own law, joys and rights – that may well have been considered hitherto to be the most outrageous of human aberrations and idolatry itself; indeed, the few who dared it always felt the need to apologize to themselves, usually as follows: 'Not I! Not I! But a *god* through me!' The wonderful art and power of creating gods – polytheism – was that through which this drive could discharge itself, purify, perfect and ennoble itself; for originally it was a base and undistinguished drive, related to stubbornness, disobedience, and envy. To be *hostile* to this drive to have one's own ideal: that was formerly the law of every morality. There was only one norm: '*the* human being' –

---

[19] Goethe, *Wilhelm Meister*, Book IV, chapter 9; *Dichtung und Wahrheit*, Book III, chapter 14

and every people believed itself to *have* this one and ultimate norm. But above and outside oneself, in a distant overworld, one got to see a *plurality of norms*: one god was not the denial of or anathema to another god! Here for the first time one allowed oneself individuals; here one first honoured the rights of individuals. The invention of gods, heroes, and overmen (*Übermenschen*) of all kinds, as well as deviant or inferior forms of humanoid life (*Neben- und Untermenschen*), dwarfs, fairies, centaurs, satyrs, demons, and devils, was the invaluable preliminary exercise for the justification of the egoism and sovereignty of the individual: the freedom that one conceded to a god in his relation to other gods one finally gave to oneself in relation to laws, customs, and neighbours. Monotheism, in contrast, this rigid consequence of the teachings of a normal human type – that is, the belief in a normal god next to whom there are only false pseudo-gods – was perhaps the greatest danger to humanity so far: it threatened us with that premature stagnation which, as far as we can tell, most other species have long reached; for all of them believe in one normal type and ideal for their species and have translated the morality of custom (*Sittlichkeit der Sitte*) definitively into flesh and blood. In polytheism the free-spiritedness and many-spiritedness of humanity received preliminary form – the power to create for ourselves our own new eyes and ever again new eyes that are ever more our own – so that for humans alone among the animals there are no eternal horizons and perspectives.

144

Religious wars. – The greatest progress of the masses up till now has been the religious war, for it proves that the mass has begun to treat concepts with respect. Religious wars start only when the finer quarrels among sects have refined common reason so that even the mob becomes subtle and takes trifles seriously, and actually considers it possible that the 'eternal salvation of the soul' might hinge on slight differences between concepts.

145

Danger for vegetarians. – A diet consisting primarily of rice leads to the use of opium and narcotics, just as a diet consisting primarily of potatoes leads to the use of liquor. But its subtler effects also include ways of thinking and feeling that work narcotically. This harmonizes with the fact that the promoters of narcotic ways of thinking and feeling, like those Indian gurus, praise precisely a diet that is purely vegetarian and would like to make that a law of the masses: thus they want to call forth and increase a need that *they* are able to satisfy.

146

German hopes. – Let us not forget that names of peoples are usually terms of abuse. The Tartars, for example, are literally 'the dogs'; that is what the Chinese called them. The 'Germans': this originally meant 'heathen'; that is what the Goths after their conversion named the great mass of their unbaptized kindred tribes, in accordance with their translation of the Septuagint[20] in which the heathens were designated with a word that in Greek means 'the nations'; see Ulfilas.[21] It would still be possible for the Germans to turn the term of abuse for them into a name of honour by becoming the first *un-Christian* nation in Europe: for which Schopenhauer honoured them as having a very strong predisposition. That would be a way of fulfilling the words of *Luther*, who taught them to be un-Roman and to say: 'Here *I* stand! *I* can do no other!'[22]

147

Question and answer. – What do savage tribes today take over first of all from the Europeans? Liquor and Christianity, the narcotics of Europe. And from what do they perish most quickly? From European narcotics.

---

[20] Translation of the Old Testament into Greek for the use of Greek-speaking Jews, produced between the third century BC and the beginning of the Christian era

[21] A fourth-century (AD) Gothic bishop who is responsible for the translation of the Bible into Gothic. Nietzsche is claiming that the German word for 'German' (*deutsch*) is etymologically related to the Gothic word *thuida* ('people'), and that Ulfilas used this word to render the Greek 'τὰ ἔθνη' in the Septuagint which originally just meant 'nations', but came to be used by Christians to refer specifically to 'heathens'. Nietzsche discusses this paragraph of the text in his letter to Peter Gast of 30 July 1882.

[22] Probably apocryphal reply Luther is said to have given at the Diet of Worms (18 April 1521) to the demand that he recant

148

Where reformations arise. – At the time of the great corruption of the Church, the Church in Germany was the least corrupt; that is why the Reformation occurred *here*, as a sign that even the beginnings of corruption were felt to be intolerable. For relatively speaking, no people has ever been more Christian than the Germans at the time of Luther; their Christian culture was ready to burst into a hundredfold splendour of blossoms – only one more night was needed, but this brought the storm that put an end to everything.

149

The failure of reformations. – That several attempts to found new Greek religions have failed testifies to the higher culture of the Greeks even in rather early times; it indicates that even early in Greece, there must have been many diverse individuals whose diverse plights could not be disposed of with a single prescription of faith and hope. Pythagoras[23] and Plato, perhaps Empedocles[24] as well, and the Orphic enthusiasts[25] much earlier yet, were out to found new religions; and the former two had souls and talents which were so much those of founders of religions that one cannot wonder enough at their failure; yet all they managed to found were sects. Every time the reformation of an entire people fails and only sects raise their heads, one may conclude that the people is already very heterogeneous and is starting to break away from crude herd instincts and the morality of custom (*Sittlichkeit der Sitte*): a notable hovering condition which one usually disparages as decay in morals and corruption, when in fact it announces the maturation of the egg and the impending breaking of the eggshell. That Luther's reformation succeeded in the North is a sign of the fact that the North was backward in comparison to the South and still had rather uniform and monochrome needs; Europe would not have been christianized at all had not the culture of the old world of the South gradually been barbarized through an excessive admixture of Germanic barbarian

---

[23] See above, Book II, footnote 23, p. 84.
[24] See above, Book II, footnote 25, p. 84.
[25] Orphism was an obscure but powerful religious movement that seems to have originated in the sixth century BC. It was often associated with the view that the soul could live on after death.

blood and its cultural superiority lost. The more general and unconditional the influence of an individual or an individual's thought can be,
the more homogeneous and the lower must the mass be that is
influenced, while counter-movements betray inner counter-needs that
also want satisfaction and recognition. Conversely, one may always infer
a high level of culture when powerful and domineering natures only
manage to have a slight and sectarian influence: this is also true of the
individual arts and the areas of knowledge. Where there is ruling, there
are masses; where there are masses, there is a need for slavery. Where
there is slavery, there are few individuals, and these have herd instincts
and conscience against them.

150

Towards a critique of saints. – Must one then, in order to have a virtue,
want to have it in its most brutal form – the way the Christian saints
wanted and needed it, as those who endured life only with the thought
that the mere sight of their virtue would destroy the self-esteem of
anyone who viewed it? But a virtue with such an effect I call brutal.

151

On the origin of religion. – The metaphysical need is not the origin of
religion, as Schopenhauer[26] has it, but only a *late offshoot* of it. Under
the rule of religious ideas, one has got used to the idea of 'another world
(behind, below, above)' and feels an unpleasant emptiness and deprivation at the annihilation of religious delusions – and from this feeling
grows now 'another world', but this time only a metaphysical and not a
religious one. But what led to the belief in 'another world' in primordial
times was *not* a drive or need, but an *error* in the interpretation of
certain natural events, an embarrassing lapse of the intellect.

152

The greatest change. – The lighting and colours of everything have
changed! We no longer fully understand how the ancients experienced

[26] In his 'Über Religion' in *Parerga und Paralipomena*, vol. II, chapter 15

what was most familiar and frequent – for example the day and waking. Because the ancients believed in dreams, waking life had a different light. The same goes for the whole of life, illuminated by a light radiated back on it from death and its significance: our 'death' is a completely different death. All experiences shone differently because a god glowed from them; all decisions and prospects concerning the distant future as well, for one had oracles and secret signs and believed in prophecy. 'Truth' was formerly experienced differently because the lunatic could be considered its mouthpiece – which makes *us* shudder and laugh. Every injustice affected feelings differently, for one feared divine retribution and not just a civil punishment and dishonour. What was joy in an age when one believed in devils and tempters! What was passion when one saw the demons lurking nearby! What was philosophy when doubt was felt as a sin of the most dangerous kind, as a sacrilege against eternal love, as mistrust of everything that is good, lofty, pure, and merciful! We have given things a new colour; we keep on painting them – but what can we nowadays accomplish in comparison to the *splendour of colour* of that old master! I mean ancient humanity.

153

Homo poeta.[27] – 'I myself, who most single-handedly made this tragedy of tragedies, insofar as it is finished; I, having first tied the knot of morality into existence and drawn it so tight that only a god can loosen it – which is what Horace demands![28] – I myself have now in the fourth act slain all gods, out of morality! What is now to become of the fifth act? From where shall I take the tragic solution? Should I start considering a comic solution?'

154

Different types of danger in life. – You have no idea what you are experiencing; you run through life as if you were drunk and once in a while fall down a staircase. But thanks to your drunkenness, you don't break your limbs in the process; your muscles are too slack and your

---

[27] 'The human being as poet'
[28] *Ars poetica*, 189ff.

head too dull for you to find the stones of these stairs as hard as the rest of us do! For us, life is a greater danger: we are made of glass – woe unto us if we *bump* against something! And everything is lost if we *fall*!

155

What we lack. – We love what is *great* in nature and have discovered it – because in our heads, great human beings are lacking. It was the other way around for the Greeks; their feeling for nature is different from ours.

156

The most influential. – That a human being resists his whole age, stops it at the gate and demands an accounting – that *must* exercise an influence! Whether he wants to is irrelevant; that he *can* is what matters.

157

Mentiri.[29] – Watch out! He's thinking; in a moment he will have a lie ready. This is a stage of culture at which entire peoples have stood. Just consider what the Romans meant by the word *mentiri*!

158

An uncomfortable trait. – To find all things deep – that is an uncomfortable trait: it makes one constantly strain one's eyes and in the end always find more than one had wished.

159

Every virtue has its age. – Whoever is unyielding these days will often have pangs of conscience because of his candour; for unyieldingness and candour are virtues that belongs to different ages.

---

[29] 'to lie' (Latin); etymologically related to *mens* ('mind') and *memini* ('bear in mind', 'remember')

160

Dealing with virtues. – To a virtue, too, one can be undignified and fawning.

161

To the lovers of the age. – The ex-priest and the ex-convict constantly make faces: what they want is a face without a past. – But have you ever seen people who know that the future is mirrored in their faces and are so polite to you, you lovers of 'the age', that they make a face without a future?

162

Egoism. – Egoism is the *perspectival* law of feeling according to which what is closest appears large and heavy, while in the distance everything decreases in size and weight.

163

After a great victory. – The best thing about a great victory is that it takes the fear of defeat out of the victor. 'Why not also be defeated once?' he says to himself; 'I'm rich enough for that now.'

164

The seekers of rest. – I recognize the spirits who seek rest by the many *dark* objects with which they surround themselves: he who wants to sleep makes his room dark or crawls into a cave. – A hint to those who don't know, but would like to know, what they actually seek most!

165

On the happiness of those who renounce something. – He who thoroughly forgoes something for a long time will, upon accidentally re-encountering it, almost think he has discovered it – and what happiness every discoverer has! Let us be wiser than the snakes who lie too long in the same sunlight.

166

Always in our company. – Everything that is of my kind, in nature and history, speaks to me, praises me, spurs me on, comforts me – everything else I don't hear or forget right away. We are always only in our own company.

167

Misanthropy and love. – One speaks of being sick of people only when one can no longer digest them and yet still has one's stomach full of them. Misanthropy is the result of an all-too-greedy love of man and 'cannibalism' – but who told you to swallow men like oysters, my Prince Hamlet?

168

About a sick man. – 'He is doing badly!' – 'What's wrong?' – 'He is suffering from the desire to be praised and finds no nourishment for it.' – 'Unbelievable! The whole world is celebrating him, and pampering him; he is on everyone's lips.' – 'Yes, but he has a bad ear for praise. If a friend praises him, it sounds to him as if the friend is praising himself. If an enemy praises him, it sounds to him as if the enemy wants be praised for that. And when finally he is praised by any of the rest – and they are not many at all; that is how famous he is! – it offends him that they don't want him as a friend or enemy; he likes to say: What do I care about people who are capable of trying to play "the just man" even towards me?'

169

Open enemies. – Courage before the enemy is one thing; it does not prevent one from being a coward and indecisive scatterbrain. That is how Napoleon judged 'the most courageous person' he knew: Murat.[30] – Which shows that open enemies are indispensable to some people if they are to rise to *their own* kind of virtue, manliness, and cheerfulness.

---

[30] French general (1767–1815). Nietzsche takes the anecdote from his usual source about Napoleon, the *Mémoires* of Madame de Rémusat (see above, Book I, footnote 16, p. 49).

170

With the crowd. – So far he is still running with the crowd and singing its praises, but one day he will become its opponent! For he is following it thinking that this will give his laziness full play, and he has not yet discovered that the crowd is not lazy enough for him! That it always pushes ahead! That it allows no one to stand still! – And he so much likes to stand still!

171

Fame. – When the gratitude of many towards one throws away all shame, fame arises.

172

The spoiler of taste. – A: 'You are a spoiler of taste – that is what everyone says!' B: 'Of course! I spoil for everyone the taste for his own party – and no party forgives that.'

173

HEGEL

Being deep and seeming deep. – Those who know they are deep strive for clarity. Those who would like to seem deep to the crowd strive for obscurity. For the crowd takes everything whose ground it cannot see to be deep: it is so timid and so reluctant to go into the water.

174

Aside. – Parliamentarianism, i.e. the public permission to choose between five basic political opinions, flatters and wins the favour of all those who like to *appear* independent and individualistic and would like to fight for their opinions. In the end, however, it is irrelevant whether the herd is commanded to have one opinion or permitted to have five. Whoever deviates from the five public opinions and steps aside will always have the whole herd against him.

175

On eloquence. – Who has had the most convincing eloquence so far? The drum roll; and as long as kings and commanders have control over that, they will remain the best orators and rabble rousers.

176

Compassion. – Those poor reigning princes! All their rights are now suddenly turning into claims, and all these claims soon begin to sound like presumptions! The moment they merely say 'We' or 'my people', wicked old Europe starts to smile. Verily, a chief master of ceremonies in the modern world would waste little ceremony on them and might perhaps decree: 'les souverains rangent aux parvenus.'[31]

177

On 'the educational establishment'. – In Germany, higher men lack one great means of education: the laughter of higher men; for in Germany, these do not laugh.

178

On moral enlightenment. – One must talk the Germans out of their Mephistopheles, and their Faust, too. They are two moral prejudices against the value of knowledge.[32]

179

Thoughts. – Thoughts are the shadows of our sensations – always darker, emptier, simpler.

Hume

---

[31] 'sovereigns rank with parvenus'
[32] In Goethe's drama *Faust*, Mephistopheles is a 'spirit who always says "no"'' (Act I, line 1338); Faust seeks for an experience so satisfying that he will wish time to stand still so that he can hold on to it (Act I, lines 1675–1706).

180

The good age for free spirits. – Free spirits take liberties even with science – and for the time being, one also allows them to – as long as the Church is still standing! To that extent they now have their good age.

181

Following and leading. – A: 'Of these two, one will always follow and the other will always lead, wherever fate may take them. And *yet* the former is superior to the other in virtue and spirit!' B: 'And yet? And yet? That was said for the others, not for me, not for us! – *Fit secundum regulam.*'[33]

182

In solitude. – When one lives alone, one neither speaks too loud nor writes too loud, for one fears the hollow echo – the criticism of the nymph Echo. And all voices sound different in solitude!

183

The music of the best future. – I would consider the foremost musician to be the one who knew only the sadness of the deepest happiness, and no other sadness at all; there has never been such a musician.

184

Justice. – I'd rather let myself be robbed than be surrounded by scarecrows – that is my taste. And in any case it is a matter of taste – nothing more!

185

Poor. – Today he is poor, not because they have taken everything away from him but because he has thrown everything away. What is that to him? He is used to *finding* things. It is the poor who misunderstand his voluntary poverty.

[33] 'This takes place according to the rule.'

186

Bad conscience. – Everything he does now is upright and orderly – and still he has a bad conscience. For the extraordinary is his task.

187

What is offensive in the presentation. – This artist offends me in the way he presents his ideas, his very good ideas: so broad and emphatic, and with such crude artifices of persuasion, as if he were speaking to a mob. Whenever we devote some time to his art, it is soon as if we were 'in bad company'.

188

Work. – How close work and the worker are now even to the most leisurely among us! The royal courtesy of the words 'We are all workers!' would still have been a cynicism and an indecency under the reign of Louis XIV.

189

The thinker. – He is a thinker: that means he knows how to make things simpler than they are.

190

Against those who praise. – A: 'One is praised only by one's peers.' B: 'Yes! And whoever praises you tells you: you are my peer!'

191

Against many a defence. – The most perfidious way of damaging a cause is deliberately to defend it with faulty arguments.

192

The good-natured. – What distinguishes those good-natured people whose faces radiate good will from the rest? They feel well in the presence of another person and quickly fall in love with him; consequently they wish him well, and their first judgement is: 'I like him.' In such people there is the following succession: the wish to appropriate (they do not scruple much over the worth of the other person), quick appropriation, delight in possession, and action for the benefit of the person possessed.

193

Kant's joke. – Kant wanted to prove, in a way that would dumbfound the whole world, that the whole world was right: that was the secret joke of this soul. He wrote against the scholars in favour of popular prejudice, but for scholars and not for the people.

194

The 'openhearted' one. – That person probably always acts according to secret reasons, for he always has communicable reasons on his tongue and virtually in his open hand.

195

Laughable. – Look! Look! He is running away from people, but they follow him because he is running *ahead* of them – that is how much they are a herd!

196

Limits of our sense of hearing. – One hears only those questions to which one is able to find an answer.

197

Better be careful! – There is nothing we like so much to impart to others as the seal of secrecy – along with what is under it.

198

Chagrin of the proud one. – The proud man feels chagrined even by those who bring him forward: he gives the horse of his carriage the evil eye.

199

Generosity. – With the rich, generosity is often just a type of shyness.

200

Laughter. – Laughter means: to gloat, but with a good conscience.

201

Applause. – In applause there is always a kind of noise – even in the applause we give ourselves.

202

A squanderer. – As yet he does not have that poverty of the rich man who has already counted his entire treasure once – he squanders his spirit with the unreason of a squandering nature.

203

Hic niger est.[34] – Usually he has no thought – but on rare occasions bad thoughts come to him.

204

Beggars and courtesy. – 'One isn't being impolite if one uses a stone to knock on a door which lacks a doorbell': that is how beggars think, and everyone who is suffering some kind of distress, but no one thinks they are right.

---

[34] 'A dangerous man, this one' (literally 'This one is black'); Horace, *Satires* 4,85

205

Need. – Need is taken to be the cause why something came to be; in reality, it is often merely an effect of what has come to be.

206

When it rains. – It is raining, and I think of the poor who now huddle together with their many troubles and without any practice at concealing them: each is ready to hurt the other and to make for himself a pitiful kind of pleasure even when the weather is bad. That and that alone is the poverty of the poor!

207

The envious one. – He is envious – let's hope he won't have any children; he would envy them because he can no longer be a child.

208

Great man! – From the fact that someone is a 'great man' one cannot infer that he is a man; he may be just a boy, or a chameleon of all stages of life, or a bewitched little woman.

209

A way of asking for reasons. – There is a way of asking us for our reasons that not only makes us forget our best reasons but also awakens in us a defiance and resistance towards reasons in general – a very stultifying mode of asking and a trick used by tyrannical people!

210

Moderation in diligence. – One should not try to surpass one's father in diligence; that makes one sick.

211

Secret enemies. – To be able to afford a secret enemy – that is a luxury for which the morality even of elevated spirits is usually not rich enough.

212

Not to let oneself be deceived. – His spirit has bad manners, is hasty and always stutters out of impatience; hence one hardly recognizes how much stamina and robustness the soul possesses in which this spirit dwells.

213

The road to happiness. – A wise man asked a fool what the road to happiness is. The latter replied without delay, like someone being asked the way to the nearest town: 'Admire yourself and live on the street!' 'Stop,' replied the sage, 'you are asking too much; it is quite enough to admire oneself!' The fool countered: 'But how can one constantly admire without constantly feeling contempt?'

214

Faith makes blessed. – Virtue gives happiness and a type of blessedness only to those who have not lost faith in their virtue – not to those subtler souls whose virtue consists of a deep mistrust of themselves and of all virtue. So in the end, here, too, 'faith makes blessed'[35] – and, mind you, *not* virtue!

215

Ideal and material. – You envisage a noble ideal, but are *you* such a noble stone that such a divine image could be fashioned out of you? And anyway – isn't all your work a barbarous sculpting? A blasphemy against your ideal?

216

Danger in the voice. – With a very loud voice in one's throat one is almost incapable of thinking subtle things.

---

[35] Gospel according to Mark 16.16

217

Cause and effect. – Before the effect one believes in causes different from those one believes in after the effect.

218

My antipathy. – I do not love people who have to explode like bombs in order to have any effect whatsoever and in whose presence one is always in danger of suddenly losing one's hearing – or more.

219

The purpose of punishment. – The purpose of punishment is to improve the one *who punishes*; that is the last resort of the apologists for punishment.

220

Sacrifice. – The sacrificial animal thinks differently about sacrifice than the spectator, but one has never let it have its say.

221

Forbearance. – Fathers and sons have much more forbearance for each other than mothers and daughters.

222

Poet and liar. – The poet sees in the liar a foster brother (*Milchbruder*) whose milk he has drunk up; that is why the latter has remained stunted and miserable and has not even got as far as having a good conscience.

223

Vicariousness of the senses. – 'Our eyes are also intended for hearing', said the old father confessor who had gone deaf, 'and among the blind he is king who has the longest ears.'

224

Animals' criticism. – I fear that the animals see man as a being like them who in a most dangerous manner has lost his animal common sense – as the insane animal, the laughing animal, the weeping animal, the miserable animal.

225

The natural. – 'Evil has always had great effects in its favour! And nature is evil! Let us therefore be natural!' That is the secret reasoning of the great effect-artists of humanity, who have all too often been considered great human beings.

226

The distrustful and style. – We say the strongest things simply, provided that we are among people who believe in our strength – such an environment breeds 'simplicity of style'. The distrustful speak emphatically; the distrustful make emphatic.

227

Bad inference; bad shot. – He cannot control himself; from that, a woman infers that it would be easy to control him and casts her net for him – the poor woman who will shortly be his slave.

228

Against mediators. – He who wants to mediate between two resolute thinkers shows that he is mediocre: he has no eye for what is unique; seeing things as similar and making things the same is the sign of weak eyes.

229

Obstinacy and faithfulness. – From defiance he clings to something he has come to see through, but he calls it 'faithfulness'.

230

Lack of silence. – His whole being fails to *persuade* – that is because he has never remained silent about any of his good deeds.

231

The 'thorough'. – Those who are slow to know think that slowness is an aspect of knowledge.

232

Dreaming. – Either one does not dream, or does so interestingly. One should learn to spend one's waking life in the same way: not at all, or interestingly.

233

The most dangerous point of view. – What I now do or omit is as important for *everything that is to come* as the greatest event of the past: seen from this tremendous perspective, from that of their effects, all actions appear equally great and small.

234

Words of comfort for a musician. – 'Your life does not reach men's ears; to them you live a mute life, and all the subtlety of melody, all tender resolution about following or leading, remain hidden from them. It is true: you are not coming down a main street with regimental music, but that does not give these good people the right to say your way of life lacks music. He who has ears to hear, let him hear!'

235

Spirit and character. – Some reach their peak as characters, but their spirit is not adequate for this height, while with others it is the other way around.

236

In order to move the crowd. – Must not he who wants to move the crowd be an actor playing the role of himself? Must he not first translate himself into the grotesquely obvious and *present* his entire person and cause in this coarsened and simplified version?

237

The polite one. – 'He is so polite!' – Yes, he always carries a cake for Cerberus[36] and is so timid that he takes everyone for Cerberus, even you and me; that is his 'politeness'.

238

Without envy. – He is quite without envy, but that has no merit because he wants to conquer a country that no one has yet possessed and hardly anyone has ever seen.

239

The joyless one. – One single joyless person is enough to create constant sullenness and dark skies for a an entire household, and only a miracle can cause that one person to be lacking! Happiness is not nearly as contagious a disease – why is that?

240

At the sea. – I wouldn't build a house for myself (and it is part of my good fortune not to be a home-owner!). But if I had to, I would, like some Romans, build it right into the sea – I certainly would like to share a few secrets with this beautiful monster.

241

Work and artist. – This artist is ambitious, nothing more: ultimately his work is just a magnifying glass that he offers everyone who looks his way.

---

[36] Three-headed dog who guarded the gates to hell. It was thought that he could sometimes be mollified by being given a honey-cake.

242

Suum cuique.[37] – However great my greed for knowledge may be, I cannot take anything else out of things than what already belongs to me – what belongs to others remains behind. How is it possible for a human being to be a thief or a robber!

243

Origin of 'good' and 'bad'. – An improvement is invented only by someone who is able to feel 'this is not good'.

244

Thoughts and words. – Even one's thoughts one cannot entirely reproduce in words.

245

Praise by choice. – The artist chooses his subjects; that is his way of praising.

246

Mathematics. – Let us introduce the subtlety and rigour of mathematics into all sciences to the extent to which that is at all possible; not in the belief that we will come to know things this way, but in order to *ascertain* our human relation to things. Mathematics is only the means to general and final knowledge of humanity.

247

Habit. – Every habit makes our hand more witty and our wit less handy.

248

Books. – What good is a book that does not even carry us beyond all books?

[37] 'To each his own'. Definition of justice found, for instance, in Cicero, *De officiis* 1.15

249

The sigh of the one who comes to know. – 'Oh, my greed! In this soul there dwells no selflessness but rather an all-desiring self that would like, as it were, to see with the eyes and seize with the hands of many individuals – a self that would like to bring back the entire past, that wants to lose nothing it could possibly possess! Oh, this flame of my greed! Oh, that I might be reborn into a hundred beings!' – Whoever does not know this sigh from experience does not know the passion of coming to know.

250

Guilt. – Although the shrewdest judges of the witches and even the witches themselves were convinced of the guilt of witchcraft, this guilt still did not exist. This is true of all guilt.

251

Misunderstood sufferers. – Great natures suffer differently from what their admirers imagine: they suffer most severely from the ignoble, petty agitations of some evil moments – in short, from their doubts about their own greatness – and not from the sacrifices and martyrdoms that their task demands from them. As long as Prometheus has pity for men and sacrifices himself for them, he is happy and great; but when he is envious of Zeus and the homage paid to him by mortals, then he suffers!

252

Better in debt. – 'Better to remain in debt than to pay with a coin that does not bear our image!' says our sovereignty.

253

Always at home. – One day we reach our goal – and now we point with pride to the long journeys we took to reach it. In truth we did not notice we were travelling. But we got so far because at each point we believed we were *at home*.

254

Against embarrassment. – Whoever is always deeply occupied is beyond all embarrassment.

255

Imitators. – A: 'What? You want no imitators?' B: 'I don't want people to imitate me; I want everyone to set his own example, which is what *I* do.' A: 'So –?'

256

Skinnedness. – All people of depth find happiness in being for once like flying fish, playing on the outermost crests of waves; what they consider best in things is that they have a surface: their skinnedness – *sit venia verbo.*[38]

257

From experience. – Some do not know how rich they are until they experience what kinds of rich people will steal from them.

258

Those who deny chance. – No victor believes in chance.

259

From paradise. – 'Good and evil are the prejudices of God' – said the snake.

260

One times one. – One is always wrong; but with two, truth begins. – One cannot prove his case, but two are already irrefutable.

---

[38] 'if you allow me to use this word'

261

Originality. – What is originality? To *see* something that still has no name; that still cannot be named even though it is lying right before everyone's eyes. The way people usually are, it takes a name to make something visible at all. – Those with originality have usually been the name-givers.

262

Sub specie aeterni.[39] – A: 'You are moving ever faster from the living: soon they will strike you out of their lists!' – B: 'That is the only way to participate in the privilege of the dead.' – A: 'What privilege?' – B: 'No longer to die.'

263

Without vanity. – When we are in love we want our defects to remain hidden – not from vanity but so the loved one won't suffer. Yes, the lover would like to be godlike – also not from vanity.

264

What we do. – What we do is never understood but always merely praised and reproached.

265

Ultimate doubt. – What, then, are man's truths ultimately? – They are the *irrefutable* errors of man.

266

Where cruelty is needed. – He who has greatness is cruel to his virtues and secondary considerations.

---

[39] 'from the point of view of eternity'

267

With a great goal. – With a great goal one is superior even to justice, not only to one's deeds and judges.

268

What makes one heroic? – To approach at the same time one's highest suffering and one's highest hope.

269

What do you believe in? – In this: that the weight of all things must be determined anew.

270

What does your conscience say? – 'You should become who you are.'[40]

271

Where lie your greatest dangers? – In compassion.

272

What do you love in others? – My hopes.

273

Whom do you call bad? – He who always wants to put people to shame.

---

[40] This is a slightly truncated version of a famous passage from a victory-ode by the early fifth-century (BC) poet Pindar, his *Second Pythian Victory-Ode* (line 73). The original Pindar passage reads: 'Become who you are *through knowing*'. The implication is that the ode should inform the victorious young aristocrat of the great deeds of his ancestors and thereby inspire him to live up to them. For Nietzsche the saying had deeper implications of self-discovery and self-realization: 'How one becomes what one is' is the sub-title of *Ecce Homo*, his reflection on his own work, which was written in 1888.

274

What is most human to you? – To spare someone shame.

275

What is the seal of having become free? – No longer to be ashamed before oneself.

Book Four
St Januarius

You who with your lances burning
Melt the ice sheets of my soul,
Speed it toward the ocean yearning
For its highest hope and goal:
Ever healthier it rises,
Free in fate most amorous: –
Thus your miracle it prizes
Fairest Januarius!

Genoa in January 1882

Januarius is the first month of the Roman civil calendar. The name might (or might not) be connected with that of the deity Janus, the god of doors and entrances. St Januarius (in Italian *San Gennaro*) was an early Christian martyr, a vial of whose dried blood is kept in a church in Naples. On certain feast days the blood is said miraculously to become fluid again.

276

For the new year. – I'm still alive; I still think: I must still be alive because I still have to think. *Sum, ergo cogito: cogito, ergo sum.*[1] Today everyone allows himself to express his dearest wish and thoughts: so I, too, want to say what I wish from myself today and what thought first crossed my heart – what thought shall be the reason, warrant, and sweetness of the rest of my life! I want to learn more and more how to see what is necessary in things as what is beautiful in them – thus I will be one of those who make things beautiful. *Amor fati:*[2] let that be my love from now on! I do not want to wage war against ugliness. I do not want to accuse; I do not even want to accuse the accusers. Let *looking away* be my only negation! And, all in all and on the whole: some day I want only to be a Yes-sayer!

277

Personal providence. – There is a certain high point in life; once we have reached it we are, for all our freedom, once more in the greatest danger of spiritual unfreedom; and no matter how much we have confronted the beautiful chaos of existence and denied it all providential reason and goodness, we still have to pass our hardest test. For it is only now that the thought of a personal providence confronts us with the most penetrating force and the best advocate, appearance, speaks for it – now that we so palpably see how everything that befalls us continually *turns out for the best*. Every day and every hour life seems to want nothing else than to prove this proposition again and again; be it what it may – bad or good weather, the loss of a friend, a sickness, slander, the absence of a letter, the spraining of an ankle, a glance into a shop, a counter-argument, the opening of a book, a dream, fraud – it shows itself immediately or very soon to be something that 'was not allowed to be lacking' – it is full of deep meaning and use precisely *for us*! Is there any more dangerous seduction than to renounce one's faith in the gods of Epicurus,[3] those carefree and unknown ones, and to believe instead in

---

[1] 'I am, therefore I think: I think, therefore I am.' In the second of his *Meditations*, Descartes argued that as long as he thought he could be sure he existed.
[2] 'love of (one's) fate'
[3] Epicurus thought common views about the gods were completely erroneous; they in fact lived a

some petty deity who is full of worries and personally knows every little hair on our heads and finds nothing nauseating in the most miserable small service? Well – I mean in spite of it all! – we should leave the gods alone as well as the genies at our service and be content with the assumption that our own practical and theoretical skill in interpreting and arranging events has now reached its apex. Nor should we think too highly of this dexterity of our wisdom when at times the wonderful harmony created by the playing of our instrument surprises us all too much – a harmony that sounds too good for us to dare to give credit to ourselves. Indeed, now and then someone plays *with* us – good old chance; occasionally chance guides our hand, and the wisest providence could not invent music more beautiful than what our foolish hand then produces.

278

The thought of death. – It gives me a melancholy happiness to live in the midst of this jumble of lanes, needs, and voices: how much enjoyment, impatience, desire; how much thirsty life and drunkenness of life comes to light every moment of the day! And yet things will soon be so silent for all these noisy, living, life-thirsty ones! How even now everyone's shadow stands behind him, as his dark fellow traveller! It's always like the last moment before the departure of an emigrant ship: people have more to say to each other than ever; the hour is late; the ocean and its desolate silence await impatiently behind all the noise – so covetous, so certain of its prey. And everyone, everyone takes the past to be little or nothing while the near future is everything; hence this haste, this clamour, this outshouting and out-hustling one another. Everyone wants to be the first in this future – and yet death and deathly silence are the only things certain and common to all in this future! How strange that this sole certainty and commonality barely makes an impression on people and that they are *farthest* removed from feeling like a brotherhood of death! It makes me happy to see that people do not at all want to think the thought of death! I would very much like to do something that would make the thought of life even a hundred times more *worth being thought* to them.

perfectly happy and contented life, and this meant that they had no interest in or involvement with the human world at all.

279

Star friendship. – We were friends and have become estranged. But that was right, and we do not want to hide and obscure it from ourselves as if we had to be ashamed of it. We are two ships, each of which has its own goal and course; we may cross and have a feast together, as we did – and then the good ships lay so quietly in one harbour and in one sun that it may have seemed as if they had already completed their course and had the same goal. But then the almighty force of our projects drove us apart once again, into different seas and sunny zones, and maybe we will never meet again – or maybe we will, but will not recognize each other: the different seas and suns have changed us! That we had to become estranged is the law *above* us; through it we should come to have more respect for each other – and the thought of our former friendship should become more sacred! There is probably a tremendous invisible curve and stellar orbit in which our different ways and goals may be *included* as small stretches – let us rise to this thought! But our life is too short and our vision too meagre for us to be more than friends in the sense of that sublime possibility. – Let us then *believe* in our star friendship even if we must be earth enemies.

280

Architecture for those who wish to pursue knowledge. – One day, and probably soon, we will need some recognition of what is missing primarily in our big cities: quiet and wide, expansive places for reflection – places with long, high-ceilinged arcades for bad or all-too-sunny weather, where no shouts or noise from carriages can penetrate and where refined manners would prohibit even priests from praying aloud: a whole complex of buildings and sites that would give expression to the sublimity of contemplation and of stepping aside. The time is past when the Church had a monopoly on contemplation, when the *vita contempla-tiva*[4] always had to be first and foremost a *vita religiosa*:[5] and everything built by the Church gives expression to that idea. I do not see how we could make do with those buildings, even if they were stripped of their churchly purposes; as houses of God and spaces for ostentatiously

---

[4] 'contemplative life'
[5] 'religious life'

displaying our intercourse with the World-Beyond, these buildings speak much that is too emotional and too partisan for us godless ones to be able to think *our thoughts* here. We want to have *us* translated into stone and plants; we want to take walks *in us* when we stroll through these hallways and gardens.

281

Knowing how to end. – Masters of the first rank are recognized by the fact that in matters great and small they know how to find an end perfectly, be it the end of a melody or a thought; of a tragedy's fifth act or an act of state. The best of the second rank always get restless toward the end, and do not fall into the sea with such proud and calm balance as do, for example, the mountains at Portofino – where the bay of Genoa finishes its melody.

282

Gait. – There are certain tricks of the spirit by which even great minds betray that they come from the mob or half-mob; the gait and stride of their thoughts especially plays the traitor: they cannot *walk*. Thus Napoleon too, was unable, to his great vexation, to walk in a princely and 'legitimate' fashion on occasions that really demanded it, such as great coronation processions; even there, he was always just the leader of a column – proud and hasty at the same time, and very conscious of it. It is laughable to behold those authors who make the ruffled robes of long sentences rustle about themselves: they are trying to hide their *feet*.

283

Preparatory human beings. – I welcome all the signs of a more virile, warlike age approaching that will above all restore honour to bravery! For it shall pave the way for a still higher age and gather the strength that the latter will need one day – the age that will carry heroism into the search for knowledge and *wage wars* for the sake of thoughts and their consequences. To this end we now need many preparatory brave human beings who surely cannot spring from nothingness any more than from the sand and slime of present-day civilization and urbanization: human beings who know how to be silent, lonely, determined, and satisfied and steadfast in invisible activities; human beings profoundly predisposed to look, in all things, for what must be *overcome*; human beings whose cheerfulness, patience, modesty, and contempt for great vanities is just as distinctive as their magnanimity in victory and patience with the small vanities of the defeated; human beings with a sharp and free judgement concerning all victors and the share of chance in every victory and glory; human beings with their own festivals, their own working days, their own periods of mourning, accustomed to command with assurance and equally prepared, when called for, to obey – in each case, equally proud, equally serving their own cause; more endangered, more fruitful, happier human beings! For – believe me – the secret for harvesting from existence the greatest fruitfulness and the greatest enjoyment is – *to live dangerously*! Build your cities on the slopes of Vesuvius! Send your ships into uncharted seas! Live at war with your peers and yourselves! Be robbers and conquerors as long as you cannot be rulers and possessors, you seekers of knowledge! Soon the time will be past in which you had to be content living hidden in forests like shy deer! Finally the search for knowledge will reach for its due; it will want to rule and possess, and you with it!

284

Faith in oneself. – Few people have faith in themselves – and of these few, some possess it as a useful blindness or partial eclipse of the mind (what would they behold if they could see the bottom of themselves!), while the rest have to acquire it. Everything good, fine, or great they do is first of all an argument against the sceptic inside them. They have to convince or persuade *him*, and that almost requires genius. These are the great self-dissatisfied people.

285

Excelsior.[6] – 'You will never pray again, never adore again, never again rest in endless trust; you refuse to let yourself stop to unharness your thoughts before any ultimate wisdom, goodness, or power; you have no perpetual guard and friend for your seven solitudes; you live without

[6] 'higher'

the view of a mountain-range with snow-capped peaks and fire in its heart; there is no avenger for you anymore, no final corrector of the text of your life; there is no more reason in what happens, no love in what will happen to you; no more resting place stands open for your heart in which to find and no longer seek; you arm yourself against any ultimate peace; you will the eternal recurrence of war and peace; – Man of renunciation, all of this you wish to renounce? Who will give you the strength to do so? No one yet has had the strength!' There is a lake that one day refused to let itself flow off and formed a dam where it used to flow off: ever since, this lake rises higher and higher. Perhaps this very renunciation will lend us the strength to bear renunciation; perhaps man will rise ever higher when he no longer *flows off* into a god.

286

Interruption. – These are hopes; but what will you see and hear of them when you have not experienced splendour, ardour, and rosy dawn in your own souls? I can only remind – more I cannot do! To move stones, to turn animals into humans – is that what you want from me? Oh, if you are still stones and animals, you had better look for your Orpheus[7] first!

287

Delight in blindness. – 'My thoughts', said the wanderer to his shadow, 'should show me where I stand, but they should not betray to me *where I am going*. I love ignorance of the future and do not want to perish of impatience and premature tasting of things promised.'

288

High spirits. – It seems to me that most people simply do not believe in elevated moods, unless it be for moments or fifteen-minute intervals at most – except for those few who experience an elevated feeling over a longer period. But to be the human being of one elevated feeling, the embodiment of a single great mood, has hitherto been a mere dream and

---

[7] See above, Book II, footnote 31, p. 88.

enchanting possibility; as yet, history does not offer us any certain examples of it. Nevertheless history might one day beget such people, too, given the creation and determination of a great many preconditions that even the dice rolls of the luckiest chance could not put together today. Perhaps the usual state for these souls would be what has so far entered our souls only as an occasional exception that made us shudder: a perpetual movement between high and low and the feeling of high and low; a continual sense of ascending stairs and at the same time of resting on clouds.

289

Get on the ships! – If one considers how an overall philosophical justification of one's way of living and thinking affects each individual – namely, like a sun, warming, blessing, impregnating, shining especially for him; how it makes him independent of praise and blame, self-sufficient, rich, generous with happiness and good will; how it incessantly turns evil into good, brings all forces to bloom and ripen and keeps the petty, great weed of melancholy and moroseness from coming up at all – one exclaims longingly, in the end: Oh, how I wish that many such new suns would yet be created! Even the evil man, the unhappy man, and the exceptional man should have their philosophy, their good right, their sunshine! Pity for them is not what is needed! We have to unlearn this arrogant notion, however long humanity has spent learning and practising it – we do not need to present them with confessors, conjurers of souls, and forgivers of sins; rather, a new *justice* is needed! And a new motto! And new philosophers! The moral earth, too, is round! The moral earth, too, has its antipodes! The antipodes, too, have their right to exist! There is another world to discover – and more than one! On to the ships, you philosophers!

290

One thing is needful. – To 'give style' to one's character – a great and rare art! It is practised by those who survey all the strengths and weaknesses that their nature has to offer and then fit them into an artistic plan until each appears as art and reason and even weaknesses delight the eye. Here a great mass of second nature has been added; there a piece of first

nature removed – both times through long practice and daily work at it. Here the ugly that could not be removed is concealed; there it is reinterpreted into sublimity. Much that is vague and resisted shaping has been saved and employed for distant views – it is supposed to beckon towards the remote and immense. In the end, when the work is complete, it becomes clear how it was the force of a single taste that ruled and shaped everything great and small – whether the taste was good or bad means less than one may think; it's enough that it was one taste! It will be the strong and domineering natures who experience their most exquisite pleasure under such coercion, in being bound by but also perfected under their own law; the passion of their tremendous will becomes less intense in the face of all stylized nature, all conquered and serving nature; even when they have palaces to build and gardens to design, they resist giving nature free rein. Conversely, it is the weak characters with no power over themselves who *hate* the constraint of style: they feel that if this bitterly evil compulsion were to be imposed on them, they would have to become *commonplace* under it – they become slaves as soon as they serve; they hate to serve. Such minds – and they may be of the first rank – are always out to shape or interpret their environment as *free* nature – wild, arbitrary, fantastic, disorderly, and surprising – and they are well advised to do so, because only thus do they please themselves! For one thing is needful: that a human being should *attain* satisfaction with himself – be it through this or that poetry or art; only then is a human being at all tolerable to behold! Whoever is dissatisfied with himself is continually prepared to avenge himself for this, and we others will be his victims if only by having to endure his sight. For the sight of something ugly makes one bad and gloomy.

291

Genoa. – I have been looking at this city for a long time, at its villas and pleasure-gardens and the wide circumference of its inhabited heights and slopes, and in the end I must say: I see *faces* that belong to past generations; this region is dotted with images of bold and autocratic human beings. They have *lived* and wish to live on – that is what they are telling me with their houses, built and adorned to last for centuries and not for the fleeting hour: they were well disposed towards life, however badly disposed they often may have been towards themselves. I

164

keep seeing the builder, how he rests his gaze on everything built near and afar as well as on city, sea, and mountain contours, and how with his gaze he is perpetrating acts of violence and conquest: he wants to fit all this into *his* plan and finally make it his *possession* by incorporating it into his plan. The whole region is overgrown with this magnificent, insatiable lust for possessions and spoils; and even as these people heeded no boundaries in distant lands and, in their thirst for what was new, placed a new world beside the old one, so, too, at home each flared up against the other and found a way to express his superiority and place his personal infinity between himself and his neighbour. Each conquered his homeland again for himself by overwhelming it with his architectural ideas and refashioning it, so to speak, into a house that was a feast for his eyes. In the North one is impressed by the law and by the general delight in lawfulness and obedience as one considers the way cities are built: this allows one to recognize the inner propensity to uniformity and conformism which must have dominated the souls of all the builders. But here you find, upon turning every corner, a separate human being who knows the sea, adventure, and the Orient; a human being averse to the law and to the neighbour as to a kind of boredom, who measures everything old and established with envious eyes: he would, with a marvellous cunning of imagination, like to establish all this anew at least in thought; to put his hand to it, his meaning into it – if only for the moment of a sunny afternoon when his insatiable and melancholy soul feels sated for once, and only what is his own and nothing alien may appear to his eye.

292

To the preachers of morals. – I do not want to moralize, but to those who do, I give this advice: if you want eventually to deprive the best things and situations of all their worth, then keep talking about them the way you have been! Place them at the top of your morality and talk from morning till night about the bliss of happiness, the tranquillity of the soul, about justice and immanent retribution – the way you carry on, all these good things will finally attain a popularity and street-clamour of their own, but at the same time all the gold that was on them will have worn off through handling, and all the gold *inside* will have turned to lead. Verily, you know the art of alchemy in reverse, the devaluation of what is most valuable! Sometime you should try a different prescription to avoid reaching the opposite of what you seek, as you have so far: *deny* these good things; withdraw from them the mob's acclaim and their easy currency; make them once again the hidden modesty of solitary souls; say that *morality is something forbidden!* That way you might win over for these things the kind of people who alone matter; I mean the *heroic.* But then there must be something in them that provokes fear and not, as hitherto, disgust! Isn't it time to say of morality what Master Eckhart said: 'I ask God to rid me of God!'[8]

293

Our air. – We know it very well: to those who glance at science as if passing it on a walk, in the manner of women and unfortunately also many artists, the severity of its service – this inexorability in matters great and small, this swiftness in weighing, judging, and passing judgement – has something dizzying and fear-inspiring. What frightens them especially is how the hardest is demanded and the best done despite the absence of praise and awards; rather, as among soldiers, what one mostly hears is almost exclusively reproaches and sharp reprimands – for doing things well is considered the rule, and failure the exception; yet here as everywhere else, the rule has a reticent mouth. Now this 'severity of science' has something in common with the form and decorum of the very best society: it frightens the uninitiated. But someone accustomed to it wants to live nowhere else than in this bright, transparent, strongly electric air – in this *masculine* air. Anywhere else is not clean and airy enough for him: he suspects that *there,* his best art would be of no real use to anyone and of no delight to himself; that among misunderstandings half his life would slip through his fingers; that much caution, much concealment and restraint would constantly be called for – ways of having large amounts of one's strength sapped uselessly! But in *this* severe and clear element he has his full strength: here he can fly! Why descend into those murky waters where one has to swim and wade and sully one's wings? No, it's too hard for us to live there; it's not our fault that we were born for the air, for clean air, we rivals of the light beam, and that we would prefer to ride on specks of

---

[8] German mystic (1260–1327). This dictum is to be found in his *Predigten und Schriften* (Frankfurt and Hamburg, 1956) p. 195.

ether, like it – not away from the sun but *towards the sun*! That, however, we cannot do. So let us do all we can do: bring light to the earth; be 'the light of the earth'! And for that, we have our wings and our speed and our severity; for that, we are masculine and even terrifying, like fire. May those be terrified of us who do not know how to gain warmth and light from us!

294

Against the slanderers of nature. – I find those people unpleasant in whom every natural inclination immediately becomes a sickness, something disfiguring or even contemptible – *they* have seduced us into the belief that man's natural inclinations are evil; *they* are the cause of our great injustice towards our nature, towards *all* nature! There are enough people who could well entrust themselves to their inclinations with grace and without care, but who do not for fear of the imagined 'evil essence' of nature! *That* is why there is so little nobility among human beings; its distinguishing feature has always been to have no fear of oneself, to expect nothing contemptible from oneself, to fly without misgivings wherever we're inclined – we free-born birds! And wherever we arrive, there will always be freedom and sunlight around us.

295

Brief habits. – I love brief habits and consider them invaluable means for getting to know *many* things and states down to the bottom of their sweetnesses and bitternesses; my nature is designed entirely for brief habits, even in the needs of its physical health and generally *as far as* I can see at all, from the lowest to the highest. I always believe *this* will give me lasting satisfaction – even brief habits have this faith of passion, this faith in eternity – and that I am to be envied for having found and recognized it, and now it nourishes me at noon and in the evening and spreads a deep contentment around itself and into me, so that I desire nothing else, without having to compare, despise, or hate. And one day its time is up; the good thing parts from me, not as something that now disgusts me but peacefully and sated with me, as I with it, and as if we ought to be grateful to each other and so shake hands to say farewell. And already the new waits at the door along with my faith – the indestructible fool and sage! – that this new thing will be the right thing, the last right thing. This happens to me with dishes, thoughts, people, cities, poems, music, doctrines, daily schedules, and ways of living. *Enduring* habits, however, I hate, and feel as if a tyrant has come near me and the air around me is *thickening* when events take a shape that seems inevitably to produce enduring habits – for instance, owing to an official position, constant relations with the same people, a permanent residence, or uniquely good health. Yes, at the very bottom of my soul I am grateful to all my misery and illnesses and whatever is imperfect in me because they provide a hundred back doors through which I can escape enduring habits. To me the most intolerable, the truly terrible, would of course be a life entirely without habits, a life that continually demanded improvisation – that would be my exile and my Siberia.

296

A firm reputation. – A firm reputation used to be a thing of utmost utility; and wherever society is still ruled by herd mentality it is still today most expedient for everyone to *act* as if his character and occupation are unchangeable, even if basically they are not. 'One can depend on him; he stays the same': wherever society is threatened this is the type of praise that means the most. Society sees in this person's virtue, in that person's ambition, in the thoughtfulness and passion of a third dependable ever-handy *instruments*. This is a source of great gratification to society, and it bestows on this *instrument-nature*, this staying-true-to-oneself, this immutability in views, aspirations, and even vices its highest honours. Such esteem, which blooms and has bloomed everywhere alongside the morality of custom (*Sittlichkeit der Sitte*), fosters 'character' and brings all change, re-learning, and self-transformation into *ill repute*. However great the advantages of this mentality may be elsewhere, to the *search for knowledge* it is the most harmful kind of general judgement, for it condemns and discredits the willingness which a seeker after knowledge must have to declare himself *against* his previous opinion and to mistrust anything that wishes to become *firm* in us. The attitude of the seeker after knowledge, which is incompatible with a 'firm reputation', is considered *dishonourable* while the petrifaction of opinions has all the honour to itself – still today we must live under the spell of such standards! How hard living is when

N. HAD ANOTE:
'A VERY PoPULAR ERROR: HAVING THE COURAGE
OF ONE'S CONVICTIONS; RATHER IT IS A MATTER OF HAVING
THE COURAGE TO ATTACK ONE'S CONVICTIONS

one feels the judgement of many millennia against and around oneself! It is probable that the search for knowledge was afflicted for many millennia with a bad conscience and that there must have been much self-contempt and secret misery in the history of the greatest spirits.

297

Being able to contradict. – Everybody knows now that being able to stand contradiction is a high sign of culture. Some even know that the higher human being desires and invites contradiction in order to receive a hint about his own injustice of which he is as yet unaware. But the *ability to* contradict, the acquired *good* conscience accompanying hostility towards what is familiar, traditional, hallowed – that is better yet than both those abilities, and constitutes what is really great, new, and amazing in our culture; it is the step of all steps of the liberated spirit: who knows that?

298

Sigh. – I caught this insight on the wing and quickly took the nearest shoddy words to fasten it lest it fly away from me. And now it has died of these barren words and hangs and flaps in them – and I hardly know any more, when I look at it, how I could have felt so happy when I caught this bird.

299

What one should learn from artists. – What means do we have for making things beautiful, attractive, and desirable when they are not? And in themselves I think they never are! Here we have something to learn from physicians, when for example they dilute something bitter or add wine and sugar to the mixing bowl; but even more from artists, who are really constantly out to invent new artistic *tours de force* of this kind. To distance oneself from things until there is much in them that one no longer sees and much that the eye must add *in order to see them at all*, or to see things around a corner and as if they were cut out and extracted from their context, or to place them so that each partially distorts the view one has of the others and allows only perspectival glimpses, or to look at them through coloured glass or in the light of the sunset, or to give them a surface and skin that is not fully transparent: all this we should learn from artists while otherwise being wiser than they. For usually in their case this delicate power stops where art ends and life begins; *we*, however, want to be poets of our lives, starting with the smallest and most commonplace details.

300

Preludes to science – So you believe the sciences would have emerged and matured, if they had not been preceded by magicians, alchemists, astrologers, and witches who with their promises and false claims created a thirst, hunger, and taste for *hidden and forbidden* powers? Indeed, infinitely more has had to be *promised* than can ever be fulfilled in order that anything at all be fulfilled in the realm of knowledge. Those things which now appear to us to be preludes and exercises preparatory to science were in the past certainly not practised and felt to be any such thing. Similarly, perhaps to a distant age the whole of *religion* will appear as an exercise and prelude. Perhaps religion could have been the strange means of making it possible one day for a few individuals to enjoy the whole self-sufficiency of a god and all his power of self-redemption. Indeed – one may ask – would man ever have learned to feel hunger for *himself* and to find satisfaction and fullness in *himself* without this religious training and prehistory? Did Prometheus[9] first have to *imagine* having *stolen* light and pay for it before he could finally discover that he had created light *by desiring light*, and that not only man but also *god* was the work of *his own* hands and clay in his hands? All mere images of the sculptor – no less than delusion, theft, the Caucasus, the vulture, and the whole tragic *Prometheia* of all those who know?

301

Delusion of the contemplative ones. – Higher human beings distinguish themselves from the lower by seeing and hearing, and *thoughtfully* seeing and hearing, immeasurably more – and just this distinguishes

9 See above, Book III, footnote 17, p. 125.

human beings from animals, and the higher animals from the lower. The world becomes ever fuller for someone who grows into the height of humanity; ever more baited hooks to attract his interest are cast his way; the things that stimulate him grow steadily in number, as do the kinds of things that please and displease him – the higher human being always becomes at the same time happier and unhappier. But a *delusion* remains his constant companion: he thinks himself placed as *spectator* and *listener* before the great visual and acoustic play that is life; he calls his nature *contemplative* and thereby overlooks the fact that he is also the actual poet and ongoing author of life – that, to be sure, he differs greatly from the *actor* of this drama, the so-called man of action, but even more so from a mere spectator and festival visitor *in front of* the stage. As the poet, he certainly possesses *vis contemplativa*[10] and a retrospective view of his work; but at the same time and above all *vis creativa*,[11] which the man of action lacks, whatever appearances and universal belief may say. It is we, the thinking-sensing ones, who really and continually *make* something that is not yet there: the whole perpetually growing world of valuations, colours, weights, perspectives, scales, affirmations, and negations. This poem that we have invented is constantly internalized, drilled, translated into flesh and reality, indeed, into the commonplace, by the so-called practical human beings (our actors). Whatever has *value* in the present world has it not in itself, according to its nature – nature is always value-less – but has rather been given, granted value, and *we* were the givers and granters! Only we have created the world *that concerns human beings*! But precisely this knowledge we lack, and when we catch it for a moment we have forgotten it the next: we misjudge our best power and underestimate ourselves just a bit, we contemplative ones. We are *neither as proud nor as happy* as we could be.

302

The danger of the happiest. – To have refined senses and a refined taste; to be accustomed to the exquisite and most excellent things of the spirit as one is to the proper and most usual food; to enjoy a strong, bold, audacious soul; to go through life with a calm eye and a firm step, always

[10] 'contemplative power'
[11] 'creative power'

prepared for the most extreme situations – as for a feast and full of yearning for undiscovered worlds and seas, people, and gods; to hearken to all cheerful music as if brave men, soldiers, seafarers were perhaps seeking a short rest and merriment there – and in the deepest pleasure of the moment to be overcome by tears and the whole crimson melancholy of the happy: who would not like all of this to be *his* possession, his state! It was the *happiness of Homer*! The happiness of the one who invented their gods for the Greeks – I mean, *his* gods for himself! But don't disregard the fact that with this Homeric happiness in one's soul one is also more capable of suffering than any other creature under the sun! Only at this price can one buy the most precious shell hitherto washed ashore by the waves of existence! As its owner, one becomes ever more refined in pain and eventually too refined; in the end, any slight discontentment and disgust was enough to spoil life for Homer. He had been unable to solve a silly little riddle posed to him by some young fishermen![12] Yes, the little riddles are the danger for those who are happiest!

303

Two happy ones. – Truly, despite his youth, this person knows how to *improvise life* and amazes even the keenest observer – for he never seems to make a mistake even though he constantly plays the riskiest game. It reminds one of those masters of musical improvisation to whose hands the listener would also like to ascribe a divine *infallibility* even though, like every mortal, they make a mistake here and there. But they are practised and inventive and always ready at any moment to incorporate into the thematic order the most accidental note to which the stroke of a finger or a mood drives them, breathing a beautiful meaning and a soul into an accident. Here is an entirely different person: basically everything he wills and plans goes wrong. What occasionally he set his heart on several times brought him to the edge of the abyss and within a hair of destruction; and if he did escape that, it was certainly not just 'with a

---

[12] Some of the ancient biographies of Homer state that at the end of his life he was deeply chagrined – some even say he died of chagrin – because he was unable to solve a riddle put to him by some young fishermen. The riddle: 'What we caught we left behind; what we didn't catch we carry with us.' (Answer: lice. Not having any luck with their fishing, they sat down to delouse each other. The lice they caught, they discarded; those they missed were still on their persons.) See *Vita Herodotea*, 492–516, *Certamen*, 321–38, *Plutarchi Vita*, 62–71 etc.

black eye.' Do you believe he is unhappy about this? He decided long ago not to take his own wishes and plans so seriously. 'If I don't succeed at this,' he says to himself, 'I might succeed at that; and on the whole I don't know whether I should be more grateful towards my failures than towards any success. Was I made to be stubborn and to have a bull's horns? That which constitutes the value and outcome of life *for me* lies elsewhere; my pride as well as my misery lie elsewhere. I know more about life because I have so often been on the verge of losing it; and precisely therefore do I *get* more out of life than any of you!'

304

By doing we forgo. – Basically I abhor every morality that says: 'Do not do this! Renounce! Overcome yourself!' But I am well disposed towards those moralities that impel me to do something again and again from morning till evening, and to dream of it at night, and to think of nothing else than doing this *well*, as well as *I* alone can! When one lives that way, one thing after another that does not belong to such a life drops off: without hate or reluctance one sees this take its leave today and that tomorrow, like the yellow leaves that every faint wisp of wind carries off a tree. Or he does not notice that it takes its leave – so sternly is his eye set on its goal, entirely forwards, not sideways, backwards, downwards. 'What we do should determine what we forgo; in doing we forgo' – that's how I like it; that is *my placitum*.[13] But I do not want to strive for my impoverishment with open eyes; I do not like negative virtues – virtues whose very essence is negation and self-denial.

305

Self-control. – Those moralists who command man first and above all to gain control of himself thereby afflict him with a peculiar disease, namely, a constant irritability at all natural stirrings and inclinations and as it were a kind of itch. Whatever may henceforth push, pull, beckon, impel him from within or without will always strike this irritable one as endangering his self-control: no longer may he entrust himself to any instinct or free wing-beat; instead he stands there rigidly with a

[13] 'opinion'

defensive posture, armed against himself, with sharp and suspicious eyes, the eternal guardian of his fortress, since he has turned himself into a fortress. Indeed, he can become *great* this way! But how insufferable he has become to others; how impoverished and cut off from the most beautiful fortuities of the soul! And indeed from all further *instruction*! For one must be able at times to lose oneself if one wants to learn something from things that we ourselves are not.

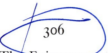

306

Stoics and Epicureans. – The Epicurean seeks out the situation, the persons, and even the events that suit his extremely sensitive intellectual constitution; he forgoes the rest – that is, almost everything – because it would be too strong and heavy a diet. The Stoic, by contrast, trains himself to swallow stones and worms, glass shards and scorpions without nausea; he wants his stomach to be ultimately insensible to everything the chance of existence pours into him – he brings to mind the Arabian sect of the Assua that one encounters in Algiers:[14] like these insensitive people, he likes to act out his insensitivity before an invited audience, which is precisely what the Epicurean gladly eschews – for he has his 'garden'![15] Stoicism may well be advisable for those with whom fate improvises and who live in violent times and depend on impulsive and changeable people. But someone who more or less *expects* fate to allow him to spin *a long thread* does well to take an Epicurean orientation; people engaged in work of the spirit have always done so! For it would be the loss of all losses, for them, to forfeit their subtle sensitivity in exchange for a hard Stoic skin with porcupine spines.

307

In favour of criticism. – Something you formerly loved as a truth or a probability now strikes you as an error; you cast it off and believe your reason has made a victory. But maybe that error was as necessary for you then, when you were still another person – you are always another

[14] For further information about this sect see P. J. André, *Contribution à l'étude des confréries musulmanes* (Algiers, 1956), pp. 216ff.
[15] Epicurus (see above, Book I, footnote 34, p. 59, and Book IV, footnote 4, p. 157), when he was about thirty-five, bought a house in Athens with a garden, setting up there a school of philosophy which came to be known as 'The Garden'.

person – as are all your present 'truths', like a skin that concealed and covered many things you weren't allowed to see yet. It is your new life, not your reason, that has killed that opinion for you: *you don't need it any more*, and now it collapses and unreason crawls out of it into the light like a worm. When we criticize, we are not doing something arbitrary and impersonal; it is, at least very often, proof that there are living, active forces within us shedding skin. We negate and have to negate because something in us *wants* to live and affirm itself, something we might not yet know or see! – This in favour of criticism.

308

The history of every day. – What is the history of your every day? Consider the habits of which it consists: are they the product of innumerable little cowardices and lazinesses or of your courage and innovative reason? Different as the two cases may be, people could conceivably give you equal praise and you might actually benefit them equally either way. However, praise and benefit and respectability may be enough for those who want merely a good conscience – but not for you who scrupulously examine the inside of things and *know about conscience*!

309

From the seventh solitude. – One day the wanderer slammed a door shut behind him, came to a halt, and wept. Then he said: 'This penchant and passion for what is true, real, non-apparent, certain – how it exasperates me! Why does this gloomy and earnest oppressor follow *me* of all people! I want to rest, but he won't allow it. How many things seduce me to linger? Everywhere there are Armida's gardens[16] for me. Thus ever again I must tear myself away and feel another new bitterness in my heart! Once again I must lift my foot, this tired, wounded foot; and having to do so often makes me cast a wrathful glance back at the most beautiful thing that could not hold me – *because* it could not hold me!'

---

[16] In the epic poem *Gerusalemme Liberata* (1575) by Torquato Tasso (1544–95), the enchantress Armida has a magic garden into which she entices men.

310

Will and wave. – How greedily this wave is approaching, as if it were trying to reach something! How it crawls with terrifying haste into the inmost crevices of the craggy gorge! It seems to be trying to arrive before someone else; something of value, of great value, seems to be hidden there. – And now it is returning, a bit more slowly but still quite white with excitement – is it disappointed? Has it found what it was seeking? Is it simulating disappointment? – But already another wave is nearing, still more greedily and wildly than the first; and its soul, too, seems full of secrets and the hunger for treasure-digging. That is how the waves live – that is how we live, we who will – I will say no more. So? You distrust me? You are angry with me, you beautiful monsters? Are you afraid I will divulge your entire secret? Well, be angry with me; raise your dangerous green bodies as high as you can; make a wall between me and the sun – as you are now! Truly, at this moment nothing remains of the world but green dusk and green thunderbolts. Carry on as you want, you high-spirited ones: roar with delight and malice – or dive again, pour your emeralds into the deepest depths, cast your endless white mane of foam and froth over them: everything is fine with me because everything suits you so well, and I love you so for everything – how could I betray *you*! For – mark my words! – I know you and your secret; I know your kind! After all, you and I are of one kind! After all, you and I have one secret!

311

Refracted light. – One is not always brave; and when one gets tired, one of us, too, is likely one day to lament: 'It is so hard to hurt people – why is it necessary! What good does it do us to live in seclusion when we don't want to keep to ourselves what gives offence? Wouldn't it be more advisable to live in the bustle and to do good to individuals as compensation for the sins that should and must be committed against everyone? To be foolish with fools, vain with the vain, fanatic with the fanatic? Wouldn't it be fair, given the extravagant degree of deviation on the whole? When I hear of other people's malice towards me, is not satisfaction the first thing I feel? Quite right! (I seem to be saying to them) I am so little in agreement with you and have so much truth on my side that you might as well have a good day at my expense whenever you can! Here are my faults and mistakes; here is my delusion, my bad taste, my confusion, my tears, my vanity, my owlish seclusion, my contradictions! Here's something for you to laugh at! So then laugh and be merry! I am not angry with the law and nature of things that want faults and mistakes to cause merriment! To be sure, there have been "more beautiful" times when one could still, with every moderately new idea, feel so *indispensable* as to take it out on the street and shout at everyone: "Behold! The kingdom of heaven is at hand!"[17] I would not miss myself if I were gone. We are all dispensable!' But as I said, this is not how we think when we are brave; then we don't think *about that.*

312

My dog. – I have named my pain and call it 'dog' – it's just as faithful, just as obtrusive and shameless, just as entertaining, just as clever as every other dog – and I can scold it and take my bad moods out on it the way others do with their dogs, servants, and wives.

313

No image of torment. – I want to follow Raphael's example and never paint another image of torment. There are enough sublime things; one does not have to seek sublimity where it lives in sisterhood with cruelty; anyway, my ambition would find no satisfaction if I wanted to make myself a sublime torturer.

314

New domestic animals. – I want my lion and eagle around so that I can always have hints and forebodings to know how great or small my strength is. Must I look down on them today and fear them? And will the hour return when they look up at me – in fear?

---

[17] Matthew 4:17

315

On the last hour. – Storms are my danger: will I have my storm of which I perish, as Cromwell perished of his storm? Or will I go out like a light that no wind blows out, but that grew tired and sated with itself – a burned-out light? Or finally: will I blow myself out lest I burn out? –

316

Prophetic human beings. – You are not sensible to the fact that prophetic human beings are full of suffering; you simply think they have been granted a beautiful 'gift' that you yourselves probably would like to have – but I will express myself in a parable. How animals can suffer from electricity in the air and clouds! We see how certain species, for example, monkeys, have a prophetic insight about the weather (as one can observe even in Europe – and not only in zoos, but also on Gibraltar). But we don't think of the fact that for them, their *pains* are prophets for them! When under the influence of an approaching, as yet far from visible cloud a strong positive electrical charge suddenly turns into negative electricity and a change in the weather is impending, these animals act as if an enemy were approaching and prepare for defence or escape. Most often they crawl into hiding – they don't see bad weather as weather, but as an enemy whose hand they can already *feel*!

317

Retrospection. – While we are living each phase of our lives we rarely recognize its true pathos, but always see it as the only state that is now possible for us and reasonable and – to use some words and a distinction of the Greeks – thoroughly an *ethos* and not a *pathos*.[18] Today a few notes of music called back to my memory a winter and a house and a most solitary life, as well as the feeling I lived with: I thought I could continue to live that way forever. But now I understand that it was pathos and passion throughout,

[18] A lasting state of character, not a temporary state of being affected one way or another

comparable to this painful, courageous music which brings certain solace – one is not allowed to possess such things for years at a time, how much the less for eternities: they would make one too 'overworldly' for this planet.

318

Wisdom in pain. – There is as much wisdom in pain as in pleasure: like pleasure, pain is one of the prime species-preserving forces. If it weren't, it would have perished long ago: that it hurts is no argument against it – it is its essence. In pain I hear the captain's command: 'Pull in the sails!' The hardy seafarer 'Man' must have learned to adjust the sails in a thousand ways; otherwise he would have gone under too quickly and the ocean would have swallowed him too soon. We have to know how to live with reduced energy, too: as soon as pain sounds its safety signal, it is time for such a reduction – some great danger, some storm is approaching, and we do well to 'inflate ourselves' as little as possible. True, there are people who hear exactly the opposite command when great pain approaches and who never look as proud, bellicose, and happy as when a storm is nearing – yes, pain itself gives them their greatest moments! They are the heroic human beings, the great *pain-bringers* of humanity, those few or rare ones who need the same apology as pain itself – and truly, they should not be denied this! They are eminently species-preserving and species-enhancing forces, if only because they resist comfort and do not hide their nausea at this type of happiness.

319

As interpreters of our experiences. – One type of honesty has been alien to all religion-founders and such: they have not made their experiences a matter of conscience for their knowledge. 'What did I really experience? What was going on inside and around me? Was my reason bright enough? Was my will turned against all deceptions of the senses and stalwart in warding off the fantastic?' None of them has asked such questions. Even today, none of our dear religious ones asks them; rather, they have a thirst for things that are *contrary to reason* and do not want to make it too hard for themselves to quench it – so they experience 'miracles' and 'rebirths' and hear the voices of the angels! But we, we others, we reason-thirsty ones, want to face our experiences as sternly as we would a scientific experiment, hour by hour, day by day! We want to be our own experiments and guinea-pigs.

320

On meeting again. – A.: Do I still understand you rightly? You are searching? Where is *your* corner and star within the real world? Where can *you* lie down in the sun so that an abundance of well-being comes to you, too, and your existence justifies itself? Let everyone do that for himself – you seem to me to be saying – and let everyone put out of his mind generalities and worries about others and about society! B: I want more than that; I am no seeker. I want to create for myself a sun of my own.

321

New caution. – Let's stop thinking so much about punishing, reproaching, and improving! We rarely change an individual; and should we succeed, something else may have been accomplished, unnoticed: *we* may have been changed through him! Let's rather make sure our own influence *on all that is to come* balances and outweighs his influence! Let's not struggle in a direct fight, which is what reproaching, punishing, and desiring to improve amount to. Let's rather raise ourselves that much higher. Let us give our own example ever more brilliant colours! Let us darken the others through our light! No – let's not become *darker* on their account, like those who punish and are dissatisfied! Let's sooner step aside! Let us look away!

322

Parable. – Those thinkers in whom all stars move in cyclical orbits are not the deepest; he who looks into himself as into a vast space and bears galaxies within also knows how irregular galaxies are; they lead into the chaos and labyrinth of existence.

323

Luck in fate – Fate bestows on us the greatest distinction when it has let us fight for a time on our opponents' side. Thus we are *predestined* for a great victory.

324

In media vita.[19] – No, life has not disappointed me. Rather, I find it truer, more desirable and mysterious every year – ever since the day the great liberator overcame me: the thought that life could be an experiment for the knowledge-seeker – not a duty, not a disaster, not a deception! And knowledge itself: let it be something else to others, like a bed to rest on or the way to one, or a diversion or a form of idleness; to me it is a world of dangers and victories in which heroic feelings also have their dance- and playgrounds. '*Life as a means to knowledge*' – with this principle in one's heart one can not only live bravely but also *live gaily and laugh gaily*! And who would know how to laugh and live well who did not first have a good understanding of war and victory?

325

What belongs to greatness – Who will attain something great if he does not feel in himself the power to *inflict* great pain? Being able to suffer is the least; weak women and even slaves often achieve mastery at that. But not to perish of inner distress and uncertainty when one inflicts great suffering and hears the cry of this suffering – that is great; that belongs to greatness.

326

Soul-doctors and pain. – All preachers of morals, and all theologians, share one bad habit: they all try to talk people into thinking they are in a very bad way and need some severe, final, radical cure. And since humanity has for centuries far too eagerly lent its ear to these doctrines, something of this superstition of being very badly off has finally stuck, so that they

---

[19] 'in mid-life'

are now only too ready to sigh and find nothing good in life and make sad faces together, as if life were really quite hard to *endure*. In reality, they are uninhibitedly sure of and in love with their lives, and are full of innumerable wiles and tricks to get rid of unpleasantness and extract the thorn of pain and misfortune. Talk of pain and misfortune always strikes me as *exaggerated*, as if it were a matter of good manners to exaggerate here while deliberately keeping quiet about the fact that there are innumerable palliatives against pain, such as an aesthetics, or the feverish haste of thoughts, or a restful position of the body, or good and bad memories, intentions, hopes, and many types of pride and sympathy, which have nearly the same effect as anaesthesia – and at the highest degrees of pain, unconsciousness automatically takes over. We know quite well how to trickle sweets onto our bitternesses, especially onto the soul's bitternesses; we find aid in our boldness and sublimity, as well as in the nobler deliriums of submission and resignation. A loss is a loss for barely an hour; somehow it also brings us a gift from heaven – new strength, for example, or at least a new opportunity for strength! What fantasies about the inner 'miseries' of evil persons the preachers of morals have concocted! How they have even *lied* to us about the unhappiness of passionate people! Yes, 'lied' is here the proper term: they knew very well about the superabundant happiness of this type of person, but kept a deathly silence about it, since it constituted a refutation of their theory on which happiness arises only with the annihilation of passion and the silencing of the will! Finally, concerning these soul-doctors' prescription and their praise for a severe, radical cure, one may ask: is our life really so painful and burdensome that it would be advantageous for us to trade it for a fossilized Stoic way of life? Things are *not bad enough* for us that they have to be bad for us in the Stoic style!

327

Taking seriously. – For most people, the intellect is an awkward, gloomy, creaking machine that is hard to start: when they want to work with this machine and think well, they call it 'taking the matter *seriously*' – oh, how taxing good thinking must be for them! The lovely human beast seems to lose its good mood when it thinks well; it becomes 'serious'! And 'where laughter and gaiety are found, thinking is good for nothing'

– that is the prejudice of this serious beast against all 'gay science'. Well then, let us prove it a prejudice!

328

To harm stupidity. – Surely the creed concerning the reprehensibility of egoism, preached so stubbornly and with so much conviction, has on the whole harmed egoism (to the advantage of, as I will repeat a hundred times, the herd instincts!) – above all, by depriving egoism of its good conscience and telling us to seek in it the true source of all unhappiness. 'Your selfishness is the reason your life is miserable (*Unheil*)' – that was preached for millennia and, as I said, harmed selfishness and deprived it of much spirit, much cheerfulness, much inventiveness, much beauty; it made selfishness stupid and ugly and poisoned it! Ancient philosophy, by contrast, taught a quite different main source of misery (*Unheil*): from Socrates onwards these thinkers never tired of preaching, 'Your thoughtlessness and stupidity, your way of living according to the rule, your subordination to the opinion of your neighbour is the reason why you so seldom achieve happiness – we thinkers are, as thinkers, the happiest.' Let us not decide here whether this sermon against stupidity had better reasons on its side than the sermon against selfishness; what is certain, however, is that it deprived stupidity of its good conscience – these philosophers *harmed* stupidity.

329

Leisure and idleness. – There is something of the American Indian, something of the savagery peculiar to the Indian blood, in the way the Americans strive for gold; and their breathless haste in working – the true vice of the new world – is already starting to spread to old Europe, making it savage and covering it with a most odd mindlessness. Already one is ashamed of keeping still; long reflection almost gives people a bad conscience. One thinks with a watch in hand, as one eats lunch with an eye on the financial pages – one lives like someone who might always 'miss out on something'. 'Rather do anything than nothing' – even this principle is a cord to strangle all culture and all higher taste. Just as all forms are visibly being destroyed by the haste of the workers, so, too, is the feeling for form itself, the ear and eye for the melody of movements. The proof of this lies in the *crude obviousness* which is universally demanded in all situations in which people want for once to be honest with others – in their relations with friends, women, relatives, children, teachers, students, leaders, and princes: one no longer has time and energy for ceremony, for civility with detours, for *esprit* in conversation, and in general for any *otium*.[20] For life in a hunt for profit constantly forces people to expend their spirit to the point of exhaustion in continual pretence or out-smarting or forestalling others: the true virtue today is doing something in less time than someone else. And thus hours in which honesty is *allowed* are rare; during them, however, one is tired and wants not only to 'let oneself go' but also to lay oneself down and *stretch oneself out* unceremoniously to one's full length and breadth. This is the way people now write *letters*, the style and spirit of which will always be the true 'sign of the times'. If sociability and the arts still offer any delight, it is the kind of delight that overworked slaves make for themselves. How frugal our educated and uneducated have become concerning 'joy'! How they are becoming increasingly suspicious of all joy! More and more, *work* gets all good conscience on its side; the desire for joy already calls itself a 'need to recuperate' and is starting to be ashamed of itself. 'One owes it to one's health' – that is what one says when caught on an excursion in the countryside. Soon we may well reach the point where one can't give in to the desire for a *vita contemplativa*[21] (that is, taking a walk with ideas and friends) without self-contempt and a bad conscience. Well, formerly it was the other way around: work was afflicted with a bad conscience. A person of good family *concealed* the fact that he worked if need compelled him to work. The slave worked under the pressure of the feeling that he was doing something contemptible: 'doing' was itself contemptible. 'Nobility and honour are attached solely to *otium* and *bellum*'[22] – that was the ancient prejudice!

330

Applause. – A thinker needs no applause and clapping of hands provided he is sure of his own clapping of hands; he cannot do without that. Are

---

[20] 'leisure'   [21] 'the contemplative life'   [22] 'war'

there people who can dispense with that, too, and altogether with every kind of applause? I doubt it; and Tacitus, who did not slander the wise, said even of the wisest of men: *quando etiam sapientibus gloriae cupido novissima excuitur*[23] – which for him means never.

331

Better deaf than deafened – Formerly one wanted to be *talked* about; that is no longer enough, since the market has grown too large – only a *shout* will do. As a result, even good voices shout themselves down, and the best goods are offered by hoarse voices; without the vendors' cry and hoarseness there is no longer any genius. That is, to be sure, a bad epoch for a thinker; he must learn how to find his own quietude even between two noises, and pretend he is deaf until he really is. As long as he has not learned this, he runs the risk of going to pieces from impatience and headaches.

332

The evil hour. – Every philosopher has probably had an evil hour when he thought: What do I matter if people don't accept my bad arguments, too? And then some malicious little bird flew over him and chirped: 'What do you matter? What do you matter?'

333

What knowing means. – *Non ridere, non lugere, neque detestari, sed intelligere!*[24] says Spinoza as simply and sublimely as is his wont. Yet in the final analysis, what is this *intelligere* other than the way we become sensible of the other three? A result of the different and conflicting impulses to laugh, lament, and curse? Before knowledge is possible, each of these impulses must first have presented its one-sided view of the thing or event; then comes the fight between these one-sided views, and occasionally out of it a mean, an appeasement, a concession to all

---

[23] 'since the desire for fame is the last thing even the wise are able to rid themselves of'; Tacitus (first century A D) *Histories* I V .6

[24] 'not to laugh at or lament over or despise, but to understand'; Spinoza (see above, Book I, footnote 28, p. 55) *Ethica*, Book III, *Praefatio*

three sides, a kind of justice and contract; for in virtue of justice and a contract all these impulses can assert and maintain themselves in existence and each can finally feel it is in the right vis-à-vis all the others. Since only the ultimate reconciliation scenes and final accounts of this long process rise to consciousness, we suppose that *intelligere* must be something conciliatory, just, and good, something essentially opposed to the instincts, when in fact *it is only a certain behaviour of the drives towards one another*. For the longest time, conscious thought was considered thought itself; only now does the truth dawn on us that by far the greatest part of our mind's activity proceeds unconscious and unfelt; but I think these drives which here fight each other know very well how to make themselves felt by and how to hurt *each other*. This may well be the source of that great and sudden exhaustion that afflicts all thinkers (it is the exhaustion of the battlefield). Indeed, there may be many hidden instances for *heroism* in our warring depths, but certainly nothing divine, eternally resting in itself, as Spinoza supposed. *Conscious* thought, especially that of the philosopher, is the least vigorous and therefore also the relatively mildest and calmest type of thought; and thus precisely philosophers are most easily led astray about the nature of knowledge.

334

One must learn to love. – This happens to us in music: first one must *learn to hear* a figure and melody at all, to detect and distinguish it, to isolate and delimit it as a life in itself; then one needs effort and good will to *stand* it despite its strangeness; patience with its appearance and expression, and kindheartedness about its oddity. Finally comes a moment when we are *used* to it; when we expect it; when we sense that we'd miss it if it were missing; and now it continues relentlessly to compel and enchant us until we have become its humble and enraptured lovers, who no longer want anything better from the world than it and it again. But this happens to us not only in music: it is in just this way that we have *learned to love* everything we now love. We are always rewarded in the end for our good will, our patience, our fair-mindedness and gentleness with what is strange, as it gradually casts off its veil and presents itself as a new and indescribable beauty. That is *its thanks* for our hospitality. Even he who loves himself will have learned it this way – there is no other way. Love, too, must be learned.

335

Long live physics! – So, how many people know how to observe? And of these few, how many to observe themselves? 'Everyone is farthest from himself'[25] – every person who is expert at scrutinizing the inner life of others knows this to his own chagrin; and the saying, 'Know thyself', addressed to human beings by a god, is near to malicious.[26] *That* self-observation is in such a bad state, however, is most clearly confirmed by the way in which *nearly everyone* speaks of the nature of a moral act – that quick, willing, convinced, talkative manner, with its look, its smile, its obliging eagerness! People seem to be wanting to say to you, 'But my dear fellow, that is precisely *my* subject! You are directing your question to the person who is *competent* to answer it: there is, as it happens, nothing I am wiser about. So: when man judges *"that is right"* and infers *"hence it must come about!"* and then *does* what he thus has recognized to be right and described as necessary – then the nature of his act is *moral*!' But, my friend, you are speaking of three acts instead of one: even the judgement 'that is right', for example, is an act. Wouldn't it be possible for a person to make a judgement in a way that would be moral or immoral? *Why* do you take this and specifically this to be right? 'Because my conscience tells me so; conscience never speaks immorally, since it determines what is to count as moral!' But why do you *listen* to the words of your conscience? And what gives you the right to consider such a judgement true and infallible? For this belief – is there no conscience? Do you know nothing of an intellectual conscience? A conscience behind your 'conscience'? Your judgement, 'that is right' has a prehistory in your drives, inclinations, aversions, experiences, and what you have failed to experience; you have to ask, '*how* did it emerge there?' and then also, '*what* is really impelling me to listen to it?' You can listen to its commands like a good soldier who heeds the command of his officer. Or like a woman who loves the one who commands. Or like a flatterer and coward who fears the commander. Or like a fool who

---

[25] Reversal of common German expression 'Everyone is closest to himself'; cf. *Andria* IV.i.12 by the Roman comedy-writer Terence (second century BC).
[26] Motto inscribed over the entrance to the oracle of Apollo at Delphi.

obeys because he can think of no objection. In short, there are a hundred ways to listen to your conscience. But *that* you hear this or that judgement as the words of conscience, i.e. *that* you feel something to be right may have its cause in your never having thought much about yourself and in your blindly having accepted what has been labelled *right* since your childhood; or in the fact that fulfilling your duties has so far brought you bread and honours – and you consider it right because it appears to you as *your own* 'condition of existence' (and that you have a *right* to existence seems irrefutable to you). For all that, the *firmness* of your moral judgement could be evidence of your personal wretchedness, of lack of a personality; your 'moral strength' might have its source in your stubbornness – or in your inability to envisage new ideals. And, briefly, had you reflected more subtly, observed better, and studied more, you would never continue to call this 'duty' of yours and this 'conscience' of yours duty and conscience. Your insight into *how such things as moral judgements could ever have come into existence* would spoil these emotional words for you, as other emotional words, for example, 'sin', 'salvation of the soul', and 'redemption' have been spoiled for you. And now don't bring up the categorical imperative, my friend! The term tickles my ear and makes me laugh despite your very serious presence. I am reminded of old Kant, who helped himself to (*erschlichen*) the 'thing in itself' – another very ridiculous thing! – and was punished for this when the 'categorical imperative' crept into (*beschlichen*) his heart and made him stray back to 'God', 'soul', 'freedom', 'immortality', like a fox who strays back into his cage. Yet it *had* been *his* strength and cleverness that had *broken open* the cage![27] What? You admire the categorical imperative within you? This 'firmness' of your so-called moral judgement? This absoluteness of the feeling, 'here everyone must judge as I do'? Rather admire your *selfishness* here! And the blindness, pettiness, and simplicity of your selfishness! For it is selfish to consider one's own judgement a universal law, and this selfishness is blind, petty,

[27] In the *Critique of Pure Reason* (1781) Kant argued that the great concepts of traditional speculation – God, the soul, freedom – did not designate objects about which it was even in principle possible for us to know anything. This seemed to spell the end of traditional metaphysics and theology. In the *Critique of Practical Reason* (1788), however, Kant seemed to argue that the morality required us to accept as 'postulates of pure practical reason' a number of principles such as the existence of God and the continuation of some form of life after death. This was thought by many to reintroduce the possibility of a version of the theology it had been the great glory of his earlier work to terminate. 'The categorical imperative' is Kant's fundamental principle of morality.

and simple because it shows that you haven't yet discovered yourself or created for yourself an ideal of your very own – for this could never be someone else's, let alone everyone's, everyone's! No one who judges, 'in this case everyone would have to act like this' has yet taken five steps towards self-knowledge. For he would then know that there neither are nor can be actions that are all the same; that every act ever performed was done in an altogether unique and unrepeatable way, and that this will be equally true of every future act; that all prescriptions of action (even the most inward and subtle rules of all moralities so far) relate only to their rough exterior; that these prescriptions may yield an appearance of sameness, *but only just an appearance;* that as one observes or recollects *any* action, it is and remains impenetrable; that our opinions about 'good' and 'noble' and 'great' can never be *proven true* by our actions because every act is unknowable; that our opinions, valuations, and tables of what is good are certainly some of the most powerful levers in the machinery of our actions, but that in each case, the law of its mechanism is unprovable. Let us therefore *limit* ourselves to the purification of our opinions and value judgements and to the *creation of tables of what is good that are new and all our own*: let us stop brooding over the 'moral value of our actions'! Yes, my friends, it is time to feel nauseous about some people's moral chatter about others. Sitting in moral judgement should offend our taste. Let us leave such chatter and such bad taste to those who have nothing to do but drag the past a few steps further through time and who never live in the present – that is, to the many, the great majority! We, however, want to *become who we are* – human beings who are new, unique, incomparable, who give themselves laws, who create themselves! To that end we must become the best students and discoverers of everything lawful and necessary in the world: we must become *physicists* in order to be creators in this sense – while hitherto all valuations and ideals have been built on *ignorance* of physics or in *contradiction* to it. So, long live physics! And even more long live what *compels* us to it – our honesty!

336

Nature's stinginess. – Why has nature been so miserly towards humans that it did not allow them to shine – one more brightly, the other less so, each according to his inner magnitude of light? Why are great human beings not as beautifully visible in their own rising and setting as the sun? How much more unambiguous this would make life among men!

337

The 'humanity' of the future. – When I view this age with the eyes of a distant age, I can find nothing odder in present-day man than his peculiar virtue and disease called 'the sense for history'. This is the beginning of something completely new and strange in history: if one gave this seed a few centuries and more, it might ultimately become a wonderful growth with an equally wonderful smell that could make our old earth more agreeable to inhabit. We present-day humans are just beginning to form the chain of a very powerful future feeling, link by link – we hardly know what we are doing. It seems to us almost as if we are dealing not with a new feeling but with a decrease in all old feelings: the sense for history is still something so poor and cold, and many are struck by it as by a frost and made even poorer and colder by it. To others it appears as the sign of old age creeping up, and they see our planet as a melancholy sick man who chronicles his youth in order to forget his present condition. Indeed, that is one colour of this new feeling: he who is able to feel the history of man altogether as his own history feels in a monstrous generalization all the grief of the invalid thinking of health, of the old man thinking of the dreams of his youth, of the lover robbed of his beloved, of the martyr whose ideal is perishing, of the hero on the eve after a battle that decided nothing but brought him wounds and the loss of a friend. But to bear and to be able to bear this monstrous sum of all kinds of grief and still be the hero who, on the second day of battle, greets dawn and his fortune as a person whose horizon stretches millennia before and behind him, as the dutiful heir to all the nobility of past spirit, as the most aristocratic of old nobles and at the same time the first of a new nobility the likes of which no age has ever seen or dreamt: to take this upon one's soul – the oldest, the newest, losses, hopes, conquests, victories of humanity. To finally take all this in one soul and compress it into one feeling – this would surely have to produce a happiness unknown to humanity so far: a divine happiness full of power and love, full of tears and laughter, a happiness which, like the sun in the evening, continually draws on its inexhaustible riches, giving them away and pouring them into the sea, a happiness which, like the evening sun, feels richest when even the poorest fisherman is rowing with a golden oar! This divine feeling would then be called – humanity!

338

The will to suffer and those who feel compassion. – Is it good for you yourselves to be above all else compassionate persons? And is it good for those who suffer if you are compassionate? But let us leave the first question unanswered for a moment. What we most deeply and most personally suffer from is incomprehensible and inaccessible to nearly everyone else; here we are hidden from our nearest, even if we eat from the same pot. But whenever we are *noticed* to be suffering, our suffering is superficially construed; it is the essence of the feeling of compassion that it *strips* the suffering of what is truly personal: our 'benefactors' diminish our worth and our will more than our enemies do. In most cases of beneficence toward those in distress there is something offensive in the intellectual frivolity with which the one who feels compassion plays the role of fate: he knows nothing of the whole inner sequence and interconnection that spells misfortune for *me* or for *you*! The entire economy of my soul and the balance effected by 'misfortune', the breaking open of new springs and needs, the healing of old wounds, the shedding of entire periods of the past – all such things that can be involved in misfortune do not concern the dear compassionate one: they want to *help* and have no thought that there is a personal necessity of misfortune; that terrors, deprivations, impoverishments, midnights, adventures, risks, and blunders are as necessary for me and you as their opposites; indeed, to express myself mystically, that the path to one's own heaven always leads through the voluptuousness of one's own hell. No, they know nothing of that: the 'religion of compassion' (or 'the heart') commands them to help, and they believe they have helped best when they have helped most quickly! Should you adherents to this religion really have the same attitude towards yourselves that you have towards your fellow men; should you refuse to let your suffering lie on you even for an hour and instead constantly prevent all possible misfortune ahead of time; should you experience suffering and displeasure as evil, hateful, deserving of annihilation, as a defect of existence, then you have besides your religion of pity also another religion in your hearts; and the latter is perhaps the mother of the former – *the religion of snug cosiness.* Oh, how little do you know of the *happiness* of man, you comfortable and good-natured ones! For happiness and misfortune (*Glück und Unglück*) are two siblings and twins who either grow up together or – as with you – *remain small* together! But now back to the first question. How is it possible to keep to *one's own* path! Some clamour is constantly calling us aside; rarely does our eye see something there that does not make it necessary to drop our own occupation instantly and spring to assistance. I know, there are a hundred decent and praiseworthy ways of losing myself *from my path*, and, verily, highly 'moral' ways! Yes, the moral teacher of compassion even goes so far as to hold that precisely this and only this is moral – to lose *one's own* way like this in order to help a neighbour. I, too, know with certainty that I need only to expose myself to the sight of real distress and I, too, *am* lost! If a suffering friend said to me, 'Look, I am about to die; please promise to die with me', I would promise it; likewise, the sight of a small mountain tribe fighting for its freedom would make me offer my hand and my life – for once to choose bad examples, for good reasons. Yes, there is a secret seduction even in all these things which arouse compassion and cry out for help, for our own way is so hard and demanding and so far from love and gratitude of others that we are by no means reluctant to escape from it, from it and our ownmost conscience – and take refuge in the conscience of the others and in the lovely temple of the 'religion of compassion'. As soon as any war breaks out, precisely the noblest men in the population immediately begin to experience a delight which is, to be sure, kept secret: they throw themselves rapturously into the new danger of *death* because it seems to offer them that long-desired permission – the permission *to deviate from their goal*; war offers them a detour to suicide, but a detour with a good conscience. And, although I will keep quiet here about some things, I do not wish to keep quiet about my morality, which tells me: Live in seclusion so that you *are able to* live for yourself! Live *in ignorance* of what seems most important to your age! Lay at least the skin of three hundred years between you and today! And let the clamour of today, the noise of war and revolutions, be but a murmur to you. You will also want to help – but only those whose distress you properly *understand* because they share with you one suffering and one hope – your *friends* – and only in the way you help yourself: I want to make them braver, more persevering, simpler, more full of gaiety. I want to teach them what is today understood by so few, least of all by these preachers of compassion (*Mitleiden*): to share not pain, but *joy* (*Mitfreude*)!

339

Vita femina.[28] – Not even all knowledge and all good will suffice for seeing the ultimate beauties of a work; it requires the rarest of lucky accidents for the clouds that veil the peaks to lift for us momentarily and for the sun to shine on them. Not only must we stand in just the right spot to see this, but our own soul, too, must itself have pulled the veil from its heights and must have been in need of some external expression and parable, as if it needed a hold in order to retain control of itself. But so rarely does all of this coincide that I am inclined to believe that the highest peaks of everything good, be it work, deed, humanity, or nature, have so far remained hidden and covered from the majority and even from the best. But what does unveil itself for us *unveils itself for us only once*! The Greeks, to be sure, prayed: 'Everything beautiful twice and thrice!'[29] Indeed, they had good reason to summon the gods, for ungodly reality gives us the beautiful either never or only once! I mean to say that the world is brimming with beautiful things but nevertheless poor, very poor in beautiful moments and in the unveilings of those things. But perhaps that is the strongest magic of life: it is covered by a veil of beautiful possibilities, woven with threads of gold – promising, resisting, bashful, mocking, compassionate, and seductive. Yes, life is a woman!

340

The dying Socrates.[30] – I admire the courage and wisdom of Socrates in everything he did, said – and did not say. This mocking, love-sick monster and pied piper of Athens, who made the most audacious youths of Athens tremble and sob, was not only the wisest chatterer of all time; he was equally great in silence. I wish he had remained silent also in

[28] 'Life – a woman'
[29] Plato, *Gorgias* 498e and *Philebus* 59e–60a
[30] See also above, § 36, p. 54.

the last moments of his life – perhaps he would then belong to a still higher order of minds. Whether it was death or the poison or piety or malice – something loosened his tongue and he said: 'O Crito, I owe Asclepius a rooster.' This ridiculous and terrible 'last word' means for those who have ears: 'O Crito, *life is a disease*.'[31] Is it possible that a man like him, who had lived cheerfully and like a soldier in plain view of everyone, was a pessimist? He had merely kept a cheerful demeanour while all his life hiding his ultimate judgement, his inmost feeling! Socrates, Socrates *suffered from life*! And then he still avenged himself – with this veiled, gruesome, pious, and blasphemous saying. Did a Socrates really need *revenge*? Was there one ounce too little magnanimity in his overabundant virtue? – O friends! We must overcome even the Greeks!

341

The heaviest weight. – What if some day or night a demon were to steal into your loneliest loneliness and say to you: 'This life as you now live it and have lived it you will have to live once again and innumerable times again; and there will be nothing new in it, but every pain and every joy and every thought and sigh and everything unspeakably small or great in your life must return to you, all in the same succession and sequence – even this spider and this moonlight between the trees, and even this moment and I myself. The eternal hourglass of existence is turned over again and again, and you with it, speck of dust!' Would you not throw yourself down and gnash your teeth and curse the demon who spoke thus? Or have you once experienced a tremendous moment when you would have answered him: 'You are a god, and never have I heard anything more divine.' If this thought gained power over you, as you are it would transform and possibly crush you; the question in each and every thing, 'Do you want this again and innumerable times again?' would lie on your actions as the heaviest weight! Or how well disposed would you have

---

[31] See Plato, *Phaedo* 116–18, esp. 118a.5–8. Asclepius was the god of healing and a rooster would have been a usual thank-offering to him from someone whom he had cured of an illness. Nietzsche's interpretation of what Socrates said was not standard in the ancient world, and became common only in the Renaissance. It is rejected by some modern scholars.

to become to yourself and to life *to long for nothing more fervently* than for this ultimate eternal confirmation and seal?

342

Incipit tragoedia.[32] – When Zarathustra[33] was thirty years old, he left his homeland and Lake Urmi and went into the mountains. There he enjoyed his spirit and solitude, and did not tire of that for ten years. But at last his heart changed – and one morning he arose with rosy dawn, stepped before the sun, and spoke to it thus: 'You great heavenly body! What would your happiness be if you did not have those for whom you shine! For ten years you have climbed up to my cave; without me, my eagle, and my snake, you would have become tired of your light and of this road; but we awaited you every morning, relieved you of your overabundance, and blessed you for it. Behold, I am sick of my wisdom, like a bee that has collected too much honey; I need outstretched hands; I would like to give away and distribute until the wise among humans once again enjoy their folly and the poor once again their riches. For that I must step into the depths, as you do in the evening when you go behind the sea and bring light even to the underworld, you over-rich heavenly body! Like you I must *go under*, as it is called by the human beings to whom I want to descend. So bless me then, you calm eye that can look without envy upon all-too-great happiness! Bless the cup that wants to overflow in order that the water may flow golden from it and everywhere carry the reflection of your bliss! Behold, this cup wants to become empty again, and Zarathustra wants to become human again.' Thus began Zarathustra's going under.

[32] 'The tragedy begins'. At this point, on completing Book IV, Nietzsche went on to write *Also Sprach Zarathustra* (*Thus Spoke Zarathustra*), the most prophetic in style among his philosophical works, in 1883–5. He added Book V to *The Gay Science* in 1887.

[33] Nietzsche takes the name from that of the Persian religious thinker of the seventh/sixth century BC who propagated a strongly dualistic doctrine, sharply distinguishing between good and evil.

Book Five
We Fearless Ones

Carcasse, tu trembles?
Tu tremblerais bien davantage, si tu savais
où je te mène.

Turenne

'Carcass, you tremble? You'd tremble even more if you knew where I'm taking you.' Henri de
Latour d'Auvergne, Vicomte de Turenne (1611–75) was one of the most successful generals of
the French King Louis XIV.

343

How to understand our cheerfulness. – The greatest recent event – that 'God is dead'; that the belief in the Christian God has become unbelievable – is already starting to cast its first shadow over Europe. To those few at least whose eyes – or the *suspicion* in whose eyes is strong and subtle enough for this spectacle, some kind of sun seems to have set; some old deep trust turned into doubt: to them, our world must appear more autumnal, more mistrustful, stranger, 'older'. But in the main one might say: for many people's power of comprehension, the event is itself far too great, distant, and out of the way even for its tidings to be thought of as having arrived yet. Even less may one suppose many to know at all *what* this event really means – and, now that this faith has been undermined, how much must collapse because it was built on this faith, leaned on it, had grown into it – for example, our entire European morality. This long, dense succession of demolition, destruction, down-fall, upheaval that now stands ahead: who would guess enough of it today to play the teacher and herald of this monstrous logic of horror, the prophet of deep darkness and an eclipse of the sun the like of which has probably never before existed on earth? Even we born guessers of riddles who are so to speak on a lookout at the top of the mountain, posted between today and tomorrow and stretched in the contradiction between today and tomorrow, we firstlings and premature births of the next century, to whom the shadows that must soon envelop Europe really *should* have become apparent by now – why is it that even we look forward to this darkening without any genuine involvement and above all without worry and fear for *ourselves*? Are we perhaps still not too influenced by the *most immediate consequences* of this event – and these immediate consequences, the consequences for *ourselves*, are the oppo-site of what one might expect – not at all sad and gloomy, but much more like a new and barely describable type of light, happiness, relief, amusement, encouragement, dawn . . . Indeed, at hearing the news that 'the old god is dead', we philosophers and 'free spirits' feel illuminated by a new dawn; our heart overflows with gratitude, amazement, forebodings, expectation – finally the horizon seems clear again, even if not bright; finally our ships may set out again, set out to face any danger; every daring of the lover of knowledge is allowed again; the sea, *our* sea, lies open again; maybe there has never been such an 'open sea'.

344

In what way we, too, are still pious. – In science, convictions have no right to citizenship, as one says with good reason: only when they decide to step down to the modesty of a hypothesis, a tentative experimental standpoint, a regulative fiction,[1] may they be granted admission and even a certain value in the realm of knowledge – though always with the restriction that they remain under police supervision, under the police of mistrust. But doesn't this mean, on closer consideration, that a conviction is granted admission to science only when it *ceases* to be a conviction? Wouldn't the cultivation of the scientific spirit begin when one permitted oneself no more convictions? That is probably the case; only we need still ask: *in order that this cultivation begin,* must there not be some prior conviction – and indeed one so authoritative and unconditional that it sacrifices all other convictions to itself? We see that science, too, rests on a faith; there is simply no 'presuppositionless' science. The question whether *truth* is necessary must get an answer in advance, the answer 'yes', and moreover this answer must be so firm that it takes the form of the statement, the belief, the conviction: '*Nothing* is *more* necessary than truth; and in relation to it, everything else has only secondary value.' This unconditional will to truth – what is it? Is it the will not to let oneself be deceived? Is it the will *not to deceive?* For the will to truth could be interpreted in this second way, too – if 'I do not want to deceive *myself*' is included as a special case under the generalization 'I do not want to deceive.' But why not deceive? But why not allow oneself to be deceived? Note that the reasons for the former lie in a completely different area from those for the latter: one does not want to let oneself be deceived because one assumes it is harmful, dangerous, disastrous to be deceived; in this sense science would be a long-range prudence, caution, utility, and to this one could justifiably object: How so? Is it really less harmful, dangerous, disasterous not to want to let oneself be deceived? What do you know in advance about the character of existence to be able to decide whether the greater advantage is on the side of the unconditionally distrustful or of the unconditionally trusting? But should both be necessary – a lot of trust *as well as* a lot of mistrust – then where might science get the

---

[1] See Kant, *Critique of Pure Reason* B 670, 799.

unconditional belief or conviction on which it rests, that truth is more important than anything else, than every other conviction? Precisely this conviction could never have originated if truth *and* untruth had constantly made it clear they they were both useful, as they are. So, the faith in science, which after all undeniably exists, cannot owe its origin to such a calculus of utility; rather it must have originated *in spite of* the fact that the disutility and dangerousness of 'the will to truth' or 'truth at any price' is proved to it constantly. 'At any price': we understand this well enough once we have offered and slaughtered one faith after another on this altar! Consequently, 'will to truth' does *not* mean 'I do not want to let myself be deceived' but – there is no alternative – 'I will not deceive, not even myself'; *and with that we stand on moral ground.* For you have only to ask yourself carefully, 'Why do you not want to deceive?' especially if it should seem – and it does seem! – as if life aimed at semblance, i.e. error, deception, simulation, blinding, self-blinding, and when life on the largest scale has actually always shown itself to be on the side of the most unscrupulous *polytropoi*.[2] Charitably interpreted, such a resolve might perhaps be a quixotism, a slight, enthusiastic folly; but it could also be something worse, namely a principle that is hostile to life and destructive. 'Will to truth' – that could be a hidden will to death. Thus the question 'Why science?' leads back to the moral problem: *Why morality at all*, if life, nature, and history are 'immoral'? No doubt, those who are truthful in that audacious and ultimate sense which faith in science presupposes *thereby affirm another world* than that of life, nature, and history; and insofar as they affirm this 'other world', must they not by the same token deny its counterpart, this world, *our* world?. . .But you will have gathered what I am getting at, namely, that it is still a *metaphysical faith* upon which our faith in science rests – that even we knowers of today, we godless anti-metaphysicians, still take *our* fire, too, from the flame lit by the thousand-year old faith, the Christian faith which was also Plato's faith, that God is truth; that truth is divine . . . But what if this were to become more and more difficult to believe, if nothing more were to turn out to be divine except error, blindness, the lie – if God himself were to turn out to be our longest lie?

---

[2] 'sly, knowing all the tricks, devious'. Nietzsche uses the plural of this word which in the singular is used in the *Odyssey* (e.g. Book I, line 1) to describe Odysseus.

345

Morality as a problem. – The lack of personality always takes its revenge: a weakened, thin, extinguished personality, one that denies itself and its own existence, is no longer good for anything good – least of all for philosophy. 'Selflessness' has no value in heaven or on earth; all great problems demand *great love*, and only strong, round, secure minds who have a firm grip on themselves are capable of that. It makes the most telling difference whether a thinker has a personal relationship to his problems and finds in them his destiny, his distress, and his greatest happiness, or an 'impersonal' one, meaning he is only able to touch and grasp them with the antennae of cold, curious thought. In the latter case nothing will come of it, that much can be promised; for even if great problems should let themselves be *grasped* by them, they would not allow frogs and weaklings to *hold on* to them; such has been their taste from time immemorial – a taste, incidentally, that they share with all doughty females. Why, then, have I never yet encountered anyone, not even in books, who approached morality in this personal way and who knew morality as a problem, and this problem as his own personal distress, torment, voluptuousness, and passion? It is clear that up to now, morality has been no problem at all but rather that on which, after all mistrust, discord, and contradiction, one could agree – the hallowed place of peace where thinkers took a rest from themselves, took a deep breath, and felt revived. I see no one who has ventured a *critique* of moral valuations; I miss even the slightest attempts of scientific curiosity, of the coddled, experimental imagination of psychologists and historians that easily anticipates a problem and seizes it in flight without knowing what it has caught. I have hardly detected a few meagre preliminary efforts to explore the *history of origins* of these feelings and valuations (which is something quite different from a critique and again different from a history of ethical systems): in one single case I did everything to encourage a sympathy and talent for this kind of history – in vain, as it seems to me today.[3] These historians of morality (particularly, the Englishmen) do not amount to much: usually they themselves unsuspectingly stand under the command of a particular morality and,

---

[3] Probably a reference to Dr Paul Rée (1849–1901), author of *Der Ursprung der moralischen Empfindungen* (1877) and *Die Entstehung des Gewissens* (1885). Nietzsche refers again to Rée in the Preface to 'On the Genealogy of Morality' (Cambridge, 1994).

without knowing it, serve as its shield-bearers and followers, for example, by sharing that popular superstition of Christian Europe which people keep repeating so naively to this day, that what is characteristic of morality is selflessness, self-denial, self-sacrifice, or sympathy (*Mitgefühl*) and compassion *(Mitleiden)*. Their usual mistaken premise is that they affirm some consensus among peoples, at least among tame peoples, concerning certain moral principles, and then conclude that these principles must be unconditionally binding also for you and me – or, conversely, they see that among different peoples moral valuations are *necessarily* different and infer from this that *no morality is binding* – both of which are equally childish. The mistake of the more subtle among them is that they uncover and criticize the possibly foolish opinions of a people about their morality, or of humanity about all human morality – opinions about its origin, its religious sanction, the myth of the free will and such things – and then think they have criticized the morality itself. But the value of the injunction 'Thou Shalt' is still fundamentally different from and independent of such opinions about it and the weeds of error that may have overgrown it – just as surely as the value of a medication for someone sick is totally independent of whether he thinks about medicine scientifically or the way an old woman thinks about it. A morality could even have grown *out of* an error, and the realization of this fact would not as much as touch the problem of its value. Thus no one until now has examined the *value* of that most famous of all medicines called morality; and for that, one must begin by *questioning* it for once. Well then! Precisely that is our task.

346

Our question mark. – But you do not understand this? Indeed, people will have trouble understanding us. We are searching for words, perhaps also for ears. Who are we anyway? If we simply called ourselves godless (to use an old expression), or unbelievers, or even immoralists, we would not think that these words came near to describing us: we are all three of them, at too advanced a stage for anyone to comprehend – for *you* to comprehend, my curious gentlemen – how it feels. No! No longer with the bitterness and passion of the one who has torn himself away and must turn his unbelief into another faith, a goal, a martyrdom! We have become hard-boiled, cold, and tough in the realization that the way of the world is not at all divine – even by human standards it is not rational, merciful, or just. We know it: the world we live in is ungodly, immoral, 'inhuman'; for far too long we have interpreted it falsely and mendaciously, though according to our wish and will for veneration, that is, according to a *need*. For man is a venerating animal! But he is also a mistrustful one; and that the world is *not* worth what we thought is about the most certain thing our mistrust has finally gotten hold of. The more mistrust, the more philosophy. We take care not to claim that the world is worth *less*; indeed, it would seem laughable to us today if man were to aim at inventing values that were supposed to *surpass* the value of the real world. That is exactly what we have turned away from, as from an extravagant aberration of human vanity and unreason that for long was not recognized as such. It found its final expression in modern pessimism, and an older and stronger expression in the teaching of Buddha; but also Christianity includes it, more doubtfully and ambiguously, to be sure, but not for that reason less seductively. The whole attitude of 'man *against* the world', of man as a 'world-negating' principle, of man as the measure of the value of things, as judge of the world who finally places existence itself on his scales and finds it too light – the monstrous stupidity of this attitude has finally dawned on us and we are sick of it; we laugh we soon as we encounter the juxtaposition of 'man *and* world', separated by the sublime presumptuousness of the little word 'and!' But by laughing, haven't we simply taken contempt for man one step further? And thus also pessimism, the contempt for that existence which is knowable to *us*? Have we not exposed ourselves to the suspicion of an opposition – an opposition between the world in which until now we were at home with our venerations – and which may have made it possible for us to *endure* life – and another world *that we ourselves are*: a relentless, fundamental, deepest suspicion concerning ourselves that is steadily gaining more and worse control over us Europeans and that could easily confront coming generations with the terrible Either/Or: 'Either abolish your venerations or – *yourselves!*' The latter would be nihilism; but would not the former also be – nihilism? That is *our* question mark.

347

Believers and their need to believe. – The extent to which one needs a *faith* in order to flourish, how much that is 'firm' and that one does not want shaken because one *clings* to it – that is a measure of the degree of one's strength (or, to speak more clearly, one's weakness). Christianity, it seems to me, is still needed by most people in old Europe even today; hence it still finds believers. For that is how man is: an article of faith could be refuted to him a thousand times; as long as he needed it, he would consider it 'true' again and again, in accordance with that famous 'proof of strength'[4] of which the Bible speaks. Metaphysics is still needed by some, but so is that impetuous *demand for certainty* that today discharges itself in scientific-positivistic form among great masses – the demand that one *wants* by all means something to be firm (while owing to the fervour of this demand one treats the demonstration of this certainty more lightly and negligently): this is still the demand for foothold, support – in short, the *instinct of weakness* that, to be sure, does not create sundry religions, forms of metaphysics, and convictions but does – preserve them. Indeed, around all these positivistic systems hover the fumes of a certain pessimistic gloom, something of a weariness, fatalism, disappointment, fear of new disappointment – or else self-dramatizing rage, a bad mood, the anarchism of exasperation and whatever other symptoms or masquerades there are of the feeling of weakness. Even the vehemence with which our cleverest contemporaries get lost in pitiful nooks and crevices such as patriotism (I refer to what the French call *chauvinisme*[5] and the Germans 'German'), or in petty aesthetic creeds such as French naturalism (which enhances and exposes only the part of nature that simultaneously disgusts and amazes – today one likes to call it *la verité vraie*[6] –), or in Petersburg-style nihilism[7] (meaning *faith in unbelief* to the point of martyrdom), always indicates primarily the *need* for faith, a foothold, backbone, support . . . Faith is

---

[4] See 1 Corinthians 2:4. Originally this seems to have referred to the view that Christianity was true because it was possible effectively to cure illnesses and drive out demons by invoking the name of Jesus. By the eighteenth century (in Germany) the doctrine had been transformed into the view that Christianity was true because firm belief in Jesus gave the believer power in the form of an optimistic attitude towards life that would make it possible to cope effectively with adversity.

[5] 'jingoistic xenophobia'

[6] 'true truth'

[7] see Turgenev (1818–83) *Fathers and Sons* (1862); Dostoyevsky, *The Possessed*.

always most desired and most urgently needed where will is lacking; for will, as the affect of command, is the decisive mark of sovereignty and strength. That is, the less someone knows how to command, the more urgently does he desire someone who commands, who commands severely – a god, prince, the social order, doctor, father confessor, dogma, or party conscience. From this one might gather that both world religions, Buddhism and Christianity, may have owed their origin and especially their sudden spread to a tremendous *sickening of the will*. And that is actually what happened: both religions encountered a demand for a 'Thou Shalt' that, through a sickening of the will, had increased to an absurd level and bordered on desperation; both religions were teachers of fanaticism in times of a slackening of the will and thereby offered innumerable people support, a new possibility of willing, a delight in willing. For fanaticism is the only 'strength of the will' that even the weak and insecure can be brought to attain, as a type of hypnosis of the entire sensual-intellectual system to the benefit of the excessive nourishment (hypertrophy) of a single point of view and feeling which is now dominant – the Christian calls it his *faith*. Once a human being arrives at the basic conviction that he *must* be commanded, he becomes 'a believer'; conversely, one could conceive of a delight and power of self-determination, a *freedom* of the will, in which the spirit takes leave of all faith and every wish for certainty, practised as it is in maintaining itself on light ropes and possibilities and dancing even beside abysses. Such a spirit would be the *free spirit* par excellence.

348

On the origin of scholars. – In Europe the scholar grows out of all kinds of classes and social conditions like a plant that requires no particular kind of soil: thus he belongs, essentially and involuntarily, to the bearers of the democratic idea. But this origin betrays itself. Once one has somewhat trained one's eye to recognize in a scholarly book, in a scientific treatise, the scholar's intellectual *idiosyncrasy* – every scholar has one – and catch it in the act, one will almost always behind it come face to face with the scholar's 'prehistory', his family, especially its occupations and crafts. Where the feeling, 'This is now proven; I am done with it,' is expressed, it is usually the ancestor in the blood and instincts of the scholar who from his standpoint approves of 'the finished job' – the faith in a proof is only the symptom of what in a hard-working family for ages has been considered 'good work'. An example: the sons of all types of clerks and office workers, whose main task was always to organize various different kinds of material, to compartmentalize and in general to schematize, when they become scholars, show a tendency to consider a problem practically solved when they have merely schematized it. There are philosophers who are basically just schematizers – for them, the formal aspect of their fathers' occupation has become content. The talent for classifications, for tables of categories, reveals something: one pays the price for being the child of one's parents. The son of a lawyer will also, as a researcher, have to be a lawyer; he primarily wants his cause to win; secondarily perhaps also for it to be right. The sons of Protestant ministers and schoolteachers one recognizes by the naive certainty with which, as scholars, they take their case already to have been proven when they have merely stated it heartily and warmly; they are thoroughly used to being *believed*, as that was part of their father's craft. A Jew, on the other hand, in keeping with the characteristic occupations and the past of his people, is not at all used to being believed. Consider Jewish scholars in this light: they all have a high regard for logic, that is for *compelling* agreement by force of reasons; they know that with logic, they are bound to win even when faced with class and race prejudices, where people do not willingly believe them. For nothing is more democratic than logic: it knows no regard for persons and takes even the crooked nose for straight. (Incidentally, Europe owes the Jews no small thanks for making its people more logical, for *cleanlier* intellectual habits – none more so than the Germans, as a lamentably *déraisonnable*[8] race that even today first needs to be given a good mental drubbing. Wherever Jews have gained influence, they have taught people to make finer distinctions, draw more rigorous conclusions, and to write more clearly and cleanly; their task was always 'to make a people "listen to *raison*" '.)

349

Once again, the origin of the scholars. – To wish to preserve oneself is a sign of distress, of a limitation of the truly basic life-instinct, which aims

---

[8] 'unreasonable'

at *the expansion of power* and in so doing often enough risks and sacrifices self-preservation. It is symptomatic that certain philosophers, such as the consumptive Spinoza, took and indeed had to take just the so-called self-preservation instinct to be decisive:[9] – they were simply people in distress. That today's natural sciences have become so entangled with the Spinozistic dogma (most recently and crudely in Darwinism with its incredibly one-sided doctrine of 'the struggle for existence' –) is probably due to the descent of most natural scientists: in this regard they belong to 'the people', their ancestors were poor and lowly folks who knew all too intimately the difficulty of scraping by. English Darwinism exudes something like the stuffy air of English overpopulation, like the small people's smell of indigence and overcrowding. As a natural scientist, however, one should get out of one's human corner; and in nature, it is not distress which *rules*, but rather abundance, squandering – even to the point of absurdity. The struggle for survival is only an *exception*, a temporary restriction of the will to life; the great and small struggle revolves everywhere around preponderance, around growth and expansion, around power and in accordance with the will to power, which is simply the will to life.

350

In honour of the homines religiosi.[10] – The struggle against the church is certainly, among other things – for it means many things – also the struggle of the baser, meaner, more cheerful, more confiding, more superficial natures against the dominion of the graver, deeper, and more contemplative, that is, more evil and distrustful individuals who, with a long-standing suspicion about the value of existence, also brooded over their own worth: the base instinct of the people, its sensuality, its 'good heart', rebelled against them. The entire Roman Church rests on a Southern distrust of human nature which is always misunderstood in the North. The European South has inherited this suspicion from the deep Orient, from ancient mysterious Asia and its contemplation. Protestantism is, to be sure, an uprising in favour of the upright, the guileless, the shallow (the North has always been more good-natured and superficial than the South); but it was the French Revolution that

---

[9] Spinoza, *Ethica*, Book IV, props. 18–25 (esp. Scholium to prop. 18)
[10] 'religious people'

finally and ceremoniously handed over the sceptre to the 'good people'
(to the sheep, the donkey, the goose, and everything that is incurably
shallow and loudmouthed and ripe for the madhouse of 'modern ideas').

351

In honour of the priestly type: – I think that what the people mean by
wisdom (and who today is not 'people'?) – that prudent, cowlike
serenity, piety and country parson meekness which lies in the meadow
and earnestly and ruminantly *observes* life – is also that from which
precisely the philosophers have always felt the most remote, probably
because they were not 'people' enough, not country parsons enough.
They will presumably also be the last to learn to believe that the people
might come to understand something of that which is most remote from
them, something of the great *passion* of the knowledge-seeker who
steadfastly lives, must live, in the thundercloud of the highest problems
and the weightiest responsibilities (and thus in no way as an observer,
outside, indifferent, secure, objective. . .). The people venerate quite
another type of person when they construct for themselves an ideal of
the 'sage', and they have a thousandfold right to adore just this type of
person with the best words and honours – the mild, serious/simple-
minded and chaste priestly natures and whatever is related to them:
they are the ones who are the objects of approbation when the common
people reveres wisdom. And towards whom would the people have more
reason to show themselves grateful than these men, who belong to and
come from them, though as consecrated, chosen, sacrificed for the
common good – they believe themselves sacrificed to God – , to whom
the people can spill their hearts with impunity and *get rid of* their
secrets, worries and worse (– for he who 'unbosoms' himself is relieved
of himself, and he who has 'confessed', forgets). Here reigns a great
necessity: drainages and their clean, cleansing waters are needed also for
the spiritual refuse; swift streams of love are needed, and strong,
humble, pure hearts who prepare and sacrifice themselves for such an
office of non-public health care – for it *is* a sacrifice; a priest is and
remains a human sacrifice. . .The people see such sacrificed, subdued,
serious persons of 'faith' as *wise*, that is, as having become knowing, as
'certain' in relation to their own uncertainty; and who would want to
deprive them of this word and of their awe? But as is conversely fair,

among philosophers a priest, too, is considered to be one of 'the people' and not a knower, primarily because philosophers do not themselves believe in 'men of knowledge' and already smell 'the people' in this belief and superstition. It was *modesty* that in Greece coined the word 'philosopher' and left the extraordinary insolence of calling oneself wise to the actors of the spirit – the modesty of such monsters of pride and conceit as Pythagoras, as Plato – .

352

The extent to which morality is hardly dispensable. – The naked human being is generally a disgraceful sight – I am talking about us Europeans (and not even about female Europeans!). Supposing that by the mischievous trick of a sorcerer, the merriest dinner party suddenly saw itself exposed and undressed; I think not only the mirth would be lost but also the strongest appetite discouraged, – it seems we Europeans are utterly unable to dispense with that masquerade called clothing. But why should there not be equally good reasons for the disguise of 'moral men', for their veil of moral formulas and notions of decency, for the whole benevolent concealment of our actions behind the concepts of duty, virtue, public spirit, respectability, self-denial? I am not supposing that something like human malice and perfidy – in short, the bad wild beast in us – is thereby disguised; my thought is, quite on the contrary, that it is precisely as *tame animals* that are we a disgraceful sight and need the disguise of morality, – that the 'inner man' in Europe is not nearly evil enough to be able to 'show himself' that way (and be *beautiful* that way –). The European disguises himself *with morality* because he has become a sick, sickly, maimed animal which has good reasons for being 'tame'; because he is almost a monstrosity, something half, weak, awkward. . .It is not the ferocity of the beast of prey that needs a moral disguise, but the herd animal with its deep mediocrity, fear, and boredom with itself. *Morality dresses up the European* – let's admit it! – into something nobler, grander, goodlier, something 'divine' –

353

On the origin of religions. – The true invention of the religion-founders is first to establish a certain way of life and everyday customs that work as a *disciplina voluntatis*[11] while at the same time removing boredom; and then to give just this life an *interpretation* that makes it appear illuminated by the highest worth, so that henceforth it becomes a good for which one fights and under certain circumstances even gives one's life. Actually, the second invention is the more important: the first, the way of life, was usually already in place, though alongside other ways of life and without any consciousness of its special worth. The significance, the originality of the religion-founder usually lies in his *seeing* and *selecting* this way of life, in his *guessing* for the first time what it can be used for and how it can be interpreted. Jesus (or Paul), for example, discovered the life of the small people in the Roman province, a humble, virtuous, depressed life: he explained it, he put the highest meaning and value into it – and thereby also the courage to despise every other way of life, the silent Moravian brotherhood[12] fanaticism, the clandestine subterranean self-confidence that grows and grows and is finally ready to 'overcome the world' (i.e. Rome and the upper classes throughout the empire). Buddha likewise discovered, scattered indeed among all classes and social strata of his people, that type of person who is good and gracious (above all, inoffensive) out of laziness and who, also from laziness, lives abstinently and with nearly no needs at all: he understood how such a type of person would inevitably, with all of his *vis inertiae*,[13] have to roll into a faith that promises to *prevent* the return of earthly toil (i.e. of work and action in general), – this 'understanding' was his genius. The religion-founder must be psychologically infallible in his knowledge of a certain average breed of souls who have not yet *recognized* one another as allies. He is the one who brings them together; and to that extent, the establishment of a religion always turns into a long festival of recognition. –

354

On 'the genius of the species'. – The problem of consciousness (or rather, of becoming conscious of something) first confronts us when we begin to realize how much we can do without it; and now we are brought to

---

[11] 'discipline of the will'
[12] A Christian religious group founded in 1722 in the town of Herrnhut (Germany). Members of the group de-emphasized technical points of religious doctrine and theology in favour of individual emotional experience and fraternal forms of living.
[13] 'force of inertia'

this initial realization by physiology and natural history (which have thus required two hundred years to catch up with *Leibniz's* precocious suspicion).[14] For we could think, feel, will, remember, and also 'act' in every sense of the term, and yet none of all this would have to 'enter our consciousness' (as one says figuratively). All of life would be possible without, as it were, seeing itself in the mirror; and still today, the predominant part of our lives actually unfolds without this mirroring – of course also our thinking, feeling, and willing lives, insulting as it may sound to an older philosopher. *To what end* does consciousness exist at all when it is basically superfluous? If one is willing to hear my answer and its possibly extravagant conjecture, it seems to me that the subtlety and strength of consciousness is always related to a person's (or animal's) *ability to communicate*; and the ability to communicate, in turn, to the *need to communicate*. The latter should not to be taken to mean that precisely that individual who is a master at expressing his needs and at making them understood must also be the most dependent on others in his needs. But for entire races and lineages, this seems to me to hold: where need and distress have for a long time forced people to communicate, to understand each other swiftly and subtly, there finally exists a surplus of this power and art of expression, a faculty, so to speak, which has slowly accumulated and now waits for an heir to spend it lavishly (the so-called artists are the heirs, as well as the orators, preachers, writers – all of them people who come at the end of a long chain, each of them 'born late' in the best sense of the term, and each of them, again, *squanderers* by nature). Assuming this observation is correct, I may go on to conjecture that *consciousness in general has developed only under the pressure of the need to communicate*; that at the outset, consciousness was necessary, was useful, only between persons (particularly between those who commanded and those who obeyed); and that it has developed only in proportion to that usefulness. Consciousness is really just a net connecting one person with another – only in this capacity did it have to develop; the solitary and predatory person would not have needed it. That our actions, thoughts, feelings, and movements – at least some of them – even enter into consciousness is the result of a terrible 'must' which has ruled over man for a long time: as the most endangered animal, he *needed* help and protection, he

---

[14] German philosopher (1646–1716) who held that we had perceptions of which we were not aware; see his *Monadology*, § 14.

needed his equals; he had to express his neediness and be able to make himself understood – and to do so, he first needed 'consciousness', i.e. even to 'know' what distressed him, to 'know' how he felt, to 'know' what he thought. For, once again: man, like every living creature, is constantly thinking but does not know it; the thinking which becomes *conscious* is only the smallest part of it, let's say the shallowest, worst part – for only that conscious thinking *takes place in words, that is, in communication symbols*; and this fact discloses the origin of consciousness. In short, the development of language and the development of consciousness (*not* of reason but strictly of the way in which we become conscious of reason) go hand in hand. One might add that not only language serves as a bridge between persons, but also look, touch, and gesture; without our becoming conscious of our sense impressions, our power to fix them and as it were place them outside of ourselves, has increased in proportion to the need to convey them *to others* by means of signs. The sign-inventing person is also the one who becomes ever more acutely conscious of himself; for only as a social animal did man learn to become conscious of himself – he is still doing it, and he is doing it more and more. My idea is clearly that consciousness actually belongs not to man's existence as an individual but rather to the community- and herd-aspects of his nature; that accordingly, it is finely developed only in relation to its usefulness to community or herd; and that consequently each of us, even with the best will in the world to *understand* ourselves as individually as possible, 'to know ourselves', will always bring to consciousness precisely that in ourselves which is 'non-individual', that which is 'average'; that due to the nature of consciousness – to the 'genius of the species' governing it – our thoughts themselves are continually as it were *outvoted* and translated back into the herd perspective. At bottom, all our actions are incomparably and utterly personal, unique, and boundlessly individual, there is no doubt; but as soon as we translate them into consciousness, *they no longer seem to be*. . .This is what *I* consider to be true phenomenalism and perspectivism: that due to the nature of *animal consciousness*, the world of which we can become conscious is merely a surface- and sign-world, a world turned into generalities and thereby debased to its lowest common denominator, – that everything which enters consciousness thereby *becomes* shallow, thin, relatively stupid, general, a sign, a herd-mark; that all becoming conscious involves a vast and thorough corruption, falsification, superficialization, and generalization. In the end, the growing consciousness is a danger; and he who lives among the most conscious Europeans even knows it is a sickness. As one might guess, it is not the opposition between subject and object which concerns me here; I leave that distinction to those epistemologists who have got tangled up in the snares of grammar (of folk metaphysics). Even less am I concerned with the opposition between 'thing in itself' and appearance: for we 'know' far too little to even be entitled to *make* that distinction. We simply have no organ for *knowing*, for 'truth': we 'know' (or believe or imagine) exactly as much as is *useful* to the human herd, to the species: and even what is here called 'usefulness' is finally also just a belief, a fiction, and perhaps just that supremely fatal stupidity of which we some day will perish.

355

The origin of our concept of 'knowledge'. – I take this explanation from the street; I heard one of the common people say 'he knew me right away' – and I asked myself: what do the people actually take knowledge to be? what do they want when they want 'knowledge'? Nothing more than this: something unfamiliar is to be traced back to something *familiar*. And we philosophers – have we really meant anything *more* by knowledge? The familiar means what we are used to, so that we no longer marvel at it; the commonplace; some rule in which we are stuck; each and every thing that makes us feel at home: – And isn't our need for knowledge precisely this need for the familiar, the will to uncover among everything strange, unusual, and doubtful something which no longer unsettles us? Is it not the *instinct of fear* that bids us to know? And isn't the rejoicing of the person who attains knowledge just rejoicing from a regained sense of security?. . .Take the philosopher who imagined the world to be 'known' when he had reduced it to the 'idea'; wasn't it precisely because the 'idea' was so familiar to him and he was so used to it? because he no longer feared the 'idea'? – How little these men of knowledge demand! Just look at their principles and their solutions to the world riddle with this in mind! When they find something in, under, or behind things which unfortunately happens to be very familiar to us, such as our multiplication table or our logic or our willing and desiring, how happy they are right away! For 'what is familiar is known': on this they agree. Even the most cautious among them assume that the familiar can at least be *more easily known* than the strange; that for example sound method demands that we start from the 'inner world', from the 'facts of consciousness', because this world is *more familiar to us*. Error of errors! The familiar is what we are used to, and what we are used to is the most difficult to 'know' – that is, to view as a problem, to see as strange, as distant, as 'outside us'. . .The great certainty of the natural sciences in comparison with psychology and the critique of the elements of consciousness – with the *unnatural* sciences, one might almost say – rests precisely on the fact that they take the *strange* as their object, while it is nearly contradictory and absurd even to *want* to take the not-strange as one's object. . .

356

The extent to which things will become ever more 'artistic' in Europe. – Even today, in this transitional period in which so many forms of coercion have lost their power, the need to make a living still forces nearly all European men to adopt a particular role – their so-called profession. A few retain the freedom, an apparent freedom, to choose this role themselves; for most of them it is chosen. The result is strange enough. Almost all Europeans, at an advanced age, confuse themselves with their role; they become the victims of their 'good performance'; they themselves have forgotten how much they were determined by accidents, moods, and arbitrariness at the time that their 'profession' was decided – and how many other roles they may have been *able* to play; for now it is too late! Upon deeper consideration, the role has actually *become* character; and artifice, nature. There were times when men believed with unyielding confidence, even with piety, in their predestination for just this business, just this way of making a living, and utterly refused to acknowledge the element of accident, role, and caprice. With the help of this faith, estates, guilds, and inherited trade privileges were able to establish those monsters, the broad-based social pyramids that distinguished the middle ages and to which one can credit at least one thing: durability (and durability is a first-rank value on earth). But there are contrary ages, the truly democratic ones, in which people unlearn this faith and a certain audacious faith and opposite viewpoint moves steadily into the foreground – the Athenian faith that first became noticeable in the

Periclean age;[15] the American faith which is increasingly becoming the European faith as well, where the individual is convinced he can do just about anything *and is up to playing any role*; and everyone experiments with himself, improvises, experiments again, enjoys experimenting, where all nature ends and becomes art. . .When the Greeks had fully accepted this *faith in roles* – the faith of artistes, if you will – they underwent, as is well known, step by step an odd metamorphosis that is not in every respect worthy of imitation: *they really became actors*; as such they captivated and overcame the whole world – finally even the 'power that overcame the whole world' itself (for it was not, as innocents tend to say, Greek culture that conquered Rome, but the *graeculus histrio*[16]). But what I fear, what even today one could grasp with one's hands if one felt like grasping it, is that we modern men are pretty much on the same road; and every time man starts to discover the extent to which he is playing a role and the extent to which he *can* be an actor, he *becomes* an actor. . .With this, a new human flora and fauna emerges that cannot grow in firmer and more limited ages – or that would at least be formally condemned and suspected of lacking honour; it is thus that the most interesting and maddest ages always emerge, in which 'the actors', *all* types of actors, are the real masters. Precisely because of this, another human type becomes ever more disadvantaged and is finally made impossible; above all, the great 'architects': the strength to build is now paralysed; the courage to make far-reaching plans is discouraged; the organizational geniuses become scarce – who still dares to undertake works that would *require* millennia to complete? For what is dying out is that fundamental faith on the basis of which someone could calculate, promise, anticipate the future in a plan on that grand scale, and sacrifice the future to his plan – namely, the basic faith that man has worth and sense only in so far as he is *a stone in a great edifice*; to this end he must be *firm* above all, a 'stone'. . .above all not an actor! To put it briefly – oh, people will keep silent about it for a long time! – what from now on will never again be built, *can* never again be built, is – a society in the old sense of the term; to build that, everything is lacking, mainly the material. *We are all no longer material for a society*; this is a timely truth!

---

[15] The mid-fifth century BC, named after Pericles, the Athenian statesman who was in power during that period and who was thought by some to embody some of its salient virtues.

[16] 'little Greek actor'. 'Graeculus' ('little Greek') was used by Romans as a term of contempt; see Juvenal 3.78.

It is a matter of indifference to me that at present the most short-sighted, perhaps the most honest, at any rate the noisiest human type that we have today – our good socialists – believe, hope, dream, and above all shout and write pretty much the opposite. For even now one reads their slogan for the future 'free society' on all tables and walls. Free society? Well, well! But surely you know, gentlemen, what one needs to build that? Wooden iron![17] The famous wooden iron! And it need not even be wooden. . .

357

On the old problem: 'What is German?' – Add up for yourself the real achievements in philosophical thinking that can be attributed to Germans: is there any legitimate sense in which one can credit them to the entire race? Can we say that they are also the work of the 'German soul', or at least symptoms of it in the same sense in which we are accustomed to take Plato's ideomania, his nearly religious lunacy about forms, as a development and testimony of 'the Greek soul'? Or would the opposite be true? Would they be just so individual, just so much *exceptions* to the spirit of the race as was, for instance, Goethe's paganism with a good conscience? Or as is Bismarck's Machiavellianism with a good conscience, his so-called *Realpolitik*, among Germans? Might our philosophers perhaps even contradict the *need* of the 'German soul'? In short, were the German philosophers really – philosophical *Germans*? I recall three cases. First, *Leibniz's* incomparable insight[18] that has been vindicated not only against Descartes but also against everyone who had philosophized before him – that conscious-ness (*Bewußtheit*)[19] is merely an *accidens*[20] of the power of representa-tion (*Vorstellung*) and *not* its necessary and essential attribute; so that what we call consciousness (*Bewußtsein*) constitutes only one state of our spiritual and psychic world (perhaps a sick state) and *by no means the whole of it* – is there something German to this idea, the profundity of which has not been exhausted to this day? Is there reason to surmise that no Latin could easily have thought of this reversal of appearances?

---

17 Common expression in German for something that cannot exist, like 'square circle'.
18 See above, Book v, footnote 14, p. 212.
19 See above, Book I, footnote 6, p. 37.
20 'accident' in the sense of 'inessential property'

For it is a reversal. Let us recall, secondly, *Kant's* colossal question mark that he placed on the concept 'causality'[21] – without, like Hume, doubting its legitimacy altogether: he started much more cautiously to delimit the realm in which this concept makes any sense whatsoever (and to this day we have not yet come to terms with this marking out of the boundaries). Let us take, thirdly, *Hegel's* astonishing move, with which he struck through all logical habits and indulgences when he dared to teach that species concepts develop *out of each other*.[22] with this proposition the minds of Europe were preformed for the last great scientific movement, Darwinism – for without Hegel there could be no Darwin. Is there anything German in this Hegelian innovation which first introduced the decisive concept of 'development' into science? Yes, without any doubt: in all three cases we feel that something in ourselves has been 'uncovered' and figured out, and we are grateful and at the same time surprised. Each of these three propositions is a thoughtful piece of German self-knowledge, self-experience, and self-conception. 'Our inner world is much richer, more comprehensive, more hidden', we feel with Leibniz. As Germans, we doubt with Kant the ultimate validity of the discoveries of the natural sciences and altogether of everything that *can* be known *causaliter*[23] – what is know*able* already seems to us of *less* value on that account. We Germans are Hegelians even had there been no Hegel, insofar as we (as opposed to all Latins) instinctively attribute a deeper meaning and greater value to becoming and development than to what 'is'; we hardly believe in the justification of the concept 'being' – and also insofar as we are not inclined to concede that our human logic is logic as such or the only kind of logic (we would rather persuade ourselves that it is only a special case and perhaps one of the oddest and stupidest). A fourth question would be whether *Schopenhauer,* too, with his pessimism – that is, the problem of the *value of existence*[24] – had to be precisely a German. I believe not. The event *after* which this problem was to be expected with certainty, so that an astronomer of the soul could have calculated the very day and hour for it – the decline of the faith in the Christian god, the triumph of scientific atheism – is a pan-European event in which all races had their

---

[21] See Kant's Preface to *Prolegomena to any Future Metaphysics* (1783).
[22] See Hegel's *Encyclopedia of Philosophical Sciences* (1830 edn), § 368 (especially the *Zusatz*).
[23] 'causally'
[24] See Schopenhauer, *World as Will and Representation* vol. I, Book 4, and vol. II, chapters 46 and 49.

share and for which all deserve credit and honour. Conversely, one might charge precisely the Germans – those Germans who were contemporaries of Schopenhauer – with having *delayed* this triumph of atheism most dangerously for the longest time. Hegel in particular was a delayer par excellence, in accordance with his grandiose attempt to persuade us of the divinity of existence, appealing as a last resort to our sixth sense, 'the historical sense'. As a philosopher, Schopenhauer was the *first* admitted and uncompromising atheist among us Germans: this was the background of his enmity towards Hegel. The ungodliness of existence counted for him as something given, palpable, indisputable; he always lost his philosopher's composure and became indignant when he saw anyone hesitate or beat around the bush on this point. This is the locus of his whole integrity; unconditional and honest atheism is simply the *presupposition* of his way of putting the problem, as a victory of the European conscience won finally and with great difficulty; as the most fateful act of two thousand years of discipline for truth that in the end forbids itself the *lie* of faith in God. . .One can see *what* it was that actually triumphed over the Christian god: Christian morality itself, the concept of truthfulness that was taken ever more rigorously; the father confessor's refinement of the Christian conscience, translated and sublimated into a scientific conscience, into intellectual cleanliness at any price. Looking at nature as if it were proof of the goodness and care of a god; interpreting history in honour of some divine reason, as a continual testimony of a moral world order and ultimate moral purposes; interpreting one's own experiences as pious people have long interpreted theirs, as if everything were providential, a hint, designed and ordained for the sake of salvation of the soul – that is *over* now; that has conscience *against* it; every refined conscience considers it to be indecent, dishonest, a form of mendacity, effeminacy, weakness, cowardice. With this severity, if with anything, we are simply *good* Europeans and heirs of Europe's longest and most courageous self-overcoming. As we thus reject Christian interpretation and condemn its 'meaning' as counterfeit, *Schopenhauer's* question immediately comes at us in a terrifying way: *Does existence have any meaning at all?* A few centuries will be needed before this question can ever be heard completely and in its full depth. What Schopenhauer himself said in answer to this question was – forgive me – something hasty, youthful, a mere compromise, a way of remaining and staying stuck in precisely those Christian and ascetic moral perspectives in which one had *renounced faith* along with the faith in God. But he *posed* the question – as a good European, as I said before, and *not* as a German. Or is it possible that at least the manner in which the Germans appropriated Schopenhauer's question proves that the Germans did have an inner affinity and relation, preparation, and *need* for this problem? That after Schopenhauer one thought and printed things in Germany, too – by the way, late enough – about the problem he had posed is certainly not sufficient to decide in favour of this closer affinity. One might rather adduce the peculiar *ineptitude* of this post-Schopenhauerian pessimism *against* the thesis; clearly the Germans did not behave in this affair as if they were in their element. This is by no means an allusion to Eduard von Hartmann.[25] On the contrary, to this day I have not shaken off my old suspicion that he is too *apt* for us. I mean that he may have been a real rogue from the start who perhaps made fun not only of German pessimism – but in the end he might even reveal to the Germans in his last will and testament to what extent it was possible to make fools of them, even in an era of economic initiative and success.[26] But let me ask you: should we perhaps consider that old humming-top Bahnsen[27] as a credit to the Germans, seeing how voluptuously he revolved his life around his real-dialectical misery and 'personal bad luck'? Might precisely that be German? (I herewith recommend his writings to the end for which I have used them myself, as an anti-pessimistic diet, especially on account of their *elegantiae psychologicae*,[28] with which, I think, they should be effective also for the most constipated bowels and temperaments.) Or could one count such dilettantes and old spinsters as that mawkish apostle of virginity, Mainländer,[29] as a genuine German? In the end he must have been a Jew (all Jews become mawkish when they moralize). Neither Bahnsen nor Mainländer, nor even Eduard von Hartmann, gives us any clear evidence regarding the question whether Schopenhauer's pessimism, his horrified look into a de-deified world

---

[25] Nineteenth-century German philosopher who drew eclectically on both Hegel and Schopenhauer to develop a pessimistic 'philosophy of the unconscious'

[26] The 1870s were a period of such economic prosperity that they are sometimes referred to as the 'Era of Foundations' (of various business enterprises).

[27] Deservedly forgotten nineteenth-century German philosopher

[28] 'psychological elegance'

[29] In his *Philosophie der Erlösung* (2 vols., 1876–7): Phillip Batz – 'Mainländer' is a pseudonym – makes much of the virtues of virginity (and of suicide). He committed suicide when the second volume of this work appeared, at the age of thirty-five.

that had become stupid, blind, crazed, and questionable, his *honest* horror. . .was not merely an exception among Germans but a *German* event. Everything else that is otherwise in the foreground – our brave politics, our merry fatherlandishness which resolutely enough consider all matters with a view to a not very philosophical principle ('Deutschland, Deutschland über alles'[30]), i.e. *sub specie speciei*,[31] namely the German species, bears emphatic witness to the opposite. No, the Germans of today are *no* pessimists. And Schopenhauer was a pessimist, to repeat, as a good European and *not* as a German. –

358

The peasant rebellion of the spirit. – We Europeans confront a world of tremendous ruins. A few things are still towering; much looks decayed and uncanny, while most things are already lying on the ground: picturesque enough – where has one ever seen more beautiful ruins? – and overgrown by large and small weeds. The Church is this city of decline: we see the religious society of Christianity shaken to its lowest foundations; faith in God has collapsed; faith in the Christian-ascetic ideal is still fighting its last battle. An edifice such as Christianity that had been built so carefully over such a long period – it was the last Roman construction! – could of course not be destroyed all at once. All kinds of earthquakes had to shake it; all kinds of minds (*Geist*) that drill, dig, gnaw, and moisten have had to help. But the oddest thing is: those who exerted themselves the most to preserve and conserve Christianity have become its best destroyers – the Germans. It seems that the Germans do not understand the nature of a church. Are they not spiritual enough for that? Not mistrustful enough? The edifice of the Church rests, at any rate, on a *Southern* freedom and liberality of the

---

[30] First line of a poem written in 1841 by Hoffmann von Fallersleben. At the time of its composition 'Germany' was no more than a geographical expression for a congeries of independent political entities. In this context the words were a call to put national unification – the creation of a 'Germany' – above all regional and local political loyalties. Once unification was attained (in 1871), the words could come to bear a more aggressive meaning in an international context ('Let Germany be above all other nations'). In 1797 Haydn had composed a melody, deriving it from an existing Croatian folktune, which he used to set the words 'Gott erhalte Franz den Kaiser' ('God Save Kaiser Franz'). Until 1918 this was the anthem of the Austro-Hungarian Empire. In 1922 Fallersleben's poem was put together with Haydn's melody and the result proclaimed the German National Anthem.

[31] 'from the point of view of the species'

mind as well as on a Southern suspicion against nature, man, and spirit; it rests on an altogether different knowledge and experience of man than the North has had. The Lutheran Reformation was, in its whole breadth, the indignation of simplicity against 'multiplicity', to speak cautiously, a crude, naively narrow-minded misunderstanding in which there is much to forgive. One failed to understand the expression of a *victorious* church and saw only corruption; one misunderstood the noble scepticism, that *luxury* of scepticism and tolerance which every victorious, self-confident power permits itself. . .Today one overlooks easily enough how in all cardinal questions of power Luther was dangerously short-sighted, superficial, incautious – mainly as a man of the common people who lacked any inheritance from a ruling caste and instinct for power; thus his work, his will to restore that work of the Romans only became the beginning of a work of destruction, without his wanting and knowing it. With honest wrath he unravelled, he tore up what the old spider had woven so carefully for such a long time. He surrendered the holy books to everyone – thus they finally ended up in the hands of the philologists, who are the destroyers of every faith that rests on books. He destroyed the concept of the 'Church' by throwing away the belief in the inspiration of the church councils; for the concept of the 'Church' retains power only under the condition that the inspiring spirit that founded the Church still lives in, builds, and continues to build its house. He gave back to the priest sexual intercourse with a woman; but three-quarters of the reverence of which the people, especially the women of the people, are capable rests on the faith that a person who is an exception in this regard will be an exception in other regards as well – it is here precisely that the popular faith in something superhuman in man, in the miracle, in the redeeming god in man, finds its subtlest and most insidious advocate. Having given the priest woman, Luther had to *take* from him auricular confession; that was psychologically right, but with that development the Christian priest was basically abolished, since his deepest utility has always been that he was a holy ear, a silent well, a grave for secrets. 'Everyone his own priest' – behind such formulas and their peasant cunning was hidden in Luther the abysmal hatred of 'the higher human beings' and the dominion of 'the higher human beings' as conceived by the Church; he smashed an ideal that he could not attain, while he seemed to fight and abhor the degeneration of this ideal. Actually he, the impossible monk, pushed away the *dominion* of the *homines religiosi*,[32] and thus he himself brought about within the *ecclesiastical* social order what in relation to the *civil* social order he attacked so intolerantly – a 'peasants' rebellion'. What grew out of his Reformation afterwards, good as well as bad, might be roughly calculated today; but who would be naive enough to praise or blame Luther on account of these consequences? He is innocent of everything; he did not know what he was doing. The flattening of the European mind, particularly in the North – its *becoming more good-natured*, if one prefers a moral term – advanced a large step with the Lutheran Reformation, there is no doubt; and owing to it also the flexibility and restlessness of the mind, its thirst for independence, its faith in a right to liberty, its 'naturalness'. If in connection with this last point one wanted to give it the credit for having prepared and favoured what we today honour as 'modern science', one must surely add that it also shares the blame for the degeneration of the modern scholar, for his lack of reverence, shame, and depth, for the whole naive guilelessness and conventionality in matters of knowledge – in short for that *plebeianism of the spirit* that is peculiar to the last two centuries and from which even pessimism has not yet liberated us. 'Modern ideas' also belong to this peasant rebellion of the North against the colder, more ambiguous, mistrustful spirit of the South that built its greatest monument in the Christian Church. Let us not forget in the end what a church is, specifically as opposed to any 'state'. A church is above all a structure for ruling that secures the highest rank to the *more spiritual* human beings and that *believes* in the power of spirituality to the extent of forbidding itself the use of all cruder instruments of force; and on that score alone the Church is under all circumstances a *nobler* institution than the state.

359

The revenge against the spirit and other ulterior motives of morality. – Morality – where do you suppose that it finds its most dangerous and insidious advocates?. . .There is a human being who has turned out badly, who does not have spirit enough to be able to enjoy it and just enough education to know this; bored, weary, a self-despiser; wealthy

---

[32] 'religious people'

through inheritance, he is deprived even of the last comfort, 'the blessings of work', self-forgetfulness in 'daily labour'. Such a person who is basically ashamed of his existence – perhaps he also harbours a few small vices – and on the other hand cannot keep himself from becoming more spoiled and touchy as a result of reading books he has no right to or through more spiritual company than he can digest: such a thoroughly poisoned human being – for spirit becomes poison, education becomes poison; ownership becomes poison, loneliness becomes poison in persons who have turned out badly in this way – eventually ends up in a state of habitual revenge, the will to revenge. . .- *What* do you think he finds necessary, absolutely necessary, to give himself in his own eyes the appearance of superiority over more spiritual people and to obtain the pleasure of an *accomplished revenge* at least in his own imagination? Always *morality*; you can bet on that. Always big moral words. Always the boom-boom of justice, wisdom, holiness, virtue. Always the Stoicism of gesture (how well Stoicism conceals what one *lacks*!). Always the cloak of prudent silence, of affability, of mildness, and whatever the other idealistic cloaks may be called under which incurable self-despisers, as well as the incurably vain, go about. Do not misunderstand me: among such born *enemies of the spirit* emerges occasionally the rare piece of humanity that the people revere under such names as saint and sage. From among such men come those monsters of morality who make noise, who make history – St Augustine[33] is among them. Fear of spirit, revenge against spirit – oh how often have these propelling vices become the roots of virtues! Indeed, *become* virtues! And, as a question asked in confidence: even that philosopher's claim to *wisdom* which has been made here and there on earth; the maddest and most immodest of all claims – was it not always, in India as well as in Greece, *primarily a hiding place*? At times perhaps a hiding place chosen with pedagogical intent, which hallows so many lies; one has a tender regard for those who are still becoming, growing – for disciples who must often be defended against themselves through faith in a person (through an error). . .In most cases, however, it is a hiding place in which the philosopher saves himself owing to weariness, age, growing cold, hardening – as a wisdom of that instinct which the animals have before death – they go off alone, become silent, choose

[33] North African rhetorician, theologian and bishop (AD 354–430)

solitude, crawl into caves, become *wise*. . .What? Wisdom as a hiding place in which the philosopher hides himself from – spirit?

360

Two kinds of causes that are often confused. – This seems to me to be one of my most essential steps forward: I learned to distinguish the cause of acting from the cause of acting in a certain way, in a certain direction, with a certain goal. The first kind of cause is a quantum of dammed-up energy waiting to be used somehow, for something; the second kind, by contrast, is something quite insignificant, mostly a small accident in accordance with which this quantum 'discharges' itself in one particular way: the match versus the powder keg. Among these small accidents and matches I consider all so-called 'purposes' as well as the even more so-called 'vocations': they are relatively random, arbitrary, nearly in-different in relation to the enormous force of energy that presses on, as I said, to be used up somehow. The usual view is different: one is used to seeing the *driving* force precisely in the goals (purposes, professions, etc.), in keeping with a very ancient error; but it is only the *directing* force – one has mistaken the helmsman for the stream. And not even always the helmsman, the driving force. . .Is the 'goal', the 'purpose', not often enough a beautifying pretext, a self-deception of vanity after the fact that does not want to acknowledge that the ship is *following* the current into which it has entered accidentally? That it 'wills' to go that way *because it – must*? That it certainly has a direction but – no helmsman whatsoever? We still need a critique of the concept of 'purpose'.

361

On the problem of the actor. – The problem of the actor has troubled me for a very long time; I was unsure (and still sometimes am) whether it is only from this angle that one can approach the dangerous concept of the 'artist' – a concept that has heretofore been treated with unpardonable generosity. Falseness with a good conscience; the delight in pretence erupting as a power that pushes aside, floods, and at times extinguishes one's so-called 'character'; the inner longing for a role and mask, for an *appearance* (*Schein*); an excess of capacities for all kinds of adaptation that can no longer be satisfied in the service of the nearest, most narrowly construed utility – perhaps all of this is distinctive not *only* of the actor? Such an instinct will have developed most easily in lower-class families who had to survive under fluctuating pressures and coercions, in deep dependency; who had nimbly to cut their coats according to their cloth, always readapting to new circumstances, always having to act and pose differently until they slowly learned to turn their coats with *every* wind and thus almost turned into coats themselves – and masters of an art which they have fully assimilated so that it is an integral part of themselves, that art of perpetually playing at self-concealment which in animals we call mimicry – until finally this capacity, accumulated from generation to generation, becomes domineering, unreasonable, intractable, an instinct that learns to command other instincts and produces the actor, the 'artist' (the buffoon, the teller of lies, the fool, the jester, the clown primarily, but also the classical servant, Gil Blas;[34] for it is in such types that we find the pre-history of the artist and often enough even of 'genius'). In more elevated social conditions, too, a similar human type develops under similar pressures; only here, the histrionic instinct is usually just barely kept in check by another instinct, as in the case of 'diplomats'. Incidentally, I would think that a good diplomat would be free at any time to become a good actor – provided, of course, that he were 'free' to do this. But as for the *Jews*, that people possessing the art of adaptability par excellence, one might, according to this train of thought, immediately see in them a world-historical organization for the cultivation of actors, a veritable breeding ground for actors; and indeed it is really high time to ask: what good actor today is *not* – a Jew? Also the Jew as a born literary man, as the true master of the European press, exercises this power by virtue of his histrionic ability, for the literary man is essentially an actor: he plays the 'expert', the 'specialist'. Finally, *women*: consider the whole history of women – *mustn't* they be actresses first and foremost? Listen to doctors who have hypnotized womenfolk; finally, love them – let yourself be 'hypnotized' by them! What is always the result? That they try to be 'taken for something' even when they are being taken. . . Woman is so artistic. . .

[34] See above, Book II, footnote 9, p. 78.

362

Our faith in the masculinization of Europe. – We owe it to Napoleon (and not at all to the French Revolution, which aimed at the 'brotherhood' of peoples and a general, blooming exchange of hearts) that a few warlike centuries, incomparable to any other in history, are likely to follow in succession – in short, that we have entered the *classic age of war*, of sophisticated yet popular war on the largest scale (in terms of weapons, talents, discipline); all coming ages will look back on this kind of war with envy and deep respect as something perfect, for the national movement out of which this war glory is growing is merely the counter-shock against Napoleon and would not exist without Napoleon. He should be credited one day for having enabled *man* in Europe to become the master over the businessman and the philistine – perhaps even over 'woman', who has been spoiled by Christianity and the enthusiastic spirit of the eighteenth century, and even more by 'modern ideas'. Napoleon, who saw something of a personal enemy in modern ideas and in civilization itself,[35] proved through this enmity to be one of the greatest continuators of the Renaissance: he brought back a whole piece, a block of granite, perhaps the decisive one, of antiquity's essence. And who knows whether this piece of antiquity's essence will finally again become master of the national movement, and whether it must not make itself the heir and protractor in an *affirmative* sense of Napoleon – who wanted one Europe, as is known, and wanted it as *mistress of the earth.* –

363

How each sex has its own prejudice about love. – Despite all the concessions I am willing to make to the prejudice favouring monogamy, I will never admit talk of *equal* rights for man and woman in love: there are none. For man and woman have different conceptions of love – and it belongs to the conditions of love in each sex that *neither* presupposes the same feeling, the same concept of 'love' in the other. What woman means by love is clear enough: total devotion (and not mere surrender) with soul and body, without any consideration or reserve, rather with shame and horror at the thought of a devotion that might be tied to

---

[35] See above, Book I, footnote 16, p. 49. In this case see vol. I, p. 112.

special clauses or conditions. In this absence of conditions her love is a *faith*: woman has no other. Man, when he loves a woman, *wants* precisely this love from her and is thus himself as far as can be from the presupposition of female love; supposing, however, that there should also be men to whom the desire for complete surrender is not alien, well, then they are – not men. A man who loves like a woman becomes a slave, but a woman who loves like a woman becomes a *more perfect* woman . . . The passion of a woman, in its unconditional renunciation of her own rights, presupposes precisely that on the other side there is *not* an equal pathos, not an equal will to renunciation; for if both should renounce themselves from love, the result would be – well, I don't know, maybe an empty space? Woman wants to be taken, adopted as a possession, wants to be absorbed in the concept 'possession', 'possessed'; consequently, she wants someone who *takes*, who does not himself give or give himself away; who on the contrary is supposed precisely to be made richer in 'himself' – through the increase in strength, happiness, and faith given him by the woman who gives herself. Woman gives herself away; man takes more – I do not believe one can get around this natural opposition through any social contracts or with the best will to justice, desirable as it may be not to remind oneself constantly how harsh, terrible, enigmatic, and immoral this antagonism is. For love, when one considers it in its perfect, fully developed state, is nature, and nature is eternally 'immoral'. Faithfulness is then implicit in woman's love, and follows from its definition; in a man's case it *could* perhaps arise as a consequence of his love, for instance as gratitude or as an idiosyncrasy of taste, a so-called 'elective affinity', but it does not belong to the *essence* of his love. Indeed this is so little the case that one might almost speak with some justification of a natural back-and-forth between love and faithfulness in a man: his love is desire for possession and *not* a renunciation or giving away, but with *possession* desire for possession always ceases . . . In fact it is the highly refined and suspicious thirst for possession on the part of a man who rarely and only after a long time admits that he has 'possession', which allows his love to endure. Thus it is possible that his love continues to grow even after surrender – he will not easily admit that a woman has nothing more to 'give up' to him.

364

The hermit speaks. – The art of dealing with people depends essentially on the skill (requiring much practice) to accept and eat a meal prepared in a kitchen you don't trust. If you come to the table ravenous, all is easy ('the worst company makes itself *felt*' – as Mephistopheles says);[36] but one is never that hungry when one needs to be! Oh, how hard it is to digest one's fellow men! First principle: as in the face of misfortune, to engage your courage, to spring boldly to action, to admire yourself in the process, to sink your teeth into your reluctance, to swallow your disgust. Second principle: to 'improve' your fellow man, e.g. by praising him so as to make him start sweating out his pleasure in himself, or by taking hold of a corner of his good or 'interesting' qualities and pulling at it until all the virtue comes out and you can hide your fellow man in its folds. Third principle: self-hypnosis. To fixate on your object of association as if on a glass button until you stop feeling pleasure and displeasure in this activity and fall asleep without noticing it, become rigid, and attain equanimity: a home remedy amply tested in marriage and friendship, praised as indispensable but not yet scientifically analysed. Its popular name is – patience.

365

The hermit speaks again. – We, too, deal with 'people'; we, too, modestly don the cloak in which (*as* which) others know us, respect us, seek us, and so we appear in company, i.e. among others who are disguised but don't want to admit it. Like all clever masks we, too, politely prop up a chair against the door when confronted with curiosity about anything but our 'cloak'. But there are other ways and tricks for 'wandering amongst', for 'associating with', people: for instance, as a ghost – which is highly advisable if one desires to get rid of them quickly and make them afraid. Example: others reach for us and can't get a hold of us. That's frightening. Or we enter through a closed door. Or when all the lights are out. Or when we're already dead. The latter is the trick of *posthumous* people par excellence. ('And what were you thinking?' one of them once said impatiently; 'Would we wish to endure this

---

[36] Goethe, *Faust I*, line 1637; the line continues: '. . . that you are a human being among humans'.

estrangement, coldness, and sepulchral silence enveloping us, this entire subterranean, hidden, mute, undiscovered loneliness that we call life but might as well be called death unless we knew what will *become* of us and that it is only after death that we come into *our* life and become alive – oh, very much alive, we posthumous ones!')

366

Faced with a scholarly book. – We are not among those who have ideas only between books, stimulated by books – our habit is to think outdoors, walking, jumping, climbing, dancing, preferably on lonely mountains or right by the sea where even the paths become thoughtful. Our first question about the value of a book, a person, or a piece of music is: 'Can they walk?' Even more, 'Can they dance?' We rarely read; but are none the worse on that account – and oh, how quickly we guess how someone has come to his ideas; whether seated before the inkwell, stomach clenched, head bowed over the paper; and oh, how soon we're done with his book! Cramped intestines betray themselves – you can bet on it – no less than stuffy air, closed ceilings, cramped spaces. – Those were my feelings just now as I closed a decent, scholarly book – grateful, very grateful, but also relieved . . . In a scholar's book there is nearly always something oppressive, oppressed: the 'specialist' emerges somehow – his eagerness, his seriousness, his ire, his overestimation of the nook in which he sits and spins, his hunchback – every specialist has his hump. Every scholarly book also reflects a soul that has become crooked; every craft makes crooked. Look at the friends of your youth again, after they have taken possession of their speciality (*Wissenschaft*) – Alas, in every case the reverse has also taken place! How they are now for all time possessed and obsessed by it! Grown into their corner, squashed beyond recognition, unfree, unstable, completely emaciated and jagged except for one spot that is paradigmatically round – one is moved and silenced when one sees them again that way. Above every craft, even one with a golden floor, is also a leaden ceiling that presses and presses on the soul until it becomes strangely and crookedly pressed. There is nothing to do about this. Don't think you can evade such crippling through some educational artifice. One pays dearly for any kind of *mastery* on earth, where perhaps one pays too dearly for everything; one is master of one's trade at the price of also being its victim. But you want things to be different – 'cheaper', above all more comfortable – not so, my dear contemporaries? Well, if so, you instantly get something different: instead of the craftsman and master, you get the man of letters, the dexterous, 'polydexterous' literary man who of course lacks the hunched back – notwithstanding the posture he assumes before you as the shop attendant of spirit and the 'bearer' of culture – the literary man of letters, who really *is* nothing but who 'represents' nearly everything, who acts and 'stands in for' the expert, who takes it upon himself in all modesty to *make* himself paid, honoured, and celebrated in place of the expert. No, my scholarly friends, I bless you even for your hunched backs! And for despising, as do I, the 'literary men' and culture parasites! And for not knowing how to make a business of the spirit! And for having opinions that cannot be translated into monetary terms! And for not representing anything that you are *not*! And because your only desire (*Wille*) is to become masters of your craft, with reverence for every type of mastery and competence and with ruthless rejection of anything specious, semi-genuine, meretricious, virtuoso-like, demagogical, or histrionic *in litteris et artibus*[37] – of anything that cannot give you proof of its unconditional *probity* in discipline and prior training. (Not even genius can compensate for such a deficiency, however much it may blind people to it. One grasps this once one has watched our most talented painters and musicians up close, who nearly without exception manage through a cunning inventiveness of manners, stop-gap devices, and even principles, to acquire artificially and belatedly the *appearance* of such probity, such solidity of schooling and culture – without, of course, managing to deceive themselves, to silence forever their bad conscience. For surely you know? All great contemporary artists suffer from a bad conscience. . .)

367

The first distinction to draw regarding artworks. – Everything that is thought, written, painted, composed, even built and sculpted, belongs either to monologue art or to art before witnesses. The second category must also include the seemingly monologue art involving faith in God, the entire lyricism of prayer; for solitude does not yet exist to the pious

---

[37] 'in arts and letters'

– this invention was first made by us, the godless. I know no deeper distinction in an artist's entire optics than this: whether he views his budding artwork ('himself') from the eye of the witness, or whether he 'has forgotten the world', which is the essential feature of all monologue art – it is based *on forgetting*; it is the music of forgetting.

368

The cynic speaks. – My objections to Wagner's music are physiological objections: why disguise them with aesthetic formulas? My 'fact' is that I stop breathing easily once this music starts affecting me; that my *foot* immediately gets angry at it and revolts – it has a need for tempo, dance, march; it demands chiefly from music the raptures found in *good* walking, striding, leaping, and dancing – but doesn't my stomach protest, too? My heart? My circulation? My intestines? Do I not unnoticeably grow hoarse as I listen? And so I ask myself: what does my whole body actually *want* from music? Its own *relief*, I believe, as if all animal functions should be quickened by easy, bold, exuberant, self-assured rhythms; as if iron, leaden life should be gilded by golden, good, tender harmonies. My melancholy wants to rest in the hiding-places and abysses of *perfection*: that's what I need music for. What is the drama to me! The cramps of its moral ecstasies that give the 'people' satisfaction! The whole hocus-pocus of gestures of the actor! You will guess that I am essentially anti-theatrical – but Wagner was, conversely, essentially a man of the theatre and an actor, the most enthusiastic mimomaniac that ever existed, also as a musician. And, incidentally, if it was Wagner's theory that 'the drama is the end; the music is always merely its means',[38] his *practice* was always, from beginning to end, 'the attitude is the end; the drama, and music, too, is always merely *its* means'. Music as a means of clarification, strengthening, internalization of the dramatic gesture and the actor's appeal to the senses; and the Wagnerian drama a mere occasion for many dramatic attitudes! Beside all other instincts, he had the commanding instinct of a great actor in absolutely everything – and, as I said, also as a musician. I once made this clear to an upright Wagnerian, with some trouble; and I had reasons to add: 'Do be a bit more honest with yourself – after all, we're not at

---

[38] Wagner, *Opera and Drama* (1850–1), Introduction

the theatre! At the theatre, one is honest only as a mass; as an individual one lies, lies to oneself. One leaves oneself at home when one goes to the theatre; one relinquishes the right to one's own tongue and choice, to one's taste, even to one's courage as one has it and exercises it within one's own four walls against god and man. No one brings the finest senses of his art to the theatre; nor does the artist who works for the theatre: there, one is people, public, herd, woman, pharisee, voting cattle, democrat, neighbour, fellow man; there, even the most personal conscience is vanquished by the levelling magic of the "greatest number"; there, stupidity breeds lasciviousness and is contagious; there, the "neighbour" reigns; there, one *becomes* a neighbour'. (I forgot to mention my enlightened Wagnerian's retort to the physiological objections: 'So, you simply aren't healthy enough for our music?')

369

Our coexistence. – Don't we have to admit to ourselves, we artists, that there exists an uncanny disparity within us; that in an odd way our taste and on the other hand our creative power stand each distinct from the other; each remains the way it is by itself, and each grows by itself; I mean each of these has completely different degrees and *tempi* of old, young, ripe, overblown, rotten? A musician, for instance, could spend a lifetime creating things that *contradict* what his spoiled listener's ear, listener's heart values, savours, prefers – he needn't even be aware of this contradiction! As experience shows with almost embarrassing regularity, one's taste can easily outgrow the taste of one's powers, even without thereby paralysing them and hindering their continued productivity. But the opposite can happen, too – and this is precisely what I'd like to call artists' attention to. A perpetually creative person, a 'mother' type in the grand sense of the term, someone who doesn't hear or know anything but the pregnancies and child-beds of his spirit anymore, who simply has no time to reflect on himself and on his work and to make comparisons, who no longer wants to exercise his taste and simply forgets it, i.e. lets it stand, lie, or fall – maybe such a person would finally produce works *that far excel his own judgement*, so that he utters inanities about them and himself – utters them and believes them. This seems to me to be almost the norm among fertile artists – nobody knows a child less well than his parents – and this is true, to take a colossal example, even in the case of the whole world of Greek art and poetry: it never 'knew' what it had done.

370

What is romanticism? – It may be recalled, at least among my friends, that initially I approached the modern world with a few crude errors and over-estimations and, in any case, with hope. I understood – on the basis of who knows what personal experiences? – the philosophical pessimism of the nineteenth century as if it were a symptom of a higher force of thought, of more audacious courage, and of more victorious *fullness* of life than had characterized the eighteenth century, the age of Hume, Kant, Condillac,[39] and the sensualists: thus, tragic insight struck me as the distinctive *luxury* of our culture, its most precious, noblest and most dangerous squandering; but still, in view of its over-richness, as its *permitted* luxury. Similarly, I explained German music to myself as the expression of a Dionysian might of the German soul: I believed I heard in it the earthquake through which some pent-up primordial force is finally released – indifferent about whether it sets everything else which is called culture atremble.[40] You see that what I misjudged both in philosophical pessimism and in German music was what constitutes its actual character – its *romanticism*. What is romanticism? Every art, every philosophy can be considered a cure and aid in the service of growing, struggling life: they always presuppose suffering and sufferers. But there are two types of sufferers: first, those who suffer from a *superabundance of life* – they want a Dionysian art as well as a tragic outlook and insight into life; then, those who suffer from an *impoverishment of life* and seek quiet, stillness, calm seas, redemption from themselves through art and insight, or else intoxication, paroxysm, numbness, madness. All romanticism in art and in knowledge fits the dual needs of the latter type, as did (and do) Schopenhauer and Richard Wagner, to name the most famous and prominent romantics that I *misunderstood* at the time – not, incidentally, to their disadvantage, one might in all fairness concede. He who is richest in fullness of life, the Dionysian god and man, can allow himself not only the sight of what is terrible and questionable but also the terrible deed and every luxury of

---

[39] French empiricist philosopher (1715–80)
[40] Nietzsche expressed these views in *The Birth of Tragedy from the Spirit of Music* (1872).

234

destruction, decomposition, negation; in his case, what is evil, non-sensical, and ugly almost seems acceptable because of an overflow in procreating, fertilizing forces capable of turning any desert into bountiful farmland. Conversely, he who suffers most and is poorest in life would need mainly mildness, peacefulness, goodness in thought and in deed – if possible, also a god who truly would be a god for the sick, a 'saviour'; as well as logic, the conceptual comprehensibility of existence – for logic soothes, gives confidence – in short, a certain warm, fear-repelling narrowness and confinement to optimistic horizons. Thus I gradually came to understand Epicurus, the antithesis of a Dionysian pessimist, and equally the 'Christian', who really is simply a kind of Epicurean and, like him, essentially a romantic; and my vision grew keener for that most difficult and insidious form of *backward inference* with which the most mistakes are made – the inference from the work to the maker, from the ideal to the one who *needs it*, from every manner of valuation to the commanding *need* behind it. Nowadays I avail myself of this primary distinction concerning all aesthetic values: in every case I ask, 'Is it hunger or superabundance that have become creative here?' At first glance, a different distinction may appear more advisable – it's far more noticeable – namely, the question of whether the creation was caused by a desire for fixing, for immortalizing, for *being*, or rather by a desire for destruction, for change, for novelty, for future, for *becoming*. However, both types of desires prove ambiguous upon closer examination, and can be interpreted under the first scheme, which seems preferable to me. The desire for *destruction*, for change and for becoming can be the expression of an overflowing energy pregnant with the future (my term for this is, as is known, 'Dionysian'); but it can also be the hatred of the ill-constituted, deprived, and underprivileged one who destroys and *must* destroy because what exists, indeed all existence, all being, outrages and provokes him. To understand this feeling, take a close look at our anarchists. The will to *immortalize* also requires a dual interpretation. It can be prompted, first, by gratitude and love; art of such origin will always be an art of apotheosis, dithyrambic perhaps like Rubens;[41] blissfully mocking like Hafis;[42] bright and gracious like Goethe, spreading a Homeric light and splendour over all things. But it

---

[41] Flemish Baroque painter (1577–1640)

[42] Persian lyric poet of the fourteenth century; especially well-known in Germany because of Goethe's great partiality for his poetry

can also be the tyrannical will of someone who suffers deeply, who struggles, is tortured, and who would like to stamp as a binding law and compulsion what is most personal, singular, narrow, the real idiosyncrasy of his suffering, and who as it were takes revenge on all things by forcing, imprinting, branding *his* image on them, the image of *his* torture. The latter is *romantic pessimism* in its most expressive form, be it Schopenhauer's philosophy of will or Wagner's music – romantic pessimism, the last *great* event in the fate of our culture. (That there *could* be a completely different pessimism, a classical one – this intuition and vision belongs to me as inseparable from me, as my *proprium*[43] and *ipsissimum*;[44] only the word 'classical' offends my ears; it has become far too trite, round, and indistinct. I call this pessimism of the future – for it is coming! I see it coming! – *Dionysian* pessimism.)

371

We incomprehensible ones. – Have we ever complained about being misunderstood, misjudged, misidentified, defamed, misheard, and ignored? This is precisely our lot – oh, for a long time yet! Let's say until 1901, to be modest – this is also our distinction; we wouldn't honour ourselves enough if we wanted it otherwise. We are misidentified – for we ourselves keep growing, changing, shedding old hides; we still shed our skins every spring; we become increasingly younger, more future-oriented, taller, stronger; we drive our roots ever more powerfully into the depths – into evil – while at the same time embracing the heavens ever more lovingly and broadly, and absorbing their light ever more thirstily with all our sprigs and leaves. Like trees we grow – it's hard to understand, like all life! – not in one place, but everywhere; not in one direction, but upwards and outwards and inwards and downwards equally; our energy drives trunk, branches, and roots all at once; we are no longer free to do anything individual, to *be* anything individual . . . This is our lot, as I have said: we grow in *height*; and even if this should be our dark fate – for we dwell ever closer to the lightning! – well, we do not honour it less on that account; it remains that which we do not want to share, to impart: the dark fate of height, *our* fate.

---

[43] '(my) own'   [44] '(my) ownmost'

372

Why we are not idealists. – Formerly, philosophers feared the senses: is it possible that we have unlearned this fear all too much? Today we are all sensualists, we philosophers of the present and future, *not* in theory but in *praxis*, in practice.[45] The former, however, saw the senses as trying to lure them away from *their* world, from the cold kingdom of 'ideas', to a dangerous Southern isle where they feared their philosophers' virtues would melt away like snow in the sun. 'Wax in the ear' was virtually a condition of philosophizing; a true philosopher didn't listen to life insofar as life is music; he *denied* the music of life – it is an old philosopher's superstition that all music is siren-music.[46] Today we are inclined to make the opposite judgement (which could itself be just as mistaken), namely, that *ideas* are worse seductresses than the senses, for all their cold, anaemic appearance and not even despite that appearance – they always lived off the 'blood' of the philosopher; they always drained his senses and even, if you believe it, his 'heart'. These old philosophers were heartless: philosophizing was always a kind of vampirism. When considering such figures, including even Spinoza, don't you feel something deeply enigmatic and strange? Don't you see the spectacle unfolding, this steady *growing paler* – this ever more ideally construed desensualization? Don't you sense in the background some long-concealed blood-sucker who starts with the senses and finally leaves behind and spares only bones and rattling? – I refer to categories, formulas, *words* (for, forgive me, what *remained* of Spinoza, *amor intellectualis dei*,[47] is mere rattle, nothing more! What is *amor*, what *deus*, when they are missing every drop of blood?). In sum: all philosophical idealism until now was something like an illness, except where, as in Plato's case, it was the caution of an overabundant and dangerous

---

[45] If Nietzsche is trying to draw a distinction here between 'praxis' and 'practice', rather than just rhetorically repeating himself, it is not clear what the distinction is.

[46] In *Odyssey* Book XII Odysseus tells how he outwitted the sirens, female singers who lure passing sailors to their death by singing irresistibly. He says he had himself bound to the mast of his ship so that he could hear the song, but could not do anything self-destructive, and that he had the ears of his crew stopped with wax so that they didn't hear the song at all, and continued to row undisturbed. Nietzsche refers to this story again in *Beyond Good and Evil* § 230, where he speaks, very puzzlingly, of man standing 'before the rest of nature, with intrepid Oedipus eyes and sealed Odysseus ears. . .' Odysseus' ears were not sealed – but equally, Oedipus' eyes, at the end, could not see.

[47] 'intellectual love of god'; see *Ethics*, Book V, props. 32–37.

health; the fear of *overpowerful* senses; the shrewdness of a shrewd Socratic. – Maybe we moderns are not healthy enough *to need* Plato's idealism? And we don't fear the senses because –

373

'Science' as prejudice. – It follows from the laws that govern rank-ordering (*Rangordnung*) that scholars, insofar as they belong to the intellectual middle class, are not even allowed to catch sight of the truly *great* problems and question marks; moreover, their courage and eyes simply don't reach that far – and above all, the need that makes them scholars, their inner expectations and wish that things might be *such and such*, their fear and hope, too soon find rest and satisfaction. What makes, for instance, the pedantic Englishman Herbert Spencer[48] rave in his own way and makes him draw a line of hope, a horizon which defines what is desirable; that definitive reconciliation of 'egoism and altruism' about which he spins fables – this almost nauseates the likes of us: a human race that adopts as its ultimate perspective such a Spencerian perspective would strike us as deserving of contempt, of annihilation! But *that* he had to view as his highest hope what to others counts and should count only as a disgusting possibility is a question mark that Spencer would have been unable to foresee. So, too, it is with the faith with which so many materialistic natural scientists rest content: the faith in a world that is supposed to have its equivalent and measure in human thought, in human valuations – a 'world of truth' that can be grasped entirely with the help of our four-cornered little human reason – What? Do we really want to demote existence in this way to an exercise in arithmetic and an indoor diversion for mathematicians? Above all, one shouldn't want to strip it of its *ambiguous* character: that, gentlemen, is what *good* taste demands – above all, the taste of reverence for everything that lies beyond your horizon! That the only rightful interpretation of the world should be one to which *you* have a right; one by which one can do research and go on scientifically in *your* sense of the term (you really mean *mechanistically?*) – one that

---

[48] English social thinker (1820–1903) who combined evolutionary beliefs with a form of utilitarianism; he believed that human history would lead to an ideal state in which egoism and altruism were reconciled.

permits counting, calculating, weighing, seeing, grasping, and nothing else – that is a crudity and naiveté, assuming it is not a mental illness, an idiocy. Would it not be quite probable, conversely, that precisely the most superficial and external aspect of existence – what is most apparent; its skin and its sensualization – would be grasped first and might even be the only thing that let itself be grasped? Thus, a 'scientific' interpretation of the world, as you understand it, might still be one of the *stupidest* of all possible interpretations of the world, i.e. one of those most lacking in significance. This to the ear and conscience of Mr Mechanic, who nowadays likes to pass as a philosopher and insists that mechanics is the doctrine of the first and final laws on which existence may be built, as on a ground floor. But an essentially mechanistic world would be an essentially *meaningless* world! Suppose one judged the *value* of a piece of music according to how much of it could be counted, calculated, and expressed in formulas – how absurd such a 'scientific' evaluation of music would be! What would one have comprehended, understood, recognized? Nothing, really nothing of what is 'music' in it!

374

Our new 'infinite'. – How far the perspectival character of existence extends, or indeed whether it has any other character; whether an existence without interpretation, without 'sense', doesn't become 'non-sense'; whether, on the other hand, all existence isn't essentially an *interpreting* existence – that cannot, as would be fair, be decided even by the most industrious and extremely conscientious analysis and self-examination of the intellect; for in the course of this analysis, the human intellect cannot avoid seeing itself under its perspectival forms, and *solely* in these. We cannot look around our corner: it is a hopeless curiosity to want to know what other kinds of intellects and perspectives there *might* be; e.g. whether other beings might be able to experience time backwards, or alternately forwards and backwards (which would involve another direction of life and a different conception of cause and effect). But I think that today we are at least far away from the ridiculous immodesty of decreeing from our angle that perspectives are *permitted* only from this angle. Rather, the world has once again become infinite to us: insofar as we cannot reject the possibility *that it includes infinite interpretations*. Once again the great shudder seizes us – but who again would want immediately to deify in the old manner *this* monster of an unknown world? And to worship from this time on the unknown (*das Unbekannte*) as 'the Unknown One' (*den Unbekannten*)? Alas, too many *ungodly* possibilities of interpretation are included in this unknown; too much devilry, stupidity, foolishness of interpretation – our own human, all too human one, even, which we know . . .

375

Why we seem to be Epicureans. – We are cautious, we modern men, about ultimate convictions; our mistrust lies in wait for the enchantments and deceptions of the conscience involved in every strong faith, every unconditional Yes and No. How can this be explained? Maybe what is to be found here is largely the caution of 'once bitten, twice shy'; of the disappointed idealist; but there is also another, superior component: the gleeful curiosity of the one who used to stand in the corner and was driven to despair by his corner and who now delights and luxuriates in the opposite of a corner, in the boundless, in 'the free as such'. Thus an almost Epicurean bent of knowledge develops that will not easily let go of the questionable character of things; also an aversion to big moral words and gestures; a taste that rejects all crude, four-square oppositions and is proudly aware of its practice in entertaining doubts. For *this* constitutes our pride, this slight tightening of the reins as our urge for certainty races ahead, this self-control of the rider on his wildest rides – for we still ride spirited and fiery animals; and when we hesitate, it is danger least of all that makes us hesitate.

376

Our slow periods. – This is how all artists and people of 'works' feel, the motherly type: at every chapter of their lives – which is always marked by a work – they always think they've reached their goal; they would always patiently take death with the feeling 'we are ripe for it'. This is not the expression of weariness – rather that of a certain autumnal sunniness and mildness that the work itself, the fact that the work has become ripe, always leaves behind in its creator. Then the pace of life slows down and becomes thick and flows like honey – to the point of a long *fermata*,[49] of the faith in *the* long *fermata*.

377

We who are homeless. – Among Europeans today there is no lack of those who have a right to call themselves homeless in a distinctive and honourable sense: it is to them in particular that I commend my secret wisdom and *gaya scienza*.[50] For their lot is hard; their hope uncertain; it is a feat to invent a form of comfort for them – but to what avail! We children of the future – how *could* we be at home in this today! We are unfavourably disposed towards all ideals that might make one feel at home in this fragile, broken time of transition; as for its 'realities', we don't believe they are *lasting*. The ice that still supports people today has already grown very thin; the wind that brings a thaw is blowing; we ourselves, we homeless ones, are something that breaks up the ice and other all too thin 'realities'. . .We 'conserve' nothing; neither do we want to return to any past; we are by no means 'liberal'; we are not working for 'progress'; we don't need to plug our ears to the market-place's sirens of the future: what they sing – 'equal rights', 'free society', 'no more masters and no servants' – has no allure for us. We hold it absolutely undesirable that a realm of justice and concord should be established on earth (because it would certainly be the realm of the most profound levelling down to mediocrity and *chinoiserie*);[51] we are delighted by all who love, as we do, danger, war, and adventure; who refuse to compromise, to be captured, to reconcile, to be castrated; we consider ourselves conquerors; we contemplate the necessity for new orders as well as for a new slavery – for every strengthening and enhancement of the human type also involves a new kind of enslavement – doesn't it? With all this, can we really be at home in an age that loves to claim the distinction of being the most humane, the mildest, and most righteous age the sun has ever seen? It is bad enough that precisely when we hear these beautiful words, we have the ugliest misgivings. What we find in

---

[49] Musical sign indicating that a note or pause may be held for longer than its value would usually prescribe

[50] See above, footnote to p. 1.

[51] European decorative style so called because it is intended to look Chinese. Because of the slight artistic value of much that was produced in this style it has the connotation of insignificant, insubstantial, vapid, frivolous.

them is merely an expression – and the masquerade – of a deep weakening, of weariness, of old age, of declining energies! What can it matter to us what sequins the sick may use to cover up their weakness? Let them parade it as their *virtue*; after all, there is no doubt that weakness makes us mild, so righteous, so inoffensive, so 'humane'! The 'religion of compassion' to which one would like to convert us – oh, we know these hysterical little men and women well enough who today need just this religion as a veil and finery. We are no humanitarians; we should never dare to allow ourselves to speak of 'our love of humanity' – our type is not actor enough for that! Or not Saint-Simonist[52] enough; not French enough. One really has to be afflicted with a *Gallic* excess of erotic irritability and enamoured impatience to approach humanity honestly with one's lust . . . Humanity! Has there ever been a more hideous old woman amongst all old women? (Unless it were 'the truth': a question for philosophers.) No, we do not love humanity; but on the other hand we are not nearly 'German' enough, in the sense in which the word 'German' is constantly used nowadays, to advocate nationalism and racial hatred and to be able to take pleasure in the national scabies of the heart and blood poisoning with which European peoples nowadays delimit and barricade themselves against each other as if with quarantines. For that, we are too uninhibited, too malicious, too spoiled, also too well-informed, too 'well-travelled': we far prefer to live on mountains, apart, 'untimely', in past or future centuries, merely in order to avoid the silent rage to which we know we should be condemned as eyewitnesses of politics that are destroying the German spirit by making it vain and which are, moreover, *petty* politics – to keep its creation from falling apart again, doesn't it need to plant it between two deadly hatreds? *Mustn't* it desire the eternalization of the European system of many petty states? We who are homeless are too diverse and racially mixed in our descent, as 'modern men', and consequently we are not inclined to participate in the mendacious racial self-admiration and obscenity that parades in Germany today as a sign of a German way of thinking and that is doubly false and indecent among the people of the 'historical sense'. In a word – and let this be our word of honour – we are *good Europeans,* the rich heirs of millennia of European spirit, with too many provisions but also too many obligations. As such, we

---

[52] Referring to Claude-Henri Saint-Simon (1760–1825), a French utopian socialist

have also outgrown Christianity and are averse to it – precisely because we have grown *out* of it, because our ancestors were Christians who in their Christianity were mercilessly upright: for their faith they willingly sacrificed possessions, blood, position, and fatherland. We – do the same. But for what? For our unbelief? For every kind of unbelief? No, you know better than that, my friends! The hidden Yes in you is stronger than all Nos and Maybes that afflict you and your age like a disease; and you must sail the seas, you emigrants, you too are compelled to this by – a *faith*!

378

'And become bright again'. – We who are generous and rich in spirit, who stand by the road like open wells with no intention to fend off anyone who feels like drawing from us – we unfortunately do not know how to defend ourselves where we want to: we have no way of preventing people from *clouding* us, from darkening us; the time in which we live throws into us what is most time-bound; its dirty birds drop their filth into us; its boys their knick-knacks; and exhausted wanderers who come to us to rest, their small and great miseries. But we will do what we have always done: we take down into our depths whatever one casts into us – for we are deep; we do not forget – *and become bright again.* . .

379

The fool's interlude. – The writer of this book is no misanthrope; today one pays too dearly for hatred of man. In order to hate the way one formerly hated *the* human being, Timonically,[53] wholly, without exception, with one's whole heart, with the whole *love* of hatred, one would have to renounce contempt. And how much fine joy, how much patience, how much graciousness even do we owe precisely to our contempt! Moreover, it makes us 'God's elect': refined contempt is our taste and privilege, our art, our virtue perhaps, and we are the most modern of moderns. . .Hatred, in contrast, places people on a par, vis-à-vis; in hatred there is honour; finally, in hatred there is *fear*, an ample

---

[53] Legendary Athenian misanthrope, who is the subject of Shakespeare's *Timon of Athens*

good piece of fear. We fearless ones, however, we more spiritual men of this age, we know our advantage well enough to live without fear of this age precisely because we are more spiritual. We will hardly be decapitated, imprisoned, or exiled; not even our books will be banned or burned. The age loves the spirit; it loves and needs us, even if we should have to make clear to it that we are artists of contempt; that every association with human beings makes us shudder slightly; that for all our mildness, patience, congeniality, and politeness, we cannot persuade our noses to give up their prejudices against the proximity of a human being; that we love nature the less humanly it behaves, and art *if* it is the artist's escape from man or the artist's mockery of man, or the artist's mockery of himself. . .

380

'The wanderer' speaks. – In order to see our European morality for once as it looks from a distance, and to measure it up against other past or future moralities, one has to proceed like a wanderer who wants to know how high the towers in a town are: he *leaves* the town. 'Thoughts about moral prejudices', if they are not to be prejudices about prejudices, presuppose a position *outside* morality, some point beyond good and evil to which one has to rise, climb, or fly – and in the present case, at least a point beyond *our* good and evil, a freedom from everything 'European', by which I mean the sum of commanding value judgements that have become part of our flesh and blood. That one *wants* to go precisely out there, up there, may be a slight rashness, a peculiar and unreasonable 'you must' – for we seekers of knowledge also have our idiosyncrasies of 'unfree will' – the question is whether one really *can* get up there. This may depend on manifold conditions. Mainly, the question is how light or heavy we are – the problem of our 'specific gravity'. One has to be *very light* to drive one's will to knowledge into such a distance and, as it were, beyond one's time; to create for oneself eyes to survey millennia and, moreover, clear skies in these eyes. One must have liberated oneself from many things that oppress, inhibit, hold down, and make heavy precisely us Europeans today. The human being of such a beyond who wants to catch a glimpse of the highest measures of value of his time must first of all 'overcome' this time in himself – this is the test of his strength – and consequently not only his time but also his aversion and

opposition *against* this time, his suffering from this time, his untimeliness, his *romanticism*.

381

On the question of being understandable. – One does not only wish to be understood when one writes; one wishes just as surely *not* to be understood. It is by no means necessarily an objection to a book when anyone finds it incomprehensible: perhaps that was part of the author's intention – he didn't *want* to be understood by just 'anybody'. Every nobler spirit and taste selects his audience when he wants to communicate; in selecting it, he simultaneously erects barriers against 'the others'. All subtler laws of a style originated therein: they simultaneously keep away, create a distance, forbid 'entrance', understanding, as said above – while they open the ears of those whose ears are related to ours. And let me say this amongst ourselves and about my own case: I want neither the inexperience nor the liveliness of my temperament to keep me from being understandable to *you*, my friends – not the liveliness, as much as it forces me to deal with a matter swiftly in order to deal with it at all. For I approach deep problems such as I do cold baths: fast in, fast out. That this is no way to get to the depths, to get deep *enough*, is the superstition of those who fear water, the enemies of cold water; they speak without experience. Oh, the great cold makes one fast! And incidentally: does a matter stay unrecognized, not understood, merely because it has been touched in flight, is only glanced at, seen in a flash? Does one absolutely have to sit firmly on it first? Have brooded on it as on an egg? *Diu noctuque incubando*,[54] as Newton said of himself? At least there are truths that are especially shy and ticklish and can't be caught except suddenly – that one must *surprise* or leave alone. Finally, my brevity has yet another value: given the questions that occupy me, I must say many things briefly so that they will be heard even more briefly. For, as an immoralist, one needs to avoid corrupting innocents – I mean, asses and old maids of both sexes to whom life offers nothing but their innocence; even more, my writing should inspire, elevate, and encourage them to be virtuous. I can't imagine a funnier sight on earth than inspired old asses and maids who get aroused by the sweet

---

[54] 'sitting upon it day and night'

sentiments of virtue: and 'this I have seen' – thus spoke Zarathustra. Enough about brevity; things stand worse with my ignorance, which I don't try to hide from myself. There are hours when I am ashamed of it – to be sure, also hours when I am ashamed of this shame. Maybe we philosophers are all in a bad position regarding knowledge these days: science is growing, and the most scholarly of us are close to discovering that they know too little. But it would be even worse if things were different – if we knew *too much*; our task is and remains above all not to mistake ourselves for someone else. We *are* different from scholars, although we are inevitably also, among other things, scholarly. We have different needs, grow differently; have a different digestion: we need more; we also need less. There is no formula for how much a spirit needs for its nourishment; but if it has a taste for independence, for quick coming and going, for wandering, perhaps for adventures of which only the swiftest are capable, it would rather live free with little food than unfree and stuffed. It is not fat but the greatest possible suppleness and strength that a good dancer wants from his nourishment – and I wouldn't know what the spirit of a philosopher might more want to be than a good dancer. For the dance is his ideal, also his art, and finally also his only piety, his 'service of God'.

382

The great health. – We who are new, nameless, hard to understand; we premature births of an as yet unproved future – for a new end, we also need a new means, namely, a new health that is stronger, craftier, tougher, bolder, and more cheerful than any previous health. Anyone whose soul thirsts to experience the whole range of previous values and aspirations, to sail around all the coasts of this 'inland sea' (*Mittelmeer*) of ideals, anyone who wants to know from the adventures of his own experience how it feels to be the discoverer or conqueror of an ideal, or to be an artist, a saint, a lawmaker, a sage, a pious man, a soothsayer, an old-style divine loner – any such person needs one thing above all – *the great health*, a health that one doesn't only have, but also acquires continually and must acquire because one gives it up again and again, and must give it up!. . .And now, after being on our way in this manner for a long time, we argonauts of the ideal – braver, perhaps, than is prudent and often suffering shipwreck and damage but, to repeat, healthier than one would like to admit, dangerously healthy; ever again healthy – it seems to us as if, in reward, we face an as yet undiscovered land the boundaries of which no one has yet surveyed, beyond all the lands and corners of the ideal heretofore, a world so over-rich in what is beautiful, strange, questionable, terrible, and divine that our curiosity and our thirst to possess it have veered beyond control – alas, so that nothing will sate us anymore! After such vistas and with such a burning hunger in our conscience and science, how could we still be satisfied with *modern-day man?* Too bad – but it's inevitable that we look at his worthiest goals and hopes with a seriousness which is difficult to maintain; maybe we don't even look at all any more. Another ideal runs before us, a peculiar, seductive, dangerous ideal to which we wouldn't want to persuade anyone, since we don't readily concede *the right to it* to anyone: the ideal of a spirit that plays naively, i.e. not deliberately but from overflowing abundance and power, with everything that was hitherto called holy, good, untouchable, divine; a spirit which has gone so far that the highest thing which the common people quite under-standably accepts as its measure of value would signify for it danger, decay, debasement, or at any rate recreation, blindness, temporary self-oblivion: the ideal of a human, superhuman well-being and benevolence that will often enough appear *inhuman* – for example, when it places itself next to all earthly seriousness heretofore, all forms of solemnity in gesture, word, tone, look, morality, and task as if it were their most incarnate and involuntary parody – and in spite of all this, it is perhaps only with it that *the great seriousness* really emerges; that the real question mark is posed for the first time; that the destiny of the soul changes; the hand of the clock moves forward; the tragedy begins.

383

Epilogue. – But as I finally slowly, slowly paint this gloomy question mark and am still willing to remind my readers of the virtues of reading in the right way – oh, what forgotten and unknown virtues! – it strikes me that I hear all around myself most malicious, cheerful, hobgoblin-like laughter: the spirits of my book are themselves descending upon me, pulling my ears and calling me to order. 'We can't stand it anymore', they shout, 'stop, stop this raven-black music! Are we not surrounded by bright mid-morning? And by soft ground and green grass, the kingdom of the dance? Was there ever a better hour for gaiety? Who will sing us a song, a morning song, so sunny, so light, so full-fledged that it does *not* chase away the crickets[55] but instead invites them to join in the singing and dancing? And even plain, rustic bagpipes would be better than the mysterious sounds, such bog-cries, voices from the crypt, and marmot whistles with which you have so far regaled us in your wilderness, my Mr. Hermit and Musician of the Future![56] No! Not such sounds! Let us rather strike up more pleasant, more joyous tones!'[57] Does it please you *now*, my impatient friends? Well then, who wouldn't like to please you? My bagpipes are already waiting; my throat, too – it may sound a bit rough, but put up with it; after all, we're in the mountains. At least what you are about to hear is new; and if you don't understand it, if you misunderstand the *singer*, what does it matter? This happens to be 'the singer's curse'.[58] You will be able to hear his music and tune so much the better, and so much the better will you be able to dance to his pipe. Is that what you *want*?

---

[55] *Grille* means both 'cricket' and 'bad mood'.
[56] Wagner referred to his own music as 'the music of the future'.
[57] from Schiller's *Ode to Joy*, used in the choral conclusion to the fourth movement of Beethoven's Ninth Symphony
[58] Title of a ballad by Ludwig Uhland (1787–1862)

Appendix: Songs of Prince Vogelfrei

To Goethe[1]

The ever-enduring
is merely your parable!
God the all-blurring
your fiction unbearable. . .

World-wheel, the turning one
spawns goals each day:
Fate – sighs the yearning one,
the fool calls it – play.

World-play, the ruling one,
blends truth and tricks: –
The eternally fooling one
blends *us* – in the mix!. . .

Vogelfrei is an archaic expression used to declare someone an outlaw, literally 'free as a bird', and therefore not to be sheltered. In German the *v* and *f* are both pronounced as *f*, adding alliteration to this name and the title Nietzsche makes of it. 'Prince Vogelfrei' here functions as Nietzsche's *nom de guerre* or pseudonym.

[1] Nietzsche is here parodying the 'Chorus Mysticus' which concludes Goethe's *Faust*. At issue are the poet's need to fictionalize, and Goethe's elevation of womanhood to a metaphysical 'eternal feminine'. In *Faust*, the 'eternal feminine' (*das Ewig-Weibliche*) represented by the blessed Gretchen succeeds in helping to redeem Faust, and to pull him up into heaven: 'Woman Eternal / Draws us on high' ('Das Ewig-Weibliche / Zieht uns hinan') (lines 12110–12111 of *Faust*).

Poet's Calling

Stopped to rest one day, while walking,
seated under shady trees,
when I heard a ticking tocking
dainty rhythm on the breeze.
I grew angry – made some faces –
but I lost my anger quick
and, as if in poet's paces,
started speaking tick tock tick.

As I sat, my verses making,
syllables and sounds did pour,
till I burst out laughing, shaking
for a quarter hour or more.
You a poet? You a poet?
Is your mind no longer good?
'Yes, my man, you are a poet'
shrugs the pecker in the wood.

Whom do I await in bushes?
Whom do I, a robber, stalk?
Proverb? Image? My rhyme rushes
after it and makes it talk.
Anything that moves, you know it
serves to fuel my poet's mood.
'Yes, my man, you are a poet'
shrugs the pecker in the wood.

Rhymes, I think, must be like arrows:
when they pierce the lizard's heart,
how he twitches, how it harrows,
how he leaps in fits and starts!
Wretched creatures, full of woe, it
kills you or it boils your blood!
'Yes, my man, you are a poet'
shrugs the pecker in the wood.

Crooked proverbs full of hurry,
drunken wordlets how you throng!
See each word and sentence scurry
to the tick tock chain so long.
Worthless souls who can't forgo it

find it fun? Are poets crude?
'Yes, my man, you are a poet'
shrugs the pecker in the wood.

Do you mock me feathered joker?
Mentally I'm in rough shape,
might my feelings too be broken?
Fear my rage you jackanapes!
Still, the poet rhymes – and though it
spoiled his mood 'twas all he could.
'Yes, my man, you are a poet'
shrugs the pecker in the wood.

In the South

I perch now midst the crooked arbour
and leave my weariness to sway.
A bird enticed me to this harbour,
within this nest I cool my ardour.
Yet where am I? Away! Away!

The sleeping sea, its colour fleeting,
a purple sail, pure indolence.
Rocks, fig trees, spires and harbour meeting,
around me idylls, sheep are bleating –
absorb me, southern innocence!

Just step by step – that is not living,
the German stride's too dull for me.
I asked the wind to lift me heaving,
with birds I soared without misgiving, –
and south I flew across the sea.

Reason! A grim preoccupation,
too soon it brings us all the way!
In flight I saw my limitation, –
now juices flow for new creation,
for life renewed and dawn of play . . .

It's wise to think in solitary,
but sing alone? – There wisdom ends!
I've come to sing your praises merry,
be still, sit down, and with me tarry
my little birds, my naughty friends!

So young so false and so beguiling,
it seems love looks upon me smiling
and offers ev'ry charm of youth?
Up north – I say it though I waver –
I loved a crone so old I quaver:
this woman bore the name of 'truth' . . .

Pious Beppa

As long as I'm curvaceous,
being pious is no test.
To young girls God is gracious,
he loves the cute ones best.
He will forgive the friar,
forgive him certainly
that he, like other friars,
so wants to be with me.

He is no grey church father!
No, young and full of sap,
hung over he'll still bother
to play the jealous chap.
I do not love the ageing,
he does not love the old:
How wondrous and engaging
when God's designs unfold!

The Church, it knows of living,
it checks us thoroughly.
And always it's forgiving –
who would not pardon me!
One whispers low and steady,
one kneels and wipes at tears,
and when the new sin's ready
the old one disappears.

Praise God who loves a maiden
as pretty as she lives,
his heart by sin is laden,
which he himself forgives.
As long as I'm curvaceous,
being pious is no test:

When old and unsalacious,
the devil take the rest!

The Mysterious Bark[2]

Yesternight, all were asleep,
how the wind with steps uncertain
sighing through the streets did creep.
Rest was not in pillow, curtain,
poppy, slumber potion deep,
nor good conscience – which unburdens.

Finally I left my bed,
dressed and ran down to the shoreline.
Tender mild the night – I met
man and bark on sand in moonshine,
sleepy both, the man and pet: –
Sleepily the bark took to the brine.

Just one hour, more than one,
or was it a year? – my thinking
and all feeling left me, sinking
down to timeless tedium.
Chasms opened, I stood shrinking,
bounds dissolved: – then it was done!

– Morning came: On blackness seeping
rests a bark, it rides the swell . . .
What took place? Thus crying, weeping
hundreds ask: what was this? Hell? – –
Nothing happened! We were sleeping,
sleeping all – so well, so well.

Declaration of Love (whereby however the poet fell into a ditch)

Oh wonder! Does he fly?
He climbs aloft, and yet his pinions rest?
What lifts and bears him high?
What are his goal and course and limit's test?

---

[2] Cf. Nietzsche's dithyramb 'The Sun Sets' ('Die Sonne sinkt') for the motif of the mysterious bark or skiff.

Star and eternity,
he lives now in the heights that living shuns,
　　forgives all jealousy – :
Who see him fly, they too are soaring ones!

　　Oh albatross! I know
that to the heights I am forever lured.
　　I thought of you: tears flow
and do not cease – I love you noble bird!

Song of a Theocritical Goatherd [3]

I lie here, stomach aching,
with bed bugs in my pants.
Close by, the noise they're making!
I hear it, how they dance . . .

She was supposed to slip away
and join me as my lover.
I wait here like a stray –
there's no sign of her.

She promised she would come,
how could she be untrue?
– Does she chase everyone
like my old goats do?

That silken dress, pray tell!
Proud girl, have you been good?
Does more than one buck dwell
in this little wood?

– Lethally love makes us wait,
it burns, it hardens!
As hot nights germinate
toadstools in gardens.

Love eats away at me
like seven deadly sins –
I'll never eat again.
Farewell, dear onions!

[3] The Greek poet Theocritus (third century BC) is considered the father of pastoral poetry. A 'theocritical' goatherd, using word play, is thus both pastoral and critical of God (*theo*). This poem, with its terse irony and irregular meter, reminds one of the lyrics of Heinrich Heine, Nietzsche's favourite lyric poet.

The moon sets in the sea,
and stars fade from the sky.
Grey dawn comes 'round for me –
I just want to die.

'These Vacillating People'

People who are vacillating
make my anger flame.
When they honour they are hating,
all their praise is self-contempt and shame.

I'm not bound by *their* convention
as I wander free,
in their gaze is apprehension,
poison-laced their hopeless jealousy.

May they curse me all to blazes,
spit for all to see!
Though they seek with helpless gazes,
none will ever find their mark in me.

Fool in Despair[4]

Oh! What I wrote on board and wall
with foolish heart and foolish scrawl,
was meant to help me decorate. . .

But *you* say: 'Foolish hands desecrate –
and we the walls must expurgate,
remove all traces big and small!'

Allow me! This I can enjoy –
I've wielded sponge and broom for all
as critic and as water boy.

But, when I've finished your employ,
I ask you, you of super wit,
your wisdom on the walls to sh—.

---

[4] 'Narrenhände beschmieren Tisch und Wände', literally 'a fool's hands smear table and walls', is a German proverb to the effect that clumsy people make a mess.

Rimus remedium, or: How sick poets console themselves[5]

Time is dour,
a witch who drools incessantly,
drips hour upon hour.
In vain, disgust cries out of me:
    'Curse, curse the power
of eternity!'

World – brazen hard:
A glowing bull – it hears no moan.
Pain shoots through me and bores like a dart
into my bone:
    'World has no heart,
and stupid he, who'd therefore groan!'

Your poppies pour,
pour, fever! poison in my brain!
Too long already you bring me pain.
What would you ask? What? 'For what *reward*?'
    – – Ha! Curse the whore
And her disdain!

No! Please don't go!
Outside it's cold, I hear it raining –
I'll cherish you without complaining.
– Here! Take my gold: it glitters so! –
    'Happiness' – No?
Fever is sustaining? –

The door panes fly!
Rain lashes in, to my bed it climbs!
The lamp blows out – havoc is nigh!
– Who did not own a hundred *rhymes*,
    betimes, betimes,
Would surely die!

---

[5] Latin for 'rhyme as remedy'. Compare the dithyramb 'Ariadne's Lament' from Nietzsche's collection of poems entitled *Dionysus Dithyrambs*. In *Zarathustra*, the poem is featured in Part IV as the song of the magician. Ariadne, lover of Theseus, is abandoned by the Greek hero, even though she rescued him from the labyrinth of the Minotaur by weaving a thread for him to follow. The 'glowing bull' refers to Phalaris of Agrigentum (570–554 BC), a tyrant who tortured his enemies by roasting them alive in a brazen bull.

'My Happiness!'[6]

I see again the pigeons of San Marco:
The square is still, all bathed in sunny leisure.
In gentle morn I idly let my songs flow
like swarms of pigeons high into the azure –
    And still caress
Them, tucking one more rhyme into their feathers
  – my happiness!

You silent, blue-lit, silky heaven's awning,
protectively above the coloured stone
I love, and fear, and *envy* – you are yawning . . .
Indeed I'd drink its soul into my own!
    Would I let it egress? –
No, silence, feast for eyes, in splendour dawning!
  – my happiness!

You tower stern, with lion force ascending
triumphantly, no effort, in full view!
Across the square your throaty peal suspending – :
In French you'd be its own accent aigu?
    To stay would be duress
like yours, a bond of silken strands unending . . .
  – my happiness!

Go, music, go! Let shadows start preparing
to grow into the brown and balmy night!
Too early in the day for chimes, the flaring
of gilded trim awaits a rosy light,
    Much does the day compress,
much time for verses, prowling, secret sharing
  – my happiness!

---

[6] The refrain of this poem, 'mein Glück! Mein Glück!' is an emphatic statement of the kind of happiness (*Glück*) Nietzsche enjoys, though in order to preserve the four beats I use 'my happiness' only once.

Toward New Seas[7]

Out there – thus I *will*; so doing
trust myself now and my grip.
Open lies the sea, its blueing
swallows my Genoese ship.

All things now are new and beaming,
space and time their noon decree – :
Only *your* eye – monstrous, gleaming
stares at me, infinity!

Sils-Maria[8]

There sat I, waiting, waiting, – yet for naught,
transcending good and evil, sometimes caught
in light, sometimes caught in shadow, all game,
all sea, all midday, all time without aim.

At once then, my friend! One turned into Two –
– and Zarathustra strode into my view . . .

To the Mistral. A Dance Song[9]

Mistral wind, you rain-cloud reaper,
sadness slayer, heaven sweeper
blustering, how I love you!
Are we not of one womb's making,
first born of one fate unbreaking,
predetermined just we two?

Here on stony pathways sliding
I run to you dancing, gliding,
dancing as you pipe and sing:
You without a ship and rudder,
you as freedom's freest brother,
over raging seas do spring.

---

[7] Nietzsche frequently used the figure of Columbus and the metaphor of seafaring to symbolize the courage of the human spirit. In *The Gay Science* § 289 he reminds us that the moral earth, too, is round, as an exhortation to explore the realm of morals just as earlier explorers had ventured around the globe. A draft of this poem was titled 'To L.' (Lou von Salomé).

[8] Sils Maria is a town in south-eastern Switzerland, in the Engadine valley, where Nietzsche spent his summers.

[9] The mistral wind of southern France is a strong north wind.

Scarce awake, I heard you calling,
rushed to where the cliffs are falling
golden walled into the sea.
Hail! You came like rapids teeming,
glitter bright and diamond gleaming
from the peaks triumphantly.

'Cross the plains of heaven dashing
I saw horses, hooves a-flashing,
saw the carriage where you stand,
saw your hand and how it quivered
when it to the steeds delivered
lightning-like the whip's command, –

Saw you toss the reins and plummet
faster from your airy summit,
diving like an arrow bright,
glowing as the distance closes,
like a ray of gold on roses
struck by daybreak's early light.

On a thousand backs we're dancing,
billow-backs and backs of chancing –
hail to dances *new*, I say!
Let us dance in every manner,
free – so shall be *our* art's banner,
And *our* science – shall be gay!

From each flower let us garner
just one blossom for our honour,
for our wreath just two leaves worth!
Then like troubadours in riches
we shall dance 'tween saints and bitches,
dance our dance 'tween God and Earth!

He who cannot dance with twisters,
bandages his wounds and blisters,
bound and old and paralysed;
he who reeks of sanctimony,
honour-fools and virtues phony,
out of our paradise!

Let us whirl the dust in doses
into sickly people's noses,

let us shoo these sickly flies!
This whole coast we must unshackle
from their shrivel-breasted cackle,
from these courage-vacant eyes!

Let us chase the overcasters,
world maligners, rain-cloud pastors,
let us tear the dark sky's veil!
Let us roar . . . Free spirits' spirit,
joy uplifts me when you're near, it
makes me bluster like a gale! –

– And to mark this joy forever,
leave a will that time can't sever,
take this wreath up where you are!
Hurl it higher, further, madder,
storm the sky on heaven's ladder,
Hang it there – upon a star!

Index

as logical 82
love of good speech 79–80
new religions 130
superficiality of xxii, 8–9
taste 81–2 (*81*)
without feelings of sin 124
guilt 149 (*250*)

habits 51, 148 (*247*), 167–8 (*295*), 175
Hafis (or Hafiz) (Shams-ed-Din Mohammad)
235
Hamlet 94, 135
happiest, the danger of the 171–2 (*302*)
happiness 11, 65, 71, 147, 150, 158, 161, 195
art and 86, 88
divine of humanity 190–1
Homeric 171–2
the road to 143 (*213*)
and suffering 59, 192
and thinking 183
of those who renounce something 134 (*165*)
and virtue 143
happy ones, two 172–3 (*303*)
Hardenberg, Friedrich Leopold von
see Novalis
harming, with what is best in oneself 51 (*28*)
Hartmann, Eduard von 220
hatred 243–4
health
defining 116–17
the great 246–7 (*382*)
and philosophy 4–7
will to 117
hearing, limits of our sense of 140 (*196*)
Hegel, Georg Wilhelm Friedrich xiv–xv, 96, 218,
219
Helvétius, Claude-Adrien 91
Heraclitus of Ephesus 90n
herd instinct 62, 114–15 (*116*), 140, 210
and conscience 115, 131
and consciousness 213–14
and harm to egoism 183
and opinions 136 (*170*)
and reputation 168
heresy, and witchcraft 54 (*35*)
hermit 229 (*364*), 229–30 (*365*), 248
heroism 153 (*268*), 160, 166, 186
hexameter 85
hic niger est 141 (*203*)
high spirits 162–3 (*288*)
Hinduism 122
history xxii, 120, 219
of every day 175 (*308*)
hidden (*historia abscondita*) 53–4 (*34*)

a sense for 83, 190
homage, learning how to pay 98–9 (*100*)
home, always at 149 (*253*)
homeless, we who are 241–3 (*377*)
Homer 37, 86, 172, 235
homines religiosi 208–9 (*350*), 223
homo poeta 132 (*153*)
honesty xvii, xviii, 98, 104, 111, 114, 179 (*319*),
184, 189, 200–1 (*344*), 232–3
hope 152
Horace 82–3, 132
horrors xiv–xv
human, what is most to you? 153 (*274*)
human beings
distinguished from animals 171
preparatory 160–1 (*283*)
prophetic 178 (*316*)
humanitarianism xiii
humanities x
humanity 77, 114, 242
ancient, colour of 132
dangers of monotheism for 128
of the future 190–1 (*337*)
naturalization of 110
no sin against 125
Hume, David xvii, 218, 234
humility, stupid 50
humour 82
hunting 52
hypocrisy 98
hypothesis 200
and faith 123–4

ideal, and material 143 (*215*)
idealism 237–8 (*372*), 240
ideals
creating one's own 127–8
'inland sea' (*Mittelmeer*) of 246–7
ideas 206–7, 214–15, 237
idleness, and leisure 183–4 (*329*)
illness, xxiii, xxiv, 4–7, 12, 117, 135
illusions x, xii, xix, 80, 95
imitators 150 (*255*)
immortality 151
imperfection, the attraction of 79 (*79*)
improvisation 46, 168, 172
in media vita 181 (*324*)
incense 127 (*142*)
incipit
parodia 4
tragoedia, 4, 195 (*342*)
incomprehensibility 236 (*371*), 245–6
Indians, diet 124, 129
individuality, as a punishment 115

Index

Cambridge texts in the history of philosophy

Titles published in the series thus far

Aristotle *Nicomachean Ethics* (edited by Roger Crisp)

Arnauld and Nicole *Logic or the Art of Thinking* (edited by Jill Vance Buroker)

Bacon *The New Organon* (edited by Lisa Jardine and Michael Silverthorne)

Boyle *A Free Enquiry into the Vulgarly Received Notion of Nature* (edited by Edward B. Davis and Michael Hunter)

Bruno *Cause, Principle and Unity* and *Essays on Magic* (edited by Richard Blackwell and Robert de Lucca with an introduction by Alfonso Ingegno)

Cavendish *Observations upon Experimental Philosophy* (edited by Eileen O'Neill)

Cicero *On Moral Ends* (edited by Julia Annas, translated by Raphael Woolf)

Clarke *A Demonstration of the Being and Attributes of God and Other Writings* (edited by Ezio Vailati)

Condillac *Essay on the Origin of Human Knowledge* (edited by Hans Aarsleff)

Conway *The Principles of the Most Ancient and Modern Philosophy* (edited by Allison P. Coudert and Taylor Corse)

Cudworth *A Treatise Concerning Eternal and Immutable Morality* with *A Treatise of Freewill* (edited by Sarah Hutton)

Descartes *Meditations on First Philosophy*, with selections from the *Objections and Replies* (edited by John Cottingham)

Descartes *The World and Other Writings* (edited by Stephen Gaukroger)

Fichte *Foundations of Natural Right* (edited by Frederick Neuhouser, translated by Michael Baur)

Hobbes and Bramhall on Liberty and Necessity (edited by Vere Chappell)

Humboldt *On Language* (edited by Michael Losonsky, translated by Peter Heath)

Kant *Critique of Practical Reason* (edited by Mary Gregor with an introduction by Andrews Reath)

Kant *Groundwork of the Metaphysics of Morals* (edited by Mary Gregor with an introduction by Christine M. Korsgaard)

Kant *The Metaphysics of Morals* (edited by Mary Gregor with an introduction by Roger Sullivan)

Kant *Religion within the Boundaries of Mere Reason and Other Writings* (edited by Allen Wood and George di Giovanni with an introduction by Robert Merrihew Adams)

La Mettrie *Machine Man and Other Writings* (edited by Ann Thomson)

Leibniz *New Essays on Human Understanding* (edited by Peter Remnant and Jonathan Bennett)

Malebranche *Dialogues on Metaphysics and on Religion* (edited by Nicholas Jolley and David Scott)

Malebranche *The Search after Truth* (edited by Thomas M. Lennon and Paul J. Olscamp)

Melanchthon *Orations on Philosophy and Education* (edited by Sachiko Kusukawa, translated by Christine Salazar)

Mendelssohn *Philosophical Writings* (edited by Daniel O. Dahlstrom)

Nietzsche *The Birth of Tragedy and Other Writings* (edited by Raymond Geuss and Ronald Speirs)

Nietzsche *Daybreak* (edited by Maudemarie Clark and Brian Leiter, translated by R. J. Hollingdale)

Nietzsche *The Gay Science* (edited by Bernard Williams, translated by Josefine Nauckhoff)

Nietzsche *Human, All Too Human* (translated by R. J. Hollingdale with an introduction by Richard Schacht)

Nietzsche *Untimely Meditations* (edited by Daniel Breazeale, translated by R. J. Hollingdale)

Schleiermacher *Hermeneutics and Criticism* (edited by Andrew Bowie)

Schleiermacher *On Religion: Speeches to its Cultured Despisers* (edited by Richard Crouter)

Schopenhauer *Prize Essay on the Freedom of the Will* (edited by Günter Zöller)

Sextus Empiricus *Outlines of Scepticism* (edited by Julia Annas and Jonathan Barnes)

Shaftesbury *Characteristics of Men, Manners, Opinions, Times* (edited by Lawrence Klein)

Voltaire *Treatise on Tolerance and Other Writings* (edited by Simon Harvey)